The Rule of Law in Central America

The Rule of Law in Central America

Citizens' Reactions to Crime and Punishment

Mary Fran T. Malone

BLOOMSBURY

NEW YORK • LONDON • NEW DELHI • SYDNEY

Bloomsbury Methuen Drama
An imprint of Bloomsbury Publishing Plc

1385 Broadway	50 Bedford Square
New York	London
NY 10018	WC1B 3DP
USA	UK

www.bloomsbury.com

Bloomsbury is a registered trade mark of Bloomsbury Publishing Plc

First published in 2012 by the Continuum International Publishing Group Inc

Paperback edition published by Bloomsbury Academic, 2014

© Mary Fran T. Malone, 2012, 2014

Library of Congress Cataloging-in-Publication Data
A catalog record for this book is available from the Library of Congress

ISBN: HB: 978-1-4411-0411-3
PB: 978-1-6289-2256-1
ePub: 978-1-4411-4066-1
ePDF: 978-1-4411-5033-2

Typeset by Newgen Imaging Systems Pvt Ltd, Chennai, India
Printed and bound in the United States of America

To Sascha

Contents

List of Figures and Tables

Figures

Tables

Acknowledgments

In my research, I have been very fortunate to have had so much assistance from many wonderful people all over the world. I wouldn't have been able to embark on this project without the guidance of three extraordinary teachers: Lisa Baglione, Jon Hurwitz, and Mitchell Seligson. These three teachers worked with me at various stages of my academic career and gave me the skills to eventually write a book on a topic I found so important. Lisa first inspired me to become a political scientist. As a sophomore undergraduate student in her class, I admired her enthusiasm for politics, even as I spent long hours studying for her exams. Lisa had the patience to work with me independently to teach me the fundamentals of research, and her help gave me the tools I needed to do well in graduate school at the University of Pittsburgh. Once at the University of Pittsburgh, Jon's classes were probably my most difficult, but they gave me a thorough background in statistical analysis and mass politics. Jon also supplied me with a ready list of good nonpolitical science books to read, recommending that I continue my outside reading to improve my writing style. I have been grateful for the reading suggestions, as well as the rationale that prevented me from feeling guilty about substituting Hildebrand and Bryson for Putnam and Dahl on occasion. While at the University of Pittsburgh, I was very fortunate to have had the opportunity to work with Mitchell Seligson before he departed for Vanderbilt University. Mitch has had extraordinary patience with me ever since I arrived on his office doorstep at the University of Pittsburgh and has worked tirelessly with me to become a well-rounded political scientist. Mitch has always been encouraging, either through reading manuscripts, offering much-needed (and valued) criticism, or going through the pros and cons of different job opportunities. His impressive work ethic has been a model for me to follow as a researcher and a teacher. Mitch has also been an extraordinarily generous scholar. By creating the Latin American Public Opinion Project (LAPOP), soliciting questions for the surveys, and widely disseminating the data, he has exponentially advanced the study of mass politics in Latin America, and in doing so provided the foundation for much of the research in this book. Lisa, Jon, and Mitch demonstrate what impact good teachers can have. Today when my students tell me how much they enjoy my classes, I realize that it is because I have learned from the best.

Also while at the University of Pittsburgh, I had the opportunity to work with an amazing group of scholars. Barry Ames, Alejandro de la Fuente, and Dietlind Stolle enhanced this project by providing insight and advice at its early stages, when they served on my dissertation committee. I was also fortunate to befriend an extraordinary group of graduate students who enriched my academic background in many ways; I am grateful for their support and friendship.

This project has benefitted from several trips to Latin America. Lucía Dammert has been a great help to me in accessing data and generously welcoming me into her home when I traveled to Chile, and our collaborations have been a great pleasure. Juliana Martinez and Jorge Nowalski greatly facilitated my work with other scholars in the field by introducing me to practitioners of criminal justice in Central America. My field research has benefitted from practitioners who have graciously shared their expertise with me: Francisco Bautista Lara, Braulio Espinoza, and Andrés Herrera.

Several other people worked hard to improve the quality of this book. My editor, Marie-Claire Antoine, provided valuable assistance at all stages of the preparation of the manuscript. My graduate and undergraduate assistants, Samantha Corti, Sophia Weeks, Elizabeth Kyriacou, Richard Barney, and Christina Ladam, pored over the pages to account for all references and minimize all errors. Christine Malone-Rowe thoroughly reviewed the final draft of the manuscript and indicated areas for improvement.

I am very grateful to my colleagues at the University of New Hampshire, who provided valuable assistance in many ways. Two chairs of the political science department, Warren Brown and Dante Scala, have worked tirelessly to make as many resources as possible available to me for this project and in my broader career as well. Ellen Cohn, Coordinator of the Justice Studies Program, has been a valuable mentor with much appreciated advice on publishing and grant writing. Deans Hoskin and Fuld of the College of Liberal Arts have ensured that I had ample opportunity to present my work to a broader academic community, providing many opportunities for travel and research. Of course, any recognition of COLA would be remiss without acknowledging the vital assistance of Dean Ted Kirkpatrick, who never met a problem he could not fix. Of course, all of us would be lost without the expert guidance of our administrative staff who work so hard behind the scenes to make us look good: Marcie Anderson, Deborah Briand, and Janis Marshall.

Several fellowships also made this work possible. At the University of New Hampshire, the Center for the Humanities graciously funded this project for a semester. The Center for International Education, the Graduate School, and the College of Liberal Arts provided summer grants for field research. I am very grateful to all my colleagues at the University of New Hampshire, particularly in the Department of Political Science and the Justice Studies Program. I am particularly appreciative of my colleagues who were generous enough to read this manuscript in part or in full and offered very valuable insights: Warren Brown, Ellen Cohn, Burt Feintuch, Stacy VanDeveer, and Sarah Wolper. I would also like to thank the anonymous reviewers who provided valuable feedback on early drafts of the manuscript.

I owe many thanks to my former foster children, Sonia, Javier, Gloria, and Carolina Luna. I was incredibly fortunate that my first experience in Latin America introduced me to such a wonderful family. When I first moved to Argentina many years ago, the Lunas welcomed me into their clan wholeheartedly, teaching me a great deal about the day-to-day practical matters of living in a new country. As they have grown over the years and started families of their own, the Lunas have kindly forgotten what a terrible job I did as a temporary foster mother, and have honored me with their friendship. One of the greatest joys I have in my travels to Latin America is the opportunity to follow their progress, and now the progress of their children.

I have also been fortunate to have had support from a generous group of working mothers. When a stomach virus makes the rounds of day care, at the same time a fall off the monkey bars means a trip to the emergency room, I am very grateful that I have such a large circle of supportive working mothers who can help me juggle illness, emergency rooms, and finishing manuscripts. Attending conferences, conducting field research, and submitting grades on time would not be possible without the help of a dedicated group of working mothers: Donna Brown, Roslyn Chavda, Molly Girard-Dorsey, Sarah Larson-Dennen, Alynna Lyon, Connie Malone, Christine Malone-Rowe, Kerry Palombaro, Cristal Partis, Jo Porter, Sharyn Potter, Rachel Rouillard, Mary Schwarzer, and Jeannie Sowers. Special thanks go to Roslyn Chavda, who saved the day on many occasions with her 5:00pm calls offering to feed my children while I worked in her study. I promise, I never taught my children to ask Roz to send home leftovers on top of it all; they just appreciated her cooking all on their own. Special thanks also go to a particularly extraordinary working mom: Christine Malone (she has waited a long time to hear this, I'm sure). In addition to ensuring I received a solid education, my mother showed me firsthand how to balance work and family, and excel at both. I've drawn on her example many times since I began to balance my own family and career, and in retrospect, I don't know how she did it all. I am grateful that she did, and in doing so, set such a high bar for me to aspire.

I am also grateful to my family for helping my research by providing extra childcare assistance when I need it most. My parents, Martin and Christine Malone, are first to claim my children when I travel to a conference or to conduct research in Latin America. Other family members are also happy to help in any way that they can: Anthony Berenato, Kathleen Kirby, Brian Malone, Christine Malone-Rowe, Joshua Rowe, and Kathleen McFadden (and baby Josh is generous to share his toys). It is much easier to spend time writing when I know my girls are having the time of their lives at Grandmom and Grandpop's famous beach house or the annual Sandyford Avenue block party. Additional thanks go to the teachers and staff of Live and Learn Early Learning Center in Lee, NH, as well as to nanny extraordinaire Kate Hayes. I never have to feel guilty about going to work, as I know my girls are in such caring and creative hands. It has truly taken a village to raise my family.

This book has also benefited greatly from the assistance of two very energetic, yet quite small, research assistants: Sonia and Eva Barth-Malone. These young girls graciously offered to liven up many drafts of this manuscript with beautiful pictures—pictures that inspired me to keep on writing until late at night, when they were fast asleep. Sonia and Eva have given me much-needed distractions as I work, and each time I interrupt a chapter to take them to the pool, I return much invigorated.

Finally, I'd like to thank my husband, Sascha Barth. Sascha has been so supportive of my work, providing assistance when I most needed it, and reminding me not to take things so seriously (also when I most needed it). Sascha's dedication to this project has rivaled my own at times; when New Hampshire storms threaten my power supply, Sascha runs to the store to get a battery backup pack for my computer to keep me from losing data. On his way home from work, he stops to make sure there is plenty of my favorite coffee on hand. Thank you so much, Sascha. You're the best.

1

The Rule of Law and
the Challenge of the Crime Crisis

*In a world in which yesterday's enemies meet to tear down walls, in a world in
which the cold war gives way to cooperation and solidarity, is not the moral force
of a nation that builds in peace more invincible than the weapons that are used
to mock the free will of the people as expressed in the ballots?*

Óscar Arias Sánchez, 1990

With these words, Costa Rican president Óscar Arias sought to encourage the
people of Panama to abolish their armed forces. In the wake of the 1989 US
invasion, Arias aimed to inspire Panama to follow Costa Rica's example and
ban the military as a permanent institution. As the "spokesman for a nation
that has found its path toward development in the abandonment of arms,"
Arias credited Costa Rica's political stability to its 1949 decision to demili-
tarize (Arias 1990, A23). Since that time, while the rest of Central America
was either engulfed in war or ruled by repressive dictatorships, Costa Ricans
never experienced repression, exile, or threats to their fundamental freedoms. Rather, Arias notes that:

> During these 41 years, when military barracks have been turned into
> schools, our symbol has been the teacher who extols intelligence. The
> youth of Latin America has the right to have new heroes, to have new lead-
> ers who cut back on arms and practice dialogue. (Arias 1990, A23)

In 1987, Arias won the Nobel Peace Prize for his efforts to secure peace in
a turbulent region, where ongoing domestic conflicts were exacerbated by
Cold War tensions. As Cold War hostilities subsided, Arias sensed an historic
opportunity to make peace a reality. In the post–Cold War era, he argued
that the military was an atavistic relic. Panama had no need for an army, even
to protect its canal, as "various practical agreements are possible—regional

or international—to insure the safety of the canal" (Arias 1990, A23). Arias proved persuasive. In 1994, constitutional reformers abolished Panama's military under Article 305. This moment was historic. A country that had long lived under military rule would now have no standing military at all.[1]

Panama's decision to abolish its armed forces epitomized the optimism of the early 1990s. Rebels could be convinced to lay down their weapons. Dictators could be persuaded to relinquish power to elected governments. The army could return to the barracks, or in the case of Panama, find new jobs altogether. The law would prove decisive, not military might. Revenues that used to flow to the military might even be free for investments in human capital, as the end of the Cold War created new possibilities to trade "rifles for books, tanks for tractors and soldiers for laborers who will build the country" (Arias 1990, A23).

Óscar Arias was not alone in his optimism. In the aftermath of the Cold War, democrats appraised political developments in Central America with a great deal of enthusiasm. The time of civil war, insurgency, and dictatorship was over. Countries turned to peace accords and constitutional reform to lay the foundations for democratic governance. Costa Rica was no longer the region's exception, as its neighbors also began to resolve disputes in the ballot box instead of the battlefield. In three countries—El Salvador, Guatemala, and Nicaragua—democracy emerged from the destruction of devastating civil wars. In El Salvador, the Chapultepec Peace Accords of 1992 ended 12 years of civil war that had resulted in approximately 75,000 casualties (Danner 1993). Four years later, the United Nations helped to broker a peace accord to end the 36-year civil war in Guatemala, which claimed over 200,000 lives (Booth, Wade, and Walker 2010). In an historic election in 1990, Nicaraguans witnessed a rare peaceful transfer of power when Violeta Chamorro replaced Daniel Ortega as president. This peaceful change stood in marked contrast to Nicaragua's recent history: in 1979 an armed revolt overthrew the Somoza dictatorship, and counter insurgents tried to dislodge the victorious Sandinistas throughout the 1980s with support from the United States. Both of these conflicts took a sobering toll: approximately 50,000 people died during the 1979 Sandinista Revolution, and an additional 31,000 perished during the subsequent Contra War (Booth et al. 2010).

In Panama, political change came on the heels of the 1989 US invasion, launched to depose the reining dictator (and former ally), General Manuel Noriega. In the aftermath of the invasion, civilians scrambled to rebuild a constitutional government, eventually resulting in democratic elections in 1994. These elections were subject to the scrutiny of international monitors and were widely considered to be free and fair. In Honduras, democratic change came even earlier, as human rights abuses declined by the mid-1980s and peaceful transfers of power occurred on the heels of competitive elections in 1986 and again in 1990.

Overall, given the intensity of political violence in the past, Guatemala, El Salvador, Nicaragua, Panama, and Honduras established competitive elections with relative ease. These countries joined what Huntington called the "third wave" of democracy, a global movement toward democratic governance that began in 1974 in Portugal and swept aside authoritarian rule throughout Latin America, Eastern Europe, and parts of Africa and Asia (Huntington 1993). As these Central American countries joined the ranks of the democratizing world, many observers hoped that these elections would be the foundation for a new era of political development in the region. After decades of authoritarian rule, citizens would finally have the chance to participate in politics and choose leaders who would respond to the many challenges facing countries in the region. Citizens welcomed the change. When a Latin American Public Opinion Project (LAPOP) survey asked people whether they preferred military solutions or dialogue to resolve political conflict, the people of Central America overwhelmingly endorsed dialogue—95 percent of respondents thought that the best way to keep the peace was through negotiation and dialogue, compared to the 5 percent who favored relying upon military force.[2] In the five countries that had armies in 1991, LAPOP also asked survey respondents to evaluate military rule, posing the following question: "Based upon what you know of military governments in this country, do you think that they have helped or harmed the ability to solve the following problems?" As Figure 1.1 indicates, respondents registered negative evaluations of military rule. Almost half of the respondents indicated that the military did a good job of enriching high-ranking officials, but was not up to the task of formulating sound economic policy. On issues related to maintaining public order, approximately one-third of respondents indicated that the military had been helpful with security problems like preventing the seizures of public buildings, removing political extremists from office, stopping guerrilla wars, and reducing crime. While sizeable, this one-third of the population was still in the minority.

The end of the Cold War marked the end of military rule in the region, and hopes were high for democratic governance. The times were clearly changing. In the past, international intervention had exacerbated domestic cleavages and intensified political violence. In the 1990s, the international community facilitated negotiations and recognized the work of activists like Guatemala's Rigoberta Menchú, who won the 1992 Nobel Peace Prize. In El Salvador, the poetry of Roque Dalton, which had been banned during the civil war, was added to the school curriculum in 1998. Imprisoned by the right-wing government and ultimately executed by left-wing guerrillas,

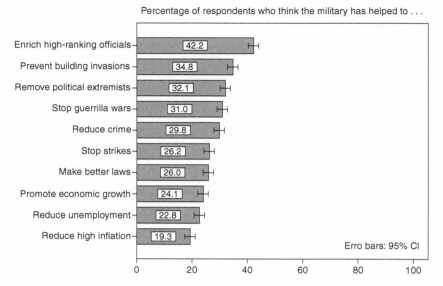

Percentage of respondents who think the military has helped to . . .

Enrich high-ranking officials	42.2
Prevent building invasions	34.8
Remove political extremists	32.1
Stop guerrilla wars	31.0
Reduce crime	29.8
Stop strikes	26.2
Make better laws	26.0
Promote economic growth	24.1
Reduce unemployment	22.8
Reduce high inflation	19.3

Erro bars: 95% CI

0   20   40   60   80   100

FIGURE 1.1 Evaluations of Military Rule in Central America (1991–1992) (excluding Costa Rica)

Dalton symbolized the violent polarization of his country during the Cold War. Six years after the Chapultepec Peace Accords, Salvadoran lawmakers unanimously declared Dalton the country's only modern "poet of great merit" (Rohter 1998, E2). In Guatemala, less than a year after the peace accords were signed, the Guatemalan Tourist Board had already planned to pave new roads to capitalize on the tourist potential of the country's Mayan history. As one correspondent frankly summarized, "At Peace, Guatemala Is Ready for Visitors" (Rohter 1997, 3).

Fifteen years have passed since the last of the peace accords ended political violence in the region. Democratic elections have become routine, and citizens are able to vote and live without fear of egregious human rights abuses. During this time, democratic governance has demonstrated remarkable resiliency. Mainwaring and Hagopian highlight the ability of elected governments to survive despite daunting social and economic challenges and point out that this very survival demonstrates that democracy "can and has lasted in hard times and inauspicious places" (Mainwaring and Hagopian 2005, 5). Democratic setbacks, such as the 2009 military coup against Honduran president Manuel Zelaya, are regarded as anomalies, rather than the typical way of doing business. Prior to the 1990s, a military coup in Honduras would not have sparked such alarm and consternation, but by 2009, such

overt military intervention was widely condemned domestically and internationally. Latin American leaders were divided in their support of President
Zelaya, but virtually unanimous in their opposition to military intervention.
The Organization of American States (OAS) suspended Honduras from the
organization, the first time such action had been taken since the 1962 sus-
pension of Cuba. President Obama quickly issued a statement calling upon
Honduran officials "to respect democratic norms, the rule of law and the
tenets of the Inter-American Democratic charter," and declared that any
"existing tensions and disputes must be resolved peacefully through dialogue free from any outside interference" (Malkin 2009, A1). The United
Nations passed a resolution (whose sponsors included both the United
States and Venezuela) by acclamation "after sustained applause in the 192-
member body," condemning the coup and demanding Zelaya's "immediate
and unconditional restoration" as president (Lacey 2009, A6). Zelaya was not
reinstated as president, but on November 29, 2009, new elections were held
to determine who would govern the country as president. Porfirio Lobo won
these elections and was peacefully inaugurated into office on January 27,
2010. The OAS reinstated Honduras's membership on June 1, 2011.

All in all, democratization has faced difficult challenges, but at the very
least elections and government respect for basic human rights have become
the norm. According to the widely cited Freedom House indicators, all of the
Central American countries were at least partly free in 2010 (Freedom House
2010). Citizens support these developments, widely regarding democracy as
the best form of government. In a 2010 LAPOP survey, over 70 percent of
Central American respondents regarded democracy as better than any other
form of government, despite its problems.[3]

The Rule of Law in Central America

Despite these important milestones, the initial enthusiasm over democratization has waned considerably. Citizens have been able to participate directly
in politics, and governments no longer engage in systematic, flagrant abuses
of basic human rights. Still, citizens face limitations on their civil liberties
and political rights and "all too often watch angrily from the sidelines as officials abuse power and partake in brazen corruption" (Sokolon and Malone
2011, 22). Democratic institutions and procedures prevail, but these fixtures
are often hollow or devoid of democratic principles. Diamond (1999) refers
to such countries as "illiberal democracies," as democratic institutions mask
undemocratic practices. Indeed, scholars have employed a host of qualifiers
to describe the ways in which democratic trappings do not necessarily signify

the prevalence of democratic practices and attitudes, referring to hollow, illiberal, or incomplete democracies. Given the plethora of qualifiers, some scholars now simply use the term "democracy with adjectives" (Smith and Ziegler 2009, 13). Citizens concur with this view. While the vast majority of citizens consider democracy to be the best form of government, as Figure 1.2 illustrates, citizens are cynical about the quality of democracy in their countries. In 2010, LAPOP posed the following question to respondents: "In your opinion, is your country very democratic, mostly democratic, a little democratic, or not at all democratic?" On average, only Costa Rican and Panamanian responses were positive. In the remaining countries, appraisals of democratic governance were significantly more pessimistic. In Honduras, El Salvador, Nicaragua, and Guatemala, more responses were concentrated at the lower end of the spectrum, indicating that more respondents viewed their countries as "not at all democratic" or only "a little democratic."[4]

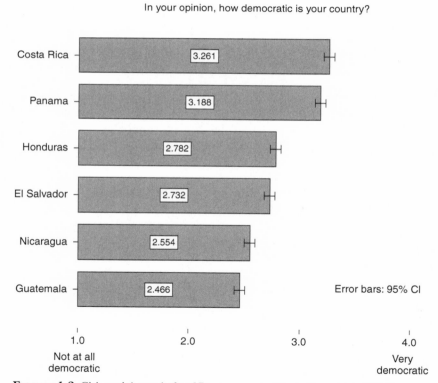

In your opinion, how democratic is your country?

FIGURE 1.2 Citizens' Appraisals of Democracy in Their Countries (2010)

At first, many observers viewed such problems as temporary—democracy was hollow because it was in transition. Many believed that democratic processes would deepen, and gradually political rights, civil liberties, and institutional accountability would entrench themselves in the political landscape. While there is some truth to this view, it is clear that many Central American democracies are not on the road to something better. Democracy has been consolidated, but in most cases the type of democracy that has taken shape falls far short of expectations. Indeed, in a longitudinal study of Latin American democratization from 1978 through 2004, Smith and Ziegler find that illiberal democracy "was the most common of all [regime] types, appearing almost 40 percent of the time" (Smith and Ziegler 2009, 15). Occasionally illiberal democracy has served as a stepping stone to full democracy, but more commonly, illiberal democracy tends to be an endpoint.

Perhaps the most glaring example of the hollowness of Central American democracy is the weakness of the rule of law (O'Donnell 1998). Many have noted that democratization has done little to change a tradition of widespread disrespect for the rule of law. Former Brazilian leader Getúlio Vargas is reported to have said "*Aos meus amigos, tudo; aos meus inimigos, a lei*" (For my friends, whatever they want; for my enemies, the law), and many observers find this phrase aptly captures current realities throughout Latin America.[5] O'Donnell even coined a new phrase, "the unrule of law," to describe the poor state of justice in the region (O'Donnell 1999). The weakness of the rule of law poses no small problem for democratization. In a seminal work, Diamond explains how liberal democracy cannot exist without the rule of law, whereby:

> legal rules are applied fairly, consistently, and predictably across equivalent cases, irrespective of the class, status, or power of those subject to the rules. Under a true rule of law, all citizens have political and legal equality, and the state and its agents are themselves subject to the law. (Diamond 1999, 11)

In other words, the rule of law comprises a set of impartial laws that effectively regulates citizens' and governments' behavior. Citizens might vary in terms of their political, economic, and social resources, but all are politically equal under the law. Appropriate institutions ensure that this legal equality is in fact a reality. For example, government officials are not above the law and follow their constitutionally prescribed roles in governance. Institutions (such as an independent judiciary, human rights ombudsman, or legislature) can constrain official abuses of power, promoting horizontal accountability by checking the power of other governmental actors. These institutions also ensure that the rights and liberties of individuals and groups are protected from arbitrary state action, as well as abuse from nonstate actors. Thus, the "rule of law protects citizens from unjustified detention, exile, terror, torture, and undue interference in their personal lives not only by the state but also by organized non-state or anti-state forces" (Diamond 1999, 12). Since the rule of law safeguards citizens' political rights and civil liberties and constrains official abuses of power, it is an indispensable cornerstone of democratic governance. Free and fair elections quickly lose their appeal if they merely offer choices between a few corrupt elites. Citizens cannot exercise their political rights and civil liberties if they are subject to arbitrary state violence. The democratic rules of the game diminish in importance if some individuals are treated differently under the law than others. Without the rule of law, democracy is hollow.

When examining Central American democracy, scholars, politicians, and the public have roundly criticized the quality of the rule of law. O'Donnell highlights a tradition of ignoring the law in the region, or when applying the law, "twisting it in favor of the powerful and for the repression or containment of the weak" (O'Donnell 1999, 312). Rather than commanding respect and compliance, the rule of law is frequently disparaged. As O'Donnell explains:

> [There is] a presumably widespread feeling that, first, to voluntarily follow the law is something that only idiots do and, second, that to be subject to the law is not to be the carrier of enforceable rights but rather a sure signal of social weakness. This is particularly true and dangerous in encounters that may unleash the violence of the state or powerful private agents, but an attentive eye can also detect it in the stubborn refusal of the privileged to submit themselves to regular administrative procedures, not to say anything of the scandalous criminal impunity they often obtain. (O'Donnell 1999, 312)

O'Donnell is not alone in his critique. There is widespread consensus that democratization has proceeded while leaving the rule of law far behind. People frequently deplore the uneven application of the law across the citizenry and the poor quality of many justice institutions. These institutional weaknesses make it difficult to curb official abuses of power, as well as protect citizens from violations of their rights at the hands of other actors (e.g., criminal organizations). In a longitudinal study of Latin American democracies, Foweraker and Krznaric measure the strength of the core elements of democracy, particularly competitive elections, respect for civil and political rights, and accountability. When contrasting the strength of vertical accountability (through free and fair elections) and horizontal accountability (through institutional checks and balances), Foweraker and Krznaric find that "third wave democracies can and do survive without a fully effective rule of law" (2009, 67).

Figure 1.3 illustrates this trend, relying upon the World Bank's Governance Indicators, which aim to describe the quality of several different facets of governance. Most importantly, the Governance Indicators distinguish among crucial elements of democracy, such as voice and accountability (i.e., meaningful citizen participation in politics), political stability and the absence of violence, and the rule of law.[6] Figure 1.3 examines these indicators from 1996 (the year the last peace accord was signed in Guatemala) through 2009. As Figure 1.3 indicates, the most recent transitions to democracy in Central America are marked by problems with the rule of law. Overall, citizens have been able to participate in politics, and the political violence of the past has subsided. However, the rule of law lags behind these other key components.

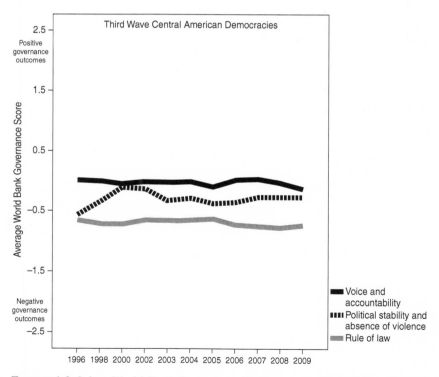

FIGURE 1.3 Select World Bank Governance Indicators for Third Wave Central American Democracies

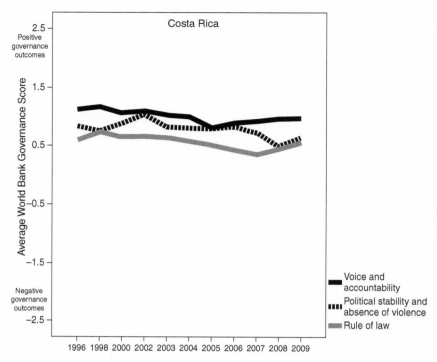

FIGURE 1.4 Select World Bank Governance Indicators for Costa Rica

Even Costa Rica, the region's longstanding democratic exception, has experienced recent difficulties in upholding the rule of law. As Figure 1.4 indicates, Costa Rica performs far better on each of these components of governance. Still, evaluations of the rule of law tend to drop below those for citizen participation in politics and political stability.[7] From 1998 through 2007 in particular, Costa Rica experienced a slight but steady decline in the rule of law, before rebounding and registering better outcomes in 2008 and 2009. Together, Figures 1.3 and 1.4 illustrate a sobering trend: the rule of law has proven to be an important yet elusive goal in newly democratizing countries, and even established democracies like Costa Rica face challenges in upholding the rule of law.

Officials have not turned a blind eye to the need for rule of law reform (Salas 2001). Given the centrality of the rule of law to both democracy and economic development, the past three decades have been marked by efforts to reform this status quo (Carothers 2006; Correa 1999). As authoritarian regimes began to weaken in the mid-1980s, reformers recognized the importance of transforming authoritarian justice systems to provide strong foundations for new democratic governments (Belton 2005). There was a pressing need to revise constitutions and legal codes, as well as train judges, lawyers, and other legal professionals to uphold these revised constitutions and laws (Carothers 2006). Institutional reform became the next priority. Under authoritarian rule, many justice institutions were kept deliberately weak so as to be unable to curb executive power. Institutions like the courts and the police required extensive updates to both their infrastructures as well as procedures, particularly since an exclusive reliance on written proceedings created extreme backlogs and delays, which opened the door for opportunities for corruption and the abuse of civil liberties. Countries needed to overhaul authoritarian justice institutions bereft of legitimacy and transform them into impartial arbiters of the rule of law. Finally, once reformers tackled legal codes and institutions, it was imperative to socialize citizens and government officials into the new democratic norms of justice.

This reform agenda was ambitious to say the least. Not surprisingly, reformers quickly encountered obstacles. The case of Guatemala highlights many of these challenges. When Guatemala began its transition to democracy, rule of law reform featured prominently on the agenda. Such reform was thought to be indispensable to addressing a history of official impunity and an unequal application of the law the latter of which was exacerbated by sharp socioeconomic and ethnic inequalities. Despite widespread attention and substantial international expenditures, democratization did little to alter these historical trends. Public officials were frequently charged with violating the law, as they engaged in corrupt activities for personal enrichment and/or violated the rights of citizens. For example, former president Alfonso Portillo (2000–2004) was arrested in 2010 on an embezzlement indictment, charged alongside his defense minister and six additional defense ministry officials (Malkin 2010). Organized crime has taken advantage of official impunity and complicity, as well as weak justice institutions (*The Economist* 2007). In 2010, two successive national police chiefs were arrested for a series of crimes stemming from their involvement in drug trafficking (*The Economist* 2010). The combination of organized crime, official impunity, and weak institutions have taken a lethal toll on Guatemalan citizens—Guatemala is one of the world's most violent countries. Hudson and Taylor provide some sobering statistics:

In 2008, 6,338 Guatemalans were violently killed, representing an average of 16 murders per day. Of those murdered, 131 homicide cases made it to trial, resulting in 83 convictions and 48 acquittals, representing a staggering conviction rate of just 2.06%. (2010, 56)

These high levels of violence, alongside concern that Guatemala was a dis-integrating narco-state, raised alarm not just within Guatemala, but in the international community as well. The United Nations declared that the Guatemalan government was infiltrated "by criminal clandestine organi-zations and the operation of violent illegal security forces outside of the control of the Guatemalan state" (Hudson and Taylor 2010, 56). To com-bat criminal organizations and promote the rule of law in Guatemala, the UN collaborated with domestic reformers to pilot an unusual experiment. On September 4, 2007, Guatemala and the United Nations established the *Comisión Internacional Contra la Impunidad en Guatemala* (The International Commission against Impunity in Guatemala), known by its Spanish acro-nym CICIG. Funded by voluntary contributions from the international community, CICIG is a unique hybrid organization comprising interna-tional and domestic actors, but operating solely within the legal framework of Guatemala. CICIG has the power to investigate government abuses of power and the activities of criminal organizations, to make policy recom-mendations, and to act as a "complimentary prosecutor" when needed (particularly in controversial or sensitive cases) (CICIG 2009). Since its inception, CICIG has focused particularly on the problem of organized crime, launching several high-profile investigations of drug trafficking and drug-related murders.

After 3 years, CICIG can boast some success. The mere fact that former president Portillo was arrested, along with several other high-ranking gov-ernment officials, is a sign that CICIG has worked with its domestic part-ners to change a status quo of impunity. CICIG has also influenced reform efforts and provided valuable technical assistance. This has resulted in the passage of important legislation such as the Law on Arms and Ammunition, as well as the strengthening of the national witness protection program and the national wiretapping system (CIGI 2009). In addition, CICIG has gar-nered support from citizens in Guatemala. In 2010, LAPOP asked survey respondents to indicate how much trust they had in a variety of institutions in Guatemala, including CICIG, the Constitutional Court, justice tribunals (lower courts), the Supreme Court, the President, Congress, and the National Police.[8] As Figure 1.5 illustrates, compared to the domestic institutions in Guatemala, respondents view CICIG in a significantly more favorable light. CICIG earns a level of legitimacy far above that of domestic institutions. In addition, when asked how much they "supported international missions like the CICIG getting involved to improve the Guatemalan political system," the majority of people registered their approval.[9]

Despite these important successes, CICIG's work has been undermined by corrupt officials, weak institutions, and recalcitrant crime lords. For

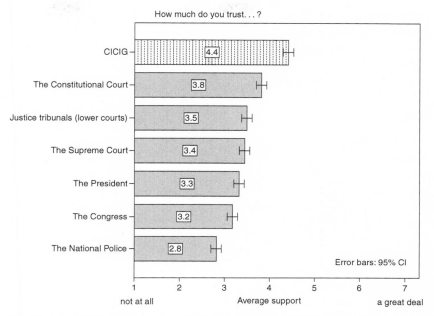

FIGURE 1.5 Public Evaluations of Institutions in Guatemala (2010)

example, the prosecution of one corrupt national police chief is a step forward, but not if another corrupt chief takes his place. Both domestic and international reformers have become frustrated with the resilience of corruption and impunity. For example, on June 7, 2010, CICIG Commissioner Carlos Castresana resigned to protest the appointment of an attorney general he charged had links to organized crime (Malkin 2010). Furthermore, given the substantial time commitment of each case, CICIG can only address around 15 cases at once (*The Economist* 2010). The ability to address high-profile cases of official impunity is laudable, and this ability has become a potent symbol of the potential for reform. However, the number of cases investigated by CICIG is a small fraction of the whole. In CICIG's first year, it discarded 49 of the 64 complaints received (Hudson and Taylor 2010, 62).[10]

The case of Guatemala highlights the many obstacles blocking the establishment of the rule of law in the region. Earnest (and sometimes not so earnest) reform efforts face a stiff uphill battle against entrenched interests, powerful officials, and in the case of organized crime, a wealthy, highly organized opponent. Even laudable domestic-international partnerships find themselves swamped by ingrained trends of impunity and corruption. Given the magnitude of the problem, and the resources of key opponents, it is easy for even sincere reforms to be overpowered by those with a stake in the status quo. Guatemala's situation is one of the gravest in the region, but its neighbors face similar problems. In particular, the problem of crime affects all the Central American countries, and has the potential to cripple efforts to promote the rule of law.

The Challenge of the Crime Crisis

To address deficiencies in the rule of law, democratizing states need to overhaul authoritarian legal codes and institutions of questionable legitimacy and transform them into respected pillars of justice. Both citizens and officials must reorient themselves in this new political system. Officials must internalize the new democratic rules of the game, designed to promote not just vertical accountability through elections, but also horizontal accountability through institutional checks and balances. Citizens must change their attitudes and behaviors toward their system of government. Rather than dismiss state actors like the courts, who served to legitimize state repression and corruption under authoritarian rule, citizens need to turn to justice institutions to redress problems and grievances. Such transformations would be a challenge for any state, but the third wave democracies of Central America have met even greater trials, as reform efforts have taken place against a backdrop of skyrocketing crime rates (Cruz 2009; Gaviria and Pages 1999; Lafree and Tseloni 2006). Cruz (2008) finds that during the era of democratization, homicide rates increased by 50 percent in Latin America on average. Just as casualties from government repression waned, fatalities due to violent crime soared, as in many cases crime has replaced civil war as the key detriment to citizens' security (Seligson 2005; Córdova, Cruz, Seligson 2007). Given the magnitude of the crime crisis and the amount of reform needed, some observers have described reform efforts as akin to "fixing a broken army in the midst of a war" (Ellingwood 2008, 1).

Figure 1.6 underscores the gravity of the current crime crisis, listing the most recent homicide rates in Latin America. Crime is a problem throughout Latin America, but as Figure 1.6 illustrates, the problem is particularly severe in Central America. Three Central American countries—Honduras, El Salvador, and Guatemala—have the highest homicide rates in the region and rank among the most violent countries in the world. Even in countries closer to the regional median, like Nicaragua and Panama, rates of violent crime are high—more than double the average homicide rate of the United States.

While Costa Rica appears to have escaped the homicide epidemic, crime is still at the forefront of national attention. Homicide rates in Costa Rica are low for the region, but they have increased steadily over time. From

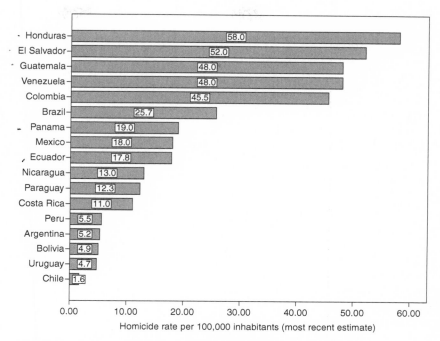

FIGURE 1.6 Homicide Rates per 100,000 (Most Recent Estimate)*
*The Appendix lists the sources and years of each homicide estimate.

1999 through 2006, homicide rates increased by 18 percent within the country (OCAVI 2006). Most Costa Ricans do not take solace in their country's ranking as the safest in Central America. Rather, the increases in homicide rates over time have provoked alarm. Public preoccupation with crime even facilitated the 2010 election of the country's first female president, Laura Chinchilla, a former minister of public security and international consultant on judicial reform and public security. Chinchilla has authored numerous articles on the problem of crime and rule of law reform in Latin America (e.g. Chinchilla 2003); these qualifications have made her an extremely appealing candidate in a fearful country.

This surge in violent crime has hampered efforts to reform the rule of law. Most obviously, crime itself is the antithesis of the rule of law. High rates of crime in and of themselves indicate a prevalence of lawbreaking behavior either by individuals or criminal organizations. However, the crime crisis in Central America has ripple effects for the rule of law as well (Whitehead 2009). First, the crime epidemic has swamped the institutions entrusted with upholding the rule of law, namely the courts and police. Even in democratic success stories like Costa Rica, the courts and police find themselves *sobrecargados* (overloaded) by the spike in crime rates.[11] Second, the institutional inability to confront crime successfully has lead many citizens to dismiss them as hopelessly ineffective and corrupt. When the public dismisses justice institutions, it further weakens their abilities to address the crime crisis. In many cases the courts and police rely upon citizens to bring crime to their attention. If a large portion of the population hesitates to turn to the law to solve problems, or registers reluctance to report crime and cooperate with police investigations, in many cases the justice system cannot act. The power of the justice system is constrained by public legitimacy. If the public does not trust these institutions, it is unlikely that they will be transformed into pillars for the rule of law. Bailey (2009) calls this situation a "security trap," whereby crime, violence, and corruption become mutually reinforcing in state -society interactions, ultimately undermining the quality of democracy. Throughout the democratization process in Central America, the crime epidemic has stymied reformers' attempts to promote the rule of law. The institutional inability to curb crime, coupled with occasional complicity in criminal acts, has led many citizens to dismiss the justice system as hopelessly ineffective, corrupt, and unfair (Cruz 2000, 2003; Pérez 2003). Even Costa Rica has not been immune to such trends, as public trust in the justice system has declined precipitously in recent years (Walker 2009).

Bailey (2009) advances our understanding of these dynamics by examining interactions among crime, civil society, and the state, and distinguishing between positive and negative equilibriums. In a positive equilibrium, the rule of law is strong, and "crime, corruption, and violence originate mainly in civil society and act on state and regime . . . The former responds primarily with corrective measures to problems that originate mainly in the latter" (Bailey 2009, 256). In contrast, under a negative equilibrium a very different pattern emerges. Under this negative equilibrium, "notions of law and norms of behavior in civil society differ markedly from formal law, the citizenry tolerates or promotes formally illegal exchanges, and state and regime themselves act as principal engines of crime, violence, and corruption" (Bailey 2009, 256). Unfortunately, all too often the reality of governance in the third wave Central American democracies approximates the negative equilibrium rather than the positive. Under this negative equilibrium, there are several characteristics that become entrenched in self-reinforcing cycles:

- Significant groups contest state notions of legality and "may ignore, evade, or openly violate formal law."
- Elected and appointed officials engage in unethical behavior and commit crimes; they take advantage of civil society "to extract resources or command obedience outside the formal law."

- Though victimized, "civil society is typically characterized by apathy, opportunism, and cynicism" and views the state (particularly the justice system) as "inefficient and ineffective." (Bailey 2009, 256)

Bailey's use of the word "equilibrium" signals why the rule of law has proven to be so elusive. Civil society and the state have fallen into a reinforcing pattern that is quite stable, and thus reproduced over time. As Bailey sums up, under a negative equilibrium "regime and civil society are unable to correct themselves and therefore unable to correct problems of public security" (Bailey 2009, 256). These negative and positive equilibriums are extreme ends on a spectrum—rather than fall discretely into one category or another, countries tend to approximate one end of the spectrum over the other. The ability to escape from the security trap will depend greatly on the severity of the crisis, resources available for reform, and the relative power of reformers in both civil society and government.

Citizens' Reactions to the Security Trap

One way in which the security trap ensnares reform efforts and undermines the rule of law is by increasing public support for undemocratic measures. Understandably, citizens have expressed growing dissatisfaction with escalating crime rates, and some have even registered support for undemocratic alternatives with the hopes that they might improve citizen security. In recent surveys, large numbers of citizens in Central America have stated that a military coup would be justified under conditions of high crime. Indeed, Cruz (2008) finds that "no other national problem raises more support for military coups than criminal violence." With the recent exception of Honduras, military intervention has largely faded from the political arena throughout Latin America (Pérez-Liñán 2007), so it seems unlikely that high crime rates would result in a reversion to the prior tradition of military rule. However, democracy advocates still have cause for concern. High rates of crime have the potential to jeopardize democracy in more subtle ways, particularly by chipping away at an already weak rule of law. As a USAID report on justice reform cautions:

> Difficult economic conditions and increasing crime are diminishing the security of person and property that the rule of law is intended to protect and are contributing to dissatisfaction with reforms that seek to safeguard civil liberties, protect political rights, and ensure due process. (United States Agency for International Development 2002, 10)

Increasingly, many popular crime-fighting measures do not bode well for the rule of law. In some cases the armed forces have renewed their engagement in internal security maintenance, even undermining peace accords to the contrary (Pérez 2003). In other cases, political leaders have called on citizens to grant more discretionary powers to public officials, arguing that the police and courts could apprehend and convict criminals more decisively if only they were not fettered by the law. Such calls have found sympathetic audiences. Desperate to break cycles of crime and violence, many people are willing to give officials carte blanche to pursue suspected criminals. In addition to allowing public officials to act on the margins of the law, some citizens have banded together to sanction suspected criminals extra-judicially through vigilante justice. Rather than rely upon legal avenues to address crime-related grievances, citizens are willing to reject the rule of law and turn to mob justice. An increasingly fearful public has also indicated it will endorse more punitive policies, such as the death penalty and harsher sentencing for even minor offenses, a trend dubbed "penal populism." In the case of wealthier citizens, walled and guarded enclaves frequently offer sanctuary from violent streets, as wealthy and middle-class people increasingly prefer to replace public officials with private security actors (Caldeira 2000).

These different measures share one common denominator: they weaken already fragile justice systems and have the potential to undermine the rule of law, thus reinforcing the hollowness of third wave democratic governance. El Salvador offers clear illustrations of this process. In El Salvador, high murder rates and gang activity turned crime into a salient political issue. Eight months before the 2004 presidential elections, President Flores and legislators from his conservative party, the National Republican Alliance (ARENA), launched *Plan Mano Dura* (the Iron Fist Plan). Included in this plan was the 2003 *Anti-Maras* Act (Anti-Gang Act), which allowed the police to arrest suspected gang members on the basis of their physical appearance (Wolf 2011). Among other things, the act criminalized an individual "wandering around without an identity document in . . . any settlement, without justified cause or who is not known by inhabitants" (Amnesty International 2003, 2). This act proved extremely popular among the public, but human rights defenders and judges roundly criticized it on the grounds that it sought to penalize "people on the basis of their appearance and social background," thus violating the Salvadoran constitution guaranteeing the right to equality before the law (Amnesty International 2003, 1). Critics of the legislation met with harsh condemnation. President Flores (1999–2004) targeted the judiciary in particular, declaring that "judges who say they cannot apply the law are siding with the criminal."[12] With this statement, Flores joined an increasingly popular trend, whereby politicians seek to maximize the electoral potency of crime by casting themselves as the allies of victims. As Dammert cautions:

> Now there is not a dichotomy between prevention and control. Now the antinomy in populist discourse is this: I am with the victims and you are with the criminals. There is no more debate between those supporting prevention and those advocating control. Now the political fight is to see who can succeed in claiming to champion the rights of victims, and who can cast their political opponents as friends of delinquents. *Garantismo* (protection of civil liberties) has become a plague in Latin America, without ever becoming a reality first. (Appialoza and Dammert 2011)

Despite concerns that such measures were unconstitutional and jeopardized civil liberties, this iron fist strategy resonated with a fearful public, and proved so popular that it was continued under Flores's successor, Antonio Saca (2004–2009). Popularity aside, Plan Mano Dura failed to lower homicide rates or quell gang activity. By the time Maurio Funes lead the *Frente Farabundo Martí para la Liberación Nacional* (FMLN) to victory in the 2009 presidential elections, homicide rates were among the highest in the world, and the gang problem "had become intractable" (Wolf 2011, 1).[13] Funes originally pledged to incorporate preventive and rehabilitative measures into his crime fighting policy, but these measures remained underfunded. In November of 2009, Funes yielded to pressure and deployed the army to fight crime, extending and strengthening its previous mandate (Wolf 2010).

Guatemala shares many similarities with the case of El Salvador, yet such problems are exacerbated by higher levels of vigilante justice. Guatemala is the most publicized site of *linchamientos* (lynchings), which in some cases have replaced state-sanctioned public executions as the most prominent human rights abuses, and frequently rely upon the same tactics to execute criminals as state forces used against suspected guerrillas in the past (Godoy 2002). Linchamientos began during the early 1990s, accelerating after the signing of the 1996 peace accords (Godoy 2002). From January through April of 2011, Guatemala made headlines for hosting 22 lynching attacks, an increase of more than 50 percent over the same period in 2010 (*Prensa Libre* 2011). Many of these attacks can be linked to former paramilitary leaders, but the public has voiced support for such attacks as well, and trends indicate this support will grow in the future in both urban and rural areas (Azpuru 2006). Often targeted criminals are members of marginalized ethnic groups and socioeconomic classes, raising the alarm that vigilante justice is a new way to abuse minority rights.

As these examples illustrate, citizen reactions to the security trap have the potential to erode the rule of law. To assess the ability of Central American countries to escape from the security trap, this book focuses on the perspective of citizens. Particularly in the third wave Central American democracies, citizens have finally obtained a voice in their governments. Will they use this voice to support measures that ultimately undermine the quality of democracy in their countries? Or will they act in ways that promote the rule of law? How do they view the security trap, and how do they evaluate their options from escaping from it?

To examine citizen reactions to crime and punishment, this book relies upon the public opinion data gathered through the Latin American Public Opinion Project (LAPOP). For more than four decades, LAPOP has gauged public attitudes toward local and national government, support for democracy, experiences and perceptions of crime and corruption, voting behavior, and civil society participation, among other things. To the author's knowledge, it is the only source of public opinion data that uses identical questions to measure public attitudes toward the law and its corresponding institutions, as well as citizens' willingness to use the law to solve everyday problems, throughout the third wave of democratization.

While the focus of this book is on citizen support for the rule of law, it is imperative to ground citizen attitudes and behaviors into their appropriate national context. The rule of law has proven to be problematic throughout the region, but countries vary dramatically in terms of the magnitude of this problem. With its low homicide rates, comparatively stronger justice institutions, and long tradition of public support for democratic norms, Costa Rica's context is drastically different from that of Honduras, with one of the highest homicide rates in the world, and recent experiences with a coup. The reality facing Costa Ricans is completely different from that of the countries in the "northern triangle" where violent crime has become commonplace. In a similar vein, like Guatemala and El Salvador, Nicaraguan history is marked by violence and poverty, but Nicaragua has not experienced the same surge in violent crime, with homicide rates on par with that of Panama. Thus, as citizens voice their views on the crime crisis, justice institutions, and ultimately the rule of law, it is important to note that they are reacting to very different realities. In order to understand citizens' preferences for escaping the security trap, it is imperative to place their views in the appropriate context. To this end, Chapter 2 provides an overview of trends in both the rule of law and crime in each country, focusing in particular on trends from the 1990s to the present. This overview aims to provide the appropriate national backdrop for contextualizing citizen attitudes and behavior toward the rule of law.

With this backdrop in place, Chapter 3 examines citizens' perceptions of crime and justice. This chapter reviews the literature on public attitudes towards the law and its corresponding institutions, noting how citizen perceptions can differ from the macro measures discussed in Chapter 2. In Chapter 4, the focus shifts to analyzing citizen support for crime-fighting measures that undermine the rule of law—support for authorities' acting on the margins of the law to apprehend criminals, as well as vigilante justice. Chapter 5 assesses public support of the law in a different vein, examining citizens' willingness to turn to the institutions of law and order to solve problems through an indicator that has not been extensively utilized as a measurement of the rule of law: reporting crimes to police. Chapter 6 also examines citizen behavior, but focuses on people's reliance on private security measures—an increasing trend in Central America. Finally, Chapter 7 discusses the results of these analyses, and their implications for democratic governance.

Since the time of Plato, discussions of the rule of law have featured prominently in political science debates. Scholars have long acknowledged that the rule of law is an indispensable feature of governance. The rule of law has been considered essential for promoting economic development, protecting human rights, curbing abuses of power, and maintaining order throughout the nation. Plato noted that "a state in which all of the citizens disobey all of the laws cannot exist." This stands in stark contrast to the more recent quotes by O'Donnell and Vargas, which highlight a tradition of disregarding and disparaging the rule of law. To understand the prospects for the rule of law in the region, and thus the future quality of democratic governance, this book aims to understand how citizens respond to the "unrule of law." Most importantly, how do people navigate the problem of crime in their everyday lives, given the constraints they face while living in their respective security traps? Ever since the end of the Cold War, the costs of violent crime and the unrule of law have been increasingly debated. Observers from all over the world have noted the high costs of violent crime and the unrule of law in terms of economic development, health, democracy, and of course the quality of human life. While it is laudable that Panama abolished its military and opened the door to democratic governance in the 1990s, this measure is futile if crime takes the military's place in undermining citizens' rights. If democracy is to have meaning in the region, it is imperative to identify the ways in which citizens can escape the security trap while preserving democratic institutions and ideals.

Notes

[1] Article 305 prohibits a standing army, but does allow for the temporary formation of special defense units in times of urgency. The exact text of the constitution is available through Georgetown University's Political Database of the Americas, at http://pdba.georgetown.edu/Constitutions/Panama/panama1994.html (last accessed March 16, 2011).

[2] These survey results are based upon the Latin American Public Opinion Project's (LAPOP) survey of urban residents in the six Central American countries. LAPOP conducted the survey in 1991 in El Salvador, Nicaragua, and Panama. LAPOP conducted the survey in Costa Rica in 1990 and Guatemala in 1992. The exact text of this survey question read: "Some people think that the best way to keep the peace is through military force. Others think that the best way to keep the peace is to sit down to talk and resolve the dispute. Which statement is closest to your point of view?" Details on the methodology of this survey and the complete questionnaire are available at: www.vanderbilt.edu/lapop/core-surveys.php (last accessed March 15, 2011).

[3] In 2010, LAPOP posed the following question to respondents: "Despite its problems, democracy is better than any other form of government. How much do you agree or disagree with this statement?" Respondents were asked to indicate the extent to which they agreed or disagreed on a scale of one (strong disagreement) through seven (strong agreement). On this scale, 70 percent of participants responded with values higher than four, indicating their agreement that democracy was the best form of government.

[4] The exact text of this survey question read: "In your opinion, is [country] very democratic (1), pretty democratic (2), a little democratic (3), or not democratic at all (4)?" Responses were recoded so that higher values corresponded to more positive appraisals of democratic governance.

[5] For example, O'Donnell (1999, 303) uses this phrase attributed to Vargas to begin his discussion of the rule of law in the region. Getúlio Vargas governed Brazil with military backing from 1930 through 1945, and later served as an elected president from 1951 through 1954.

[6] Each of these elements is ranked on a scale of +2.5 (positive governance outcome) through -2.5 (negative development outcome). For these five countries, the average during this time frame was -.027 for voice and accountability, -.300 for political stability and absence of violence, and -.696 for the rule of law. See Kaufmann, Kraay, and Mastruzzi (2009) for a thorough discussion of the methodology of the Governance Indicators. The dataset in its entirety is available for download at http://info.worldbank.org/governance/wgi/index.asp (last accessed March 8, 2011).

[7] For this time frame, the average scores in Costa Rica were 1.00414 for voice and accountability, .78550 for political stability, and .56183 for the rule of law.

[8] In the 2010 LAPOP survey, a battery of questions gauged the legitimacy of several institutions. This battery of questions was preceded by the following introduction: "Now we are going to use a card. This card has a scale of seven points; each one indicates a range that goes from one (that means none) through seven (much). For example, if you were to ask how much you trusted

the news on television, if you did not trust it at all you would choose the number one. If on the contrary you trusted it a lot, you would choose number seven. If your opinion was between none at all and a lot, you would select an intermediate point." Respondents then answered a series of follow up questions in a similar format, including items measuring trust in domestic and international institutions.

9   On the same 1–7 scale, 55 percent of people gave responses of five or higher.

10 In the first year, this number was particularly high as there was confusion within CICIG as well as the broader Guatemalan political system over which cases fell within CICIG's mandate, and which cases did not.

11 Author interview with Lara Blanco, technical coordinator for *Política Integral y Sostenible de Seguridad Ciudadana y Promoción de la Paz Social para Costa Rica* (POLSEPAZ) (Integral and Sustainable Politics for Citizen Security and Promotion of Social Peace for Costa Rica), United Nations Development Program, San José, Costa Rica.

12 *Diario de Hoy*, 21 October 2003, as cited in Amnesty International's Open Letter on the Anti-Maras Act (2003).

13 Maurio Funes was the first member of the FMLN, the former guerrilla group, to be elected to the presidency, thus ending the conservative string of presidential victories that had marked Salvadoran democratization.

2

National Trends in Crime and Justice

LEY

Panel in the *Salón Dorado* (Golden Room) in the Museum of Costa Rican Art, by
Luis Féron Parizot (1901–1998). This panel is part of a mural depicting scenes
from Costa Rican history, ranging from Pre-Colombian times through 1940.
Featuring prominently is this tablet with the inscription "*Ley*" (law), highlighting
the importance of the law in the formative years of contemporary Costa Rican
democracy.

Photo by José Carrasquillo

Insecurity affects all of us today; it is a complex problem which we must seriously consider. Insecurity has deep roots and requires action in two areas: Social Security and Public Safety.

Laura Chinchilla, President of Costa Rica[1]

The situation of violence and insecurity in which we are living shows that we will need to take advantage of any resources that are available. The army is a resource of the state.

Otto Pérez Molina, former Guatemalan military general
and frequent presidential candidate[2]

Despite some regional similarities, the Central American countries vary substantially in terms of the rule of law. When examining whether a set of impartial laws effectively regulates the behavior of citizens and governments, it is clear that all the countries face challenges, but in some cases these challenges are dire. Sometimes the law itself is not impartial, as evidenced by El Salvador's 2003 Anti-Maras Act. Other times the law might be impartial and offers a good foundation for the rule of law, but justice institutions are too weak to uphold and enforce it. For example, the judiciary might prove incapable of prosecuting government officials for breaking the law, or the police might be unable to solve homicides or keep gangs from demanding protection money from average citizens. Citizens themselves might refuse to comply with the law, or favor extralegal venues for redressing grievances instead of legal ones.

As the above quotes from Chinchilla and Pérez Molina highlight, countries also differ in terms of their responses to the twin challenges of justice reform and crime. As a long-time public security expert, Chinchilla has emphasized the need for a holistic response to problems of crime in Costa Rica. Costa Rica registers the lowest rates of violent crime when compared to other countries in the region, but these rates are at historic highs within the country. Pérez Molina occupies the opposite end of the spectrum, advocating the militarization of internal security and harsh mano dura crackdowns as the only viable ways to confront crime in a country with one of the highest rates of homicide in the world. These diametrically opposed examples illustrate that in addition to the different realities of Central American countries, politicians in these countries also offer their people different policy options for improving public security and reforming the justice system.

In order to understand citizens' political attitudes and behaviors toward the law, it is imperative to ground them in their appropriate contexts. The Central American countries might share some fundamental characteristics, but it is important to note the ways in which they differ, and how these differences might make some "escapes" from the security trap more desirable than others. For example, if the police have a long track record of failing to prevent crime or apprehend perpetrators, citizens might not think that further police reform is viable and turn to other mechanisms to protect themselves. These alternate mechanisms can range from supporting military engagement in public security to hiring private security guards. The mechanisms might differ markedly, but their effects are the same—they do not challenge the negative equilibrium that has emerged in state-society relations, and thus they further undermine the rule of law. In order to understand citizens' respect (or disregard) for the rule of law, it is imperative to comprehend the reality in which public attitudes are formed, and in which state-society interactions take place.

Historical Overview of National Political Development

Costa Rica has long been touted as the peaceful oasis of the Central American region. Seligson quips that the extensive emphasis on Costa Rica's exceptionalism, exemplified by descriptions such as "the Switzerland of Central America," might lead some first-time visitors to be "surprised to find a Central American nation, not an alpine one" (Seligson 2006, 450). Costa Rican exceptionalism is frequently traced back to its 1949 decision to abolish its military after the 1948 civil war. This six-week war was brief, but with approximately 4,000 casualties, it was the bloodiest political event in Costa Rican history (Palmer and Molina 2006, 139). In the aftermath of the war, political elites famously abolished the standing army and increased investment in social welfare programs, proclaiming their preference for an army of teachers. Thus, the subsequent 1949 constitution was famous not only for eliminating the military, but also for establishing a social welfare state that prioritized near universal education and health care. A half century later, this investment would pay off. With approximately one-third of the income of advanced industrial democracies, Costa Rica boasts health and education indicators on par with wealthier democracies, even surpassing Switzerland with its proportion of college age students attending an institution of higher education (Seligson 2006, 450).

The 1949 constitution has earned its revered space in Costa Rican history, but Costa Rica's tradition of civilian rule and investment in human capital predates the 1949 constitution. Booth (1998, 41) points out that only 36 percent of the 1824–1905 period was governed under military rule, and this percentage drops to 7 percent in the 1906–1949 period. In 1940, artist Luis Féron Parizot (1901–1998) highlighted the importance of the law in Costa Rican political development in his mural depicting pivotal scenes from Costa Rican history. In the *Salón Dorado* (Golden Room) of the former diplomatic room of the international airport (now part of the Museum of Costa Rican Art),

Féron Parizot portrayed historical milestones, ranging from the arrival of Christopher Columbus to the introduction of coffee cultivation. Featured prominently in this tableau are public officials holding large tablets with the inscriptions of "*Ley*" (law) and "*Déclaration des Droits de L'Homme et du Citoyen*" (Declaration of the Rights of Man and of the Citizen)—images that highlight the importance of the law in the formative years of contemporary Costa Rican democracy. In a thorough review of historical documents ranging from electoral registers to citizen petitions, Palmer and Molina note that:

> By the end of the colonial period, a pattern of legal and institutional mediation of individual and collective conflicts had already been set, and the Costa Rican state reinforced this tendency after independence. Despite the authoritarian nature of presidential succession in certain periods, electoral practices were rarely interrupted during the nineteenth century. (Palmer and Molina 2006, 140)

In addition to highlighting the longevity of elections, Palmer and Molina (2006) also underscore the importance of the law in Costa Rica. Indeed, one of the cornerstones of Costa Rican exceptionalism has been the reliance on the law. Respect for civilian rule and the law it upholds have been historically facilitated by several factors. To begin, under colonial rule Costa Rica's lack of exportable resources and geographic isolation effectively insulated it from the tumultuous politics of its neighbors, a trend that continued after independence in 1821. Isolation continued to be a blessing throughout the nineteenth and early twentieth century, as "the dictatorial rule and foreign invasions that plagued the region had little direct impact on Costa Rica" (Seligson 2006, 453). In particular, Costa Rica is the only Central American country that has never been invaded by the United States.[3]

Domestic factors were also more conducive to civilian government and the rule of law than in other countries. In Costa Rica, few indigenous people survived Spanish colonization, rendering the resultant population more socially homogeneous than elsewhere on the isthmus. Most importantly, the lack of an indigenous labor force meant that the economic system did not depend upon a large pool of exploited laborers, and the military did not evolve to suppress resistance domestically (Booth 1998, 19). In the other Central American countries, military involvement in politics stunted the growth of civilian political institutions. In nineteenth-century Costa Rica, such institutions emerged given the military's irregular participation in politics. This is not to say that Costa Rica was completely immune to the problems of inequality, exploitation, and militarization. Particularly during the coffee export boom of the late nineteenth and early twentieth centuries, the distribution of wealth and land became more unequal in Costa Rica. During this time frame, authoritarian rule did interrupt electoral cycles. As Booth points out, "Costa Rica does not escape Central America's worst social problems, but it experiences them less severely" (1998, 27). These differences in degree, however, have been substantial enough to make civilian governance and the rule of law viable alternatives to the military rule and "rapacious elite culture" of its northern neighbors (Booth 1998, 19). It is easier to rely upon the law to govern and settle disputes when the distances between socioeconomic actors is smaller, and the economy does not depend upon the exploitation of a poor underclass. Despite some challenges, all in all the quality of the rule of law has historically approximated that of advanced industrialized countries.

The other Central American countries have historically lacked this legacy of civilian rule and respect for the rule of law. As a former province of Colombia, Panama was also isolated from the postcolonial fighting of the northern Central American countries, but it experienced extensive foreign intervention due to its international importance as a canal site. The United States facilitated a Panamanian independence movement in 1903 and remained heavily involved in Panamanian affairs long after the canal's completion.[4] Indeed, international influence has long shaped Panamanian politics and society, as its geographic location makes it an ideal transit route for both legal and illegal goods. Even under colonial times, elites built their power base around the control of illicit activities; for example, the slave trade offered numerous opportunities for enrichment and served to stimulate further investments in local real estate and business ventures (Pérez 2000, 150). In the postcolonial period, the economy continued to revolve around the transfer of goods and a consensus emerged within the Panamanian elite on the importance of upholding classic liberal economic ideals to facilitate such activities (Pérez 2000). Merchants became the most powerful economic and political class, and to protect their interests, the commercial elite monopolized control of government and excluded the popular sectors from power. Under this arrangement, the government served not to uphold an impartial rule of law, but rather, as a means of personal enrichment, particularly by protecting one's economic stake in illicit and/or licit commerce. The military later adopted this style of governance and reinforced it through "repression, manipulation of elections, and general corruption including heavy involvement in drug trafficking and other illicit enterprises" (Pérez 2000, 138).

Given the potential for accumulating both wealth and power, the military increased its involvement in governance and trade throughout the mid-twentieth century. The 1968 coup, led by General Omar Torrijos, solidified the military's control over the government apparatus and accompanying illicit trade. After General Torrijos's death in 1981, his successor, General Manuel Noriega, increased the military's role in illicit activities. Pérez notes that "By

1982, Noriega was working with the Medellín Cartel—smuggling drugs, protecting traffickers, guarding cocaine-processing plants in Panama, and laundering money" (2000, 152). Panama's strong international banking center, its use of the US dollar, and its lax foreign exchange regulations also made it an appealing site for money laundering. Given the military's firm grip on government and active participation in illicit activities, Pérez refers to this style of governance as a "mafiacracy" (2000, 138).

Noriega failed to spread this wealth around, and his monopolization of revenue and power caused dissension among commercial and military elites. By the late 1980s, the United States also sought to distance itself from its long time ally, as the end of the Cold War diminished Noriega's value. The situation came to a head when the United States Department of Justice issued a warrant for Noriega's arrest on several charges, including drug trafficking and collaboration with notorious drug lord Pablo Escobar. Once Noriega refused to bargain with the United States and annulled the 1989 presidential elections, the US prepared to remove him by force. The United States invaded Panama on December 20, 1989. It quickly destroyed the Panamanian Defense Forces. Fourteen days later, Noriega surrendered and became the United States' only Prisoner of War at that time.

The US invasion of Panama destroyed the Panamanian army and captured Noriega; however, the problems of corruption and illicit trade proved intractable. In the early 1990s, drug trafficking actually increased in Panama (Sullivan 1997). The abolition of a standing army in 1994 solidified civilian rule, and from a human rights standpoint, some progress was made toward improving the rule of law. Citizens were relatively free from egregious human rights abuses at the hands of the state. Still, such progress continued to occur under the shadow of a vibrant illicit sector, which thrived with the help of corrupt elites (Sullivan 2011).

Guatemala, El Salvador, and Nicaragua experienced far more political violence throughout their histories. The roots of these conflicts were similar—a small, wealthy oligarchy ruled over the impoverished majority. Colonialism had established a class structure marked by extreme inequality, as the Spanish crown granted large tracts of land to early colonists, who relied upon coerced indigenous and mestizo people to extract commodities cheaply for export (Booth 1998, 19). Independence did not alter these socioeconomic structures, and the new political systems frequently wielded repression to preserve the status quo. Since these economies relied upon coerced labor, governance typically depended upon the military. The history of these three countries is marked by popular uprisings against this status quo, as well as ruthless repression of these uprisings, frequently with the assistance of foreign powers like the United States. By the early twentieth century, these uprisings had evolved into widespread revolts, which met with fierce repression. In El Salvador, the repression of the rebellion was "so ferocious that it came to be known simply as *la matanza*" (the killing) (Danner 1993, 26). In 1931 and 1932, the military massacred approximately 30,000 peasants to stamp out dissent (Booth 1998). After eliminating the opposition, the military ruled El Salvador either directly or indirectly until the 1980s. In Nicaragua, the US marines had frequently intervened in politics, but by 1927, they had trouble defeating the nationalist uprising led by Augusto Sandino. After 6 years the US marines bequeathed the struggle to a leader popular in US circles, Anastasio Somoza. Somoza promptly murdered Sandino, and in 1936 overthrew the shaky constitutional order in favor of his own personalistic (and dynastic) dictatorship. The Somoza family ruled Nicaragua with the help of the repressive US-trained National Guard, until overthrown in 1979. In Guatemala, inequality and unrest were exacerbated by an ethnic divide, as the Guatemalan indigenous communities remained ethnically and culturally distinct from the wealthy landino minority (Booth 1998, 19). Cycles of rebellion and repression were interrupted briefly by democratic elections in the 1940s and 1950s; however, democratic governance was interrupted by a US-backed coup in 1954 and the country plunged into civil war until the 1990s.

By the 1970s, Guatemala, El Salvador, and Nicaragua were all engulfed in civil wars. These countries differed tremendously in terms of the outcomes of these wars, however. In Nicaragua, the *Frente Sandinista de Liberación Nacional* (FSLN), or simply the Sandinistas, led a successful popular revolution against the Somoza dynasty. The Sandinistas had little time to savor their victory, however, as the United States retrained the defeated National Guard to fight a counterrevolution against the victorious Sandinistas. The National Guard rechristened itself as the *Contras* and aimed to destabilize the Sandinista government through a series of small-scale (but incredibly violent) attacks throughout the 1980s, predominantly in rural areas. In El Salvador, US aid primarily kept the guerrilla forces, organized under the umbrella of the *Frente Farabundo Martí para la Liberación Nacional* (FMLN), from overthrowing the government. By the late 1980s, the civil war had settled into a stalemate. Guerrillas were also unable to overthrow the government in Guatemala. For almost four decades, guerrilla groups challenged government forces, eventually unifying under the umbrella group *Unidad Revolucionaria Nacional Guatemalteca* (URNG). In addition to the longest conflict, Guatemala also suffered the most atrocious human rights violations during its civil war, and the United Nations considered some massacres in the war to be acts of genocide.

Peace came to Guatemala, El Salvador, and Nicaragua in the 1990s. The end of the Cold War created opportunities for democratic governance, as domestic conflicts were no longer exacerbated by Cold War rivalries and ideological crusades. In 1990, the Sandinistas peacefully turned over power to the opposition after their electoral defeat, leaving the Contras without their raison d'être.[5] Peace accords ended the fighting in El Salvador in 1992, and in Guatemala in 1996. Thus, by the 1990s, these war-torn countries began to install democratic governments under conditions of peace. Little from their histories prepared them for this step. The unequal socioeconomic structures that had historically precipitated political unrest remained untouched for the most part. Despite some notable experiments, by and large these three countries had little experience with civilian governance and the rule of law. Furthermore, the institutions entrusted with upholding the rule of law were unprepared for the task. Under authoritarian rule, courts were deliberately kept weak so that they could not oppose the government. In El Salvador and Guatemala, the police and military were inherently repressive, and had thoroughly alienated their respective citizenries with notorious human rights abuses. Nicaragua did deviate from this trend in important ways, however. While the courts remained weak, the police experienced a complete overhaul under Sandinista rule. After the overthrow of the Somoza dynasty in 1979, the Sandinistas completely abolished the repressive police force. While the Sandinista government generated a great deal of controversy, there is consensus that its new police system was a vast improvement over its notorious predecessor, particularly in the arena of human rights. Article 97 of the 1987 constitution explicitly stated that the police's role would be preventive, not repressive.

Honduran history is also marked by military rule and human rights violations, but on a much smaller scale. As Booth succinctly summarizes, "Honduras, less party-polarized, less integrated into the world economy, and with less concentration of wealth than elsewhere in Central America, also experienced less turmoil in the early twentieth century than its neighbors" (Booth 1998, 20). Labor strikes were frequent during the early twentieth century, but "the Honduran governments felt less inclined to forcibly suppress workers and the companies more willingly made wage concessions" than in other countries (Booth et al. 2010, 160). The Honduran military did not begin to intervene regularly in politics until the 1950s. This decade ushered in land shortages, accompanied by tensions between socioeconomic classes and "increasing peasant mobilization" (Booth et al. 2010, 161). The beginning of the Cold War also increased political polarization by casting long-standing disputes in a new light. For example, the frequent labor unrest on banana plantations was no longer a simple matter of workers protesting for better wages and working conditions, but a problem of a global communist movement seeking to spread its tentacles to Central American countries like Honduras. The United States dramatically increased its military aid to

Honduras during the Cold War, from an annual average of less than half a million US dollars in the 1950s to an annual average of over \$57 million at the end of the 1980s (Booth et al. 2010, 272).

With this new influx of foreign funds and training, the Honduran military grew steadily more powerful throughout the Cold War and began to use this power to intervene in politics. The 1956 army coup signaled this change toward the greater militarization of politics. While the military intensified its engagement in politics throughout the 1960s and 1970s, it did so more benignly than in Guatemala, El Salvador, and Nicaragua, acting "more as an arbiter between other political groups than as an agent of a ruling class" (Booth et al. 2010, 162). To address increasing unrest and peasant mobilization, the military did rely on repression, but also employed populist measures to reduce poverty, such as agrarian reform. The press retained some of its freedoms, and human rights violations never reached the same level of atrocity as in Guatemala, El Salvador, and Nicaragua. By 1983, however, this benign period of military rule changed dramatically. This year marked the inception of death squads to target political opponents; political disappearances and murders rose precipitously, as did the numbers of the comparatively small guerrilla forces. Despite this rise in repression and resistance, Honduras avoided the civil wars that had plagued its neighbors. As Booth, Wade, and Walker argue, "the state never sufficiently repressed legitimate mass mobilization to the point of triggering armed resistance as a last resort, as had been true in Nicaragua, El Salvador, or Guatemala" (2010, 167). Rather than unleash civil war, the military chose to turn over power to civilians, but still retained the power to repress dissent and influence political elites. As the Cold War ended, military support from the United States dwindled, and the Honduran military increasingly entrusted political matters to civilians and reduced repression. Starting in 1986, presidential elections resulted in the peaceful transfer of power from one civilian government to the next. In 1990, the new commander of the military reduced and punished abuses of power and infringements on human rights, and subsequently reconciled the military with opposition forces (Booth et al. 2010, 170). By 1996, constitutional reforms solidified civilian control over the military, bolstering Honduras's commitment to democracy.

As the Cold War ended, Costa Rica was no longer the exception to regional trends; the remaining Central American countries all joined the global democratization movement. This push toward democratization marched hand in hand with efforts to promote the rule of law. However, as this historical overview highlights, in the wake of the Cold War only Costa Rica had a respectable track record in terms of civilian governance and the rule of law. The other countries faced stiff challenges as they joined the third wave of democratization. However, given the centrality of the rule of law to both democracy and economic development, reformers throughout the 1990s aimed to change this status quo, promoting the rule of law as a panacea to the political and economic problems of the region (Carothers 2006).[6]

The Rule of Law and Justice Institutions: Reform after the Cold War

Technically, interest in justice reform actually predates the widespread democratization of the Central American region. Lip service was given to reform as early as the 1960s, as domestic leaders and the international community began to promote the rule of law (Carothers 2006). The wave of military coups in the 1970s interrupted these efforts, as authoritarian governments either ignored the rule of law completely, or twisted it to legitimize their regimes. By the 1980s, the third wave of democratization sparked a renewed interest in rule of law promotion, and foreign aid began to trickle into the region for justice reform (Carothers 2006).

Reformers quickly noted that rule of law promotion had several facets. Democratization underscored the importance of revising constitutions and legal codes, or writing new ones altogether. Once the law itself was addressed, institutional reform became the next priority. Institutions like the courts and police required extensive updates to both their infrastructures as well as procedures. In many cases, the police faced the additional challenges of demilitarization and depoliticization (Call 2003; Chinchilla 2003). Even in Costa Rica, there were clear efforts to reform justice institutions (Chinchilla 2003). Once reformers tackled legal codes and institutions, it was imperative to train judges, lawyers, police detectives, and other legal professionals to uphold these new features (Carothers 2006). Citizens also needed to be socialized into these norms, in order to view the law and justice institutions as mechanisms for resolving conflict and settling disputes (Belton 2005; Carothers 2003). This would be a particularly difficult challenge in the postconflict countries, where the human rights abuses of the past had given citizens reason to fear their governments.

Reforming Constitutions and Legal Codes

To promote democracy, constitutions and legal codes required extensive overhaul to ensure that the law itself was impartial, and could equitably govern relationships among citizens, and between citizens and their governments. Constitutions and legal codes also needed to include mechanisms to enhance horizontal accountability in order to check the power of government officials. To this end, constitutional reform featured prominently during democratic transitions throughout Latin America, with reforms addressing a wide array of issues, ranging from indigenous rights to presidential term limits. While the most recent wave of reforms was largely inspired by democratization trends, Schor (2005) reminds us that constitutional reform has a long history in Latin America. From the time of independence, elites have historically regarded constitutions as quite malleable. Elites have a long tradition of viewing constitutions as a means for entrenching their own power, rather than formal mechanisms delineating the political rules of the game. Indeed, some have regarded constitutional reform as a national pastime in the region.

In many cases, democratization increased the popularity of constitutional reform. As Table 2.1 indicates, the 1980s ushered in new constitutions in Guatemala, El Salvador, Honduras, and Nicaragua. In Honduras and El Salvador, these constitutions were subject to rigorous revision, a trend continuing to the present day. Constitutional reform was more limited in Nicaragua, picking up momentum in the mid-2000s. Constitutional revision

TABLE 2.1 Constitutional Reform in Central America

Country	Year of current constitution	Years of constitutional revisions
Guatemala	1985	1993
El Salvador	1983	1991, 1992, 1993, 1994, 1996, 1999, 2000, 2003, 2009
Honduras	1982	1982, 1984, 1985, 1986, 1987, 1988, 1989, 1990, 1991, 1993, 1994, 1995, 1996, 1997, 1998, 1999, 2000, 2001, 2002, 2003, 2004, 2005, 2006
Nicaragua	1987	1995, 2000, 2005, 2007
Costa Rica	1949	1954, 1956, 1957, 1958, 1959, 1961, 1963, 1965, 1968, 1969, 1971, 1975, 1977, 1981, 1982, 1984, 1987, 1989, 1993, 1994, 1995, 1996, 1997, 1999, 2000, 2001, 2002, 2003
Panama	1972	1978, 1983, 1993, 1994, 2004

Source: Political Database of the Americas, Georgetown University. This database contains the text of the constitutions for all members of the Organization of American States, and notes the years of constitutional amendments and revisions: http://pdba.georgetown.edu/Constitutions/constudies.html.

was rarer in Guatemala, where the constitution was revised only once in 1993, and additional provisions failed to pass a popular referendum in 1999. In Panama, the 1972 constitution was subject to major revisions even before the advent of democracy in the early 1990s and was modified three times under democratic governance. With the longest continuous constitutional history, Costa Rica also features the largest number of reforms, with 28 revisions from 1949 to the present, and more changes potentially pending.

Some constitutional reforms introduced major changes to countries' political systems, and consequently promoted the rule of law. Panama's 1994 constitutional reforms aimed to ensure that governance would be a strictly civilian affair, whereby politics would follow legally inscribed norms rather than military might. To this end, the 1994 constitutional reform abolished the standing armed forces under Article 305, allowing only for the temporary formation of special defense units in times of urgency. The 1991 and 1992 constitutional reforms of El Salvador focused extensively on the justice system, detailing major reorganizations of the judiciary, military tribunals, and the police, in addition to creating the new office of the Human Rights Ombudsman.[7] Together with the 1992 Peace Accords, El Salvador's constitutional reforms aimed to confront a legacy of human rights abuses by dismantling the prior repressive security apparatus and creating a new national police force, led by civilians (Call 2003).

In some cases, constitutional reforms ultimately weakened the rule of law instead of strengthening it, however. For example, the 2000 reforms in Nicaragua resulted when two long-time enemies and former presidents, Daniel Ortega (1985–1990) of the FSLN and Arnoldo Alemán (1997–2002) of the Liberal Constitutionalist Party (PLC), agreed on a series of measures to parcel out power to their respective political parties. This alliance was called *El Pacto* (the Pact). Ortega and Alemán have described El Pacto as a bipartisan effort designed to promote political stability through compromise. Critics have countered that many of these compromises are self-serving, involving agreements on issues such as shielding the presidency from prosecution at a time when both former presidents faced legal troubles. For example, amendments to Article 130 of the constitution granted the president of Nicaragua immunity from arrest or prosecution, which can be revoked only by a two-thirds vote in the National Assembly (Pallais 2009, 3). Additional amendments further strengthened the immunity of public officials, rendering it more difficult for other branches of government to promote horizontal accountability by checking the power of the executive branch and prosecuting abuses of power. For example, amendments to Article 133 gave outgoing presidents and vice-presidents immediate membership to the legislature, the National Assembly, a change that "essentially allows ex-presidents to remain immune from prosecution for crimes committed during their administration for an additional five years, often long enough to exceed the statute of limitations for those crimes" (Pallais 2009, 3).

Opponents of El Pacto tried to block constitutional changes by appealing to the Central American Court of Justice (CCJ), which ruled that many constitutional revisions violated the Nicaraguan Constitution and regional treaties. In 2002, President Bolaños (2002–2007) tried to repeal some of these constitutional changes, such as the amnesty law for ex-presidents. As part of his anticorruption campaign, Bolaños convinced the National Assembly to strip Alemán of his immunity and charge him with money laundering and embezzlement. Alemán was convicted of these charges in 2004 and sentenced to a 20-year jail term; however, a newly reformed (and consequently very supportive) Nicaraguan Supreme Court overturned his conviction in 2009 (Booth et al. 2010). Joining forces against Bolaños, Ortega and Alemán convinced the National Assembly to pass another series of constitutional reforms, this time designed to undermine the authority of the president.

The confrontation between President Bolaños and his rivals resulted in a highly charged deadlock. Responding to Bolaños's call, the OAS intervened, dispatching a mission and ultimately ruling against the constitutional reforms. In 2005, the OAS issued a resolution declaring that the institutional changes driven by El Pacto were detrimental to building democracy and the rule of law. In resolution 892, the OAS asserted that:

> the escalation of the institutional and political crisis in Nicaragua threatens the country's democratic governance, the legitimate exercise of power, and the rule of law, with serious social and economic consequences, both now and in the future, for the people of Nicaragua . . . the critical developments in Nicaragua severely jeopardize the separation of powers and the independence of the branches of government, which are essential elements of representative democracy. (OAS 2005, resolution 892)

The OAS ultimately called on all parties to cease and desist their efforts to alter the constitution and its institutional configurations and use the mechanisms of the OAS to resolve the political crisis that undermined governance in the country. Once again, backed by the newly reformed (and very supportive) Nicaraguan Supreme Court of Justice, Ortega and Alemán ignored such calls. Ortega went on to win the presidency in the 2006 elections.

Upon assuming the presidency, Ortega launched a series of new programs to provide social services and address the endemic poverty of the country. He also began to reexamine the constitutional measures barring him from a second presidential term. The key to the success of such endeavors was control over the judiciary. In September of 2010, Ortega decreed a public holiday. While the country enjoyed a vacation, he reprinted the constitution that included a law "that was left dead 20 years ago" (Rogers 2010). The resurrected law permitted judges, electoral magistrates, and other officials to stay in office beyond their term limits until the appointment of new officials. Legal analysts criticizing the measure argued "that the law was a 'transitory' provision in the 1987 Constitution and expired more than two decades ago. That's why it wasn't included in the current Constitution, which was printed after the reforms of 1995" (Rogers 2010). However, reinstating this law allowed Ortega to take advantage of the legislative deadlock that had delayed new judicial appointments and keep his own supporters in office.

These maneuvers proved successful for Ortega. Despite a constitutional ban on presidential election, in March of 2011 Ortega inscribed his candidacy for the 2011 presidential elections. Support from the judiciary made this possible, as a ruling by a group of loyal judges in 2009 determined that "Article 147 of the Constitution is 'inapplicable' because it violates Ortega's right to equal treatment under the law" (Rogers 2011). The Supreme Court of Justice, packed with Ortega's supporters, upheld the ruling in 2010. Some of the magistrates, such as Rafael Solís, are Ortega supporters serving in the Supreme Court of Justice even though their terms have expired.

This example from Nicaragua illustrates the other side of constitutional reform. In some cases constitutional reform can succeed in transforming a biased and inefficient justice system to promote the rule of law. Alternatively, elites can use constitutional reform as a means to undermine the rule of law in order to consolidate power or misappropriate funds for personal use. The example from Nicaragua is not an isolated one. The 2009 military intervention in Honduras was precipitated by a dispute over the constitution and bans on presidential reelection. In cases where the constitution itself is not altered, political actors can still find ways to undermine the spirit of the law. In Guatemala, President Álvaro Colom and his wife, Sandra Torres, have employed creative techniques to circumvent the constitutional law on presidential succession. The Guatemalan constitution bans presidential reelection, along with prohibiting the president's close relatives for running for president too. In March of 2011, Colom and Torres announced that they would seek a divorce so that their marriage would not keep Torres from running for president to succeed Colom. A court injunction in April 2011 put the couple's divorce plans on hold, as several opposition groups have mounted legal challenges to the divorce proceedings, arguing that such moves are unconstitutional (BBC 2011a).

Enjoying a much lower profile are reforms that seek to revise legal codes. Rather than overhaul the constitution or reorganize the political system, reforms targeting legal codes aim to introduce transparency and efficiency into legal proceedings. The need for improved transparency and efficiency are tied to the reliance on code law. The Central American justice systems are based upon civil or code law, an inheritance from Spanish colonialism. Under code law, the legislature compiles a body of laws, or legal codes, and the courts apply these laws in a systematic fashion. Courts apply the law to individual cases, but these decisions do not set legal precedent as in the common law systems of Britain and the United States. Some argue that this inability to set precedent can weaken the courts' power. For example, Correa notes, "If the law in the codes is clear, operative, just, effective, and capable of regulating almost any relevant case, then the judges' role is reduced to a largely mechanical one" (Correa 1999, 274n9).

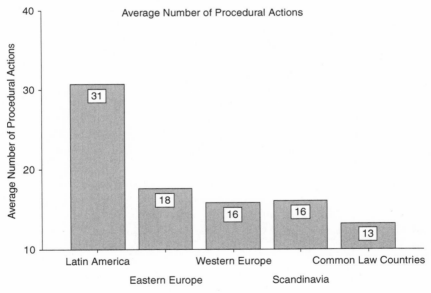

FIGURE 2.1 Average Number of Procedural Actions in Global Perspective
Notes Common law counries include: Australia, Canada, United Kingdom, and the United States. The only Latin American country not included was Nicaragua. The remaining regions included: Eastern Europe (Czech Republic, Hungary, Poland, Romania, Russia); Western Europe (Austria, France, Germany, Italy, the Netherlands, Switzerland); Scandinavia (Denmark, Finland, Norway, Sweden).
For a more thorough discussion of the Lex Mundi study, see Djankov et al. (2001) and Malone (2004).

Civil law countries also tend to regulate court proceedings more heavily than their common law counterparts (Djankov, La Porta, Lopez-de-Silanes, and Shleifer 2001). Extensive regulation reduces the discretionary power of members of the judicial branch, as it specifies more stringently how the judiciary should adjudicate disputes. Such regulations can also create many delays. In a global study of court procedures, Djankov et al. (2001) compare the number of procedures regulating two civil disputes: the eviction of a residential tenant for failure to pay rent and the collection of a returned check. As Figure 2.1 points out, for this type of dispute, Latin American countries on average have far more procedural requirements than in other global regions. Extensive regulation leads to delayed justice. In Djankov et al.'s study, in the Latin American countries it took 241 days to resolve these two disputes on average, compared to 145 days in the common law countries.

While civil law countries tend to be more heavily regulated than common law systems, in Central America there is also a strong tradition of relying on written proceedings rather than oral ones. Written measures are more time-consuming, which increases the average duration of both civil and criminal proceedings. Justice moves slowly due to the written formalities of filing motions, gathering evidence, and complying with legal justifications for complaints and statutory regulations. In criminal cases, delayed justice has severe ramifications, as the amount of time some defendants spend in pretrial detention can even exceed the maximum sentence allotted for the crimes of which they are accused. According to the 2010 US State Department's *Human Rights Reports*, this problem of excessive pretrial detention was particularly acute in El Salvador, Honduras, and Panama (see Table 2.2). The prevalence of written forms of communication can create

TABLE 2.2 Prisoners Awaiting Trial in Central America

Country	Percentage unsentenced prison population (%)
Guatemala	50
El Salvador	34
Honduras	51
Nicaragua	17
Costa Rica	26
Panama	63

Sources: Data are from the 2010 US Department of State *Human Rights Reports*, with the exception of Nicaragua. Nicaraguan data are based upon 2004 estimates in Duce et al. (2010).

additional problems, such as police misconduct. If the police are frequently ill-trained in investigative techniques and are encouraged to seek written documentation of suspects' guilt, incentives arise to extract written confessions from suspects, frequently engaging in human rights violations to do so (Correa 1999; Rodley 1999). Such glaring problems made reform of the penal codes a priority throughout the region at the end of the twentieth and beginning of the twenty-first centuries (Hammergren 2007). In many cases the goals of penal reform were to streamline and modernize an outdated system that was prone to corruption. However, it is important to remember that reform is always a political process, and political actors use reforms as a means to serve their own interests. For example in El Salvador, the 1999 reforms of the criminal code created new categories of crime and broadened police and prosecutorial powers (Amaya 2006, 145).

To address the inefficiencies and injustices caused by an overreliance on written proceedings, all the Central American countries have implemented reforms introducing oral proceedings, replacing the inquisitorial model with adversarial or mixed models (Chinchilla 2003; Espinoza 2004). Domestic civil society has been an active participant in such reforms, frequently aided by foreign governments, international organizations, and foreign civil society associations. For example, the United States Agency for International Development (USAID) assisted with the transition to oral proceedings in Nicaragua and Honduras in 2002, and the American Bar Association has cooperated with civil society groups in Panama to adjust to oral proceedings. Throughout the 1990s and 2000s, oral proceedings began to replace written ones, but given the extensive nature of such reforms, the success of implementation has been uneven.

In addition to reforming constitutions and legal codes, reformers have also targeted the institutions and actors entrusted with upholding the law. Constitutions and legal codes establish a foundation for the rule of law, but the ultimate outcomes of this foundation depend heavily upon institutions and actors. Thus, changes in constitutions and legal codes have been accompanied by a variety of measures designed to improve the functioning of institutions like the courts and police, as well as train and socialize actors such as judges and lawyers.

Reforming Institutions

When discussing the rule of law, attention gravitates to two key institutions, the courts and police. More recently, a third institution has been increasing in prominence—the human rights ombudsmen. Within these institutions, a wide array of actors engages in various stages of the justice process, including inter alia: police officers, detectives, defense lawyers, prosecutors, judges, legal aides, and judicial councils.[8] Within the justice system, the courts and the police feature most prominently. Human rights ombudsmen are less visible, but are increasingly important as they provide alternate venues for people to voice grievances on a variety of matters, including problems with obtaining justice. In a recent study documenting grievances addressed to ombudsmen, Pegram (2008, 6–7) finds that complaints pertaining to justice delays, due process, access to justice, and crime were at the top of the list.

It is important to note that these institutional actors represent distinct stages of the justice process. For example, the police are most visible in the stage of prevention, apprehension, and investigation. These "street-level bureaucrats" are the actors with whom citizens are likely to have the most contact. The lower courts are naturally the cornerstone of a different stage of the justice process—detention, trial, and appeals. High courts serve an additional function, as they are responsible for applying the law to government officials. The Central American high courts have the potential to play an important role in promoting horizontal accountability by checking official malfeasance such as corruption or abuse of power. Finally, the human rights ombudsmen are involved at various stages of the justice system, as they respond to citizens' grievances.

The judiciary tends to take center stage in many rule of law promotion efforts. Reformers have focused on improving three distinct yet interrelated components of the judicial process: independence, efficiency, and equality.[9] Independence refers to the ability of the judiciary to act without facing constraints or pressure from other actors. Independence is crucial for promoting horizontal accountability; if the judiciary is not independent, it is typically unable to sanction the executive or members of the legislature for malfeasance. In contrast, efficiency refers to the basic functioning of the court system, such as the length of trials, ability to solve disputes, and administrative organization. Finally, equality refers to the ability to make justice accessible and distribute it fairly to all citizens. That is, can all citizens access the courts? Are interpreters provided for those speaking indigenous languages? Does socioeconomic status influence both access to justice and court outcomes?

Given the political nature of the reform process, reformers typically find it slightly easier to tackle problems of efficiency first. Reforms targeting efficiency tend to be mechanistic in nature, concentrating on the basic administration of justice. Such reforms focus on the lack of resources of the judicial branch and seek to remedy this through "the selective addition of a few missing elements" (Hammergren 2002, 8). To address efficiency problems, international donors have purchased hardware (computers, case management systems, tools for evaluating evidence, etc.); instituted common juridical training programs; and developed new administrative systems (USAID 2002).

Alternatively, some reforms have sought to alleviate the workload of an over-burdened judiciary by creating alternative dispute resolution (ADR) mechanisms. Given the recognition that the judiciary is presently ill-equipped to manage increases in civil litigation and criminal prosecutions, some countries have sought to reduce courts' caseloads by relegating some civil disputes to ADR arenas. For example, Costa Rica has pursued ADR mechanisms through constitutional provisions, which encourage less costly means of settling disputes, such as arbitration and out-of-court settlements (Correa 1999).

Tackling equality is arguably a more difficult task, as inequality in the legal process reflects long-standing patterns of socioeconomic inequality within each country. Transforming the judiciary into a vehicle for challenging such inequality, instead of a crucible for reinforcing it, is no easy task. Prillaman (2000, 18) notes that unequal access to justice is tightly intertwined to "persistent social, ethnic, linguistic, and cultural cleavages that serve as barriers to the poor or socially marginal," as well as "more tangible factors such as geographic remoteness." In addition, extensive bureaucratic requirements create procedural biases against citizens of lower socioeconomic status, as they do not typically have access to legal services, language interpretation, and basic information on the law (disseminated in terms the uneducated can understand). Lengthy bureaucratic procedures also open the doors to corruption, as the wealthy frequently seek to bypass time-consuming delays with their bank accounts. Reforms have tried to challenge this unequal status quo, with measures ranging from providing legal counsel to the poor to launching anticorruption campaigns to reduce the prevalence of bribery. Despite notable efforts, entrenched inequality in the justice system has proven difficult to eradicate.

Judicial independence is the most politically sensitive type of reform. A wide array of actors have long bemoaned the lack of independence in Central American judiciaries, and dismissed both judges and courts as notoriously ineffective agents of horizontal accountability (Dodson and Jackson 2001). Independence is widely recognized as an essential component of horizontal accountability, and Central American judiciaries are notoriously ill-equipped to fulfill this duty, yet most reforms have not seriously challenged this subpar status quo. The issue of independence is politically sensitive, as it typically requires the executive and legislative branches of government to empower the judiciary to keep them in check (Finkel 2008). Not surprisingly, independence is consequently difficult to achieve. To be sure, the post–Cold War era was punctuated by provisions designed to enhance the independence of the judiciary. For example, in El Salvador, Panama, and Costa Rica, constitutional provisions created *Consejos de Magistratura* (Magistrate Councils), which aimed to improve the independence and professionalism of the judiciary. These councils were charged with deciding superior judicial appointments, disciplining members of the judicial branch, preparing judicial budgets, supervising juridical education, and overseeing court administration (Correa 1999). Despite such efforts, the judiciary tends to be swayed by partisanship and is frequently unable to check the power of the other branches of government, particularly in cases of corruption.

In addition to reforming the judiciary, police systems also required extensive overhaul. Bailey and Dammert (2006) provide a thorough overview of several different types of police reform, ranging from the demilitarization of police forces (e.g., Colombia, Chile, and El Salvador) to the formation of business-oriented nongovernmental organizations to promote police reform (e.g., São Paulo). Their comprehensive study makes clear that the nature and scope of police reforms vary a great deal, but generally speaking, reformers have recognized the need to address the same three dimensions: independence, efficiency, and equality. Reformers have recognized that it is imperative to create an independent police force under civilian leadership and divorced from partisanship or the power of individual leaders (Candina 2006). Particularly in Guatemala, El Salvador, and Honduras, the poor human rights records of previous dictatorships have tainted police forces, rendering citizens less likely to turn to the police to address problems under democratic governance. An independent police force is needed to convince such skeptical citizens that the police will enforce the law, not special interests.

El Salvador provides one of the clearest examples of reforms that aimed to create an independent police force. Historically, security forces had served the interests of the upper classes and landed oligarchy, evolving from the forces that kept order on coffee plantations (Cruz 2006). Rather than existing to protect the life and property of the citizenry as a whole, security forces served as "an instrument to discipline, dominate, and control the population and, especially, to contain societal conflict" (Amaya 2006, 132). The 1992 Peace Accords sought to make a break from this past by demilitarizing and depoliticizing the police, and placing police forces squarely under civilian control. This new police force, the National Civilian Police (PNC), was entrusted with upholding internal security, and the Peace Accords aimed to restrict the military to their barracks to wait for external threats. The PNC was designed for civilian leadership, and civilians (with no prior combat experience) were to comprise 60 percent of personnel. The remaining 40 percent were to be comprised equally of previous government and guerrilla forces (Call 2003). Implementation of the peace accords hit several snags, mainly due to the political interests of the ruling party and opposition. Cruz notes that political elites took advantage of the escalating rates of violent crime during the transition to democracy "to resist changes in the public-security system, and this posed a major obstacle to creating a more professional and transparent police force" (Cruz 2006, 154). The 2002 National Defense Law illustrated the ability of elites to resist change, as it reversed the trends of demilitarization of internal security ushered in by the Peace Accords. The 2002 National Defense Law mixed domestic and external security, creating a space for the military to return to the streets and engage in internal security (Amaya 2006). In the name of fighting crime, elites succeeded in maneuvering around the Peace Accords and grafting former militarized structures onto the new democratic police force; however, there is little evidence that this militarization was successful in combating crime. Many observers argued that the manipulation of police reform ultimately subordinated it to political interests, thus weakening "its capacity to fulfill its duties" (Cruz 2006, 158).

Despite this setback, overall police reform in El Salvador is considered to be one of the more successful cases in Central America. Police reform might not uphold the promise of the Peace Accords, but it has created a new civilian police force (despite some authoritarian artifacts) that is capable of curbing human rights abuses perpetrated by paramilitary groups, such as the Sombra Negra (Dark Shadow) (Cruz 2006, 165). Still, El Salvador illustrates the problems of creating an independent civilian police force. Unfortunately over the past 20 years, in many countries the police's track record has made many citizens doubt its independence. In some cases, police forces remain tied to a militarized organizational structure, often acting at the discretion of the ruling party. In other cases the armed forces and the police work together on internal security patrols, blurring the line between military and civilian roles. More recently, organized crime has compromised the independence of police forces, using bribes and intimidation to ensure that police action is conducive to their interests.

In addition to problems of independence, critics charge that the police frequently do not enforce the law equally, and sometimes act as "border guards" shielding the middle and upper classes of society from the lower classes. Chevigny (1999) argues that there is a "shoot first, ask questions later" mentality among police officers in the region that has led to the arbitrary use of excessive and deadly violence, particularly in poor neighborhoods. In many cases police do not view themselves as part of the communities they patrol and are trained to subdue citizens rather than protect them. Such trends are reinforced by insufficient resources. Under democracy, police have faced "uncertain funding, poor coordination, and growing demands from both government and citizens" (Ungar 2002, 63). Given limitations in crime prevention and investigation, police routinely rely upon blunt force to deter infractions against the law and devote less attention to other functions, such as prevention patrol and investigation. Furthermore, police force is yielded almost exclusively against the lower classes. Such misconduct is reinforced by the courts, which decline to prosecute misuses of power and even ignore evidence of police misbehavior when pursuing convictions against defendants (Ungar 2002, 84).

Efficiency is also a critical problem, as in most cases, police lack training in investigation and prevention, and consequently have been unable to prevent the occurrence of crime and/or apprehend the correct suspects (Chevigny 1999; Ungar 2002). Despite reform efforts, the police remain underfunded and lacking in the basic requisite materials to do their jobs. The impact of scant resources manifests itself in different ways. Low salaries frequently lead police to engage in corruption to supplement their income; a lack of basic forensics equipment can lead police to overstep the law and use force to extract confessions. While independence, equality, and efficiency are separate dimensions, they overlap in mutually reinforcing ways.

In addition to the courts and the police, another actor began to engage in the justice system throughout the 1990s—the *Defensoría del Pueblo* (literally the Defender of the People), or the human rights ombudsmen. Table 2.3 lists the exact names and founding years of the Central American human rights ombudsmen. These national human rights ombudsmen agencies are designed to help protect constitutional guarantees on human rights. These agencies investigate rights abuses, address citizens' complaints, initiate legal proceedings, and formulate policy (Ungar 2002, 36). Defensorías have the

TABLE 2.3 Human Rights Ombudsmen in Central America

Country	Official name of office	Year created	Official website
Guatemala	Procuraduría de Derechos Humanos	1985	www.pdh.org.gt/
El Salvador	Procuraduría para la Defensa de los Derechos Humanos	1992	www.pddh.gob.sv/index.php
Honduras	Comisionado Nacional de los Derechos Humanos	1994	www.conadeh.hn/Joomla/
Nicaragua	Procuraduría para la Defensa de los Derechos Humanos	1995	www.procuraduriaddhh.gob.ni/nosotros.asp
Costa Rica	Defensoría de los Habitantes*	1993	www.dhr.go.cr/
Panama	Defensoría del Pueblo	1997	www.defensoriadelpueblo.gob.pa/

* The Procuraduría de Derechos Humanos was a precursor to the Defensoría, created in 1982 as an organ of the Procuraduría General de la República.

potential to become viable mechanisms by which citizens can challenge unequal applications of the law. As Ungar notes:

> Either on its own initiative or on behalf of an aggrieved individual, the Defensoría . . . investigates abuses by the police, prisons, and judiciary. When denouncing specific violations and advocating prosecution, it has at its disposal the range of legal processes: habeas corpus, amparo (the general recourse against illegal state actions), and in some cases, challenges to the laws' unconstitutionality or enforcement mechanisms. (Ungar 2002, 38)

Initial evidence indicates that these agencies enjoy a substantial amount of public legitimacy and could provide a valuable resource, particularly for the poor, to address unequal applications of justice. To date, their ability to fulfill this potential is mixed, however. In Costa Rica, the *Defensoría de los Habitantes* is very active in investigating citizens' recriminations and plays a valuable role in ensuring that state action conforms to the law. In cases such as Guatemala and El Salvador, however, the high hopes of the early 1990s have not been realized, and the human rights ombudsmen have not been able to fulfill their functions as a check on state power, nor ensure that citizens have access to justice and respect for their rights as prescribed by law (Dodson and Jackson 2004).

Track Record of Reform

All in all, considerable domestic and international resources have been invested in rule of law reform. The governments of Central America have aimed to increase funding to the justice system. For example, all of these countries have legal provisions reserving percentages of the national budget for the judicial branch (Correa 1999; Justice Studies Center of the Americas 2008–2009). This measure aims to ensure that the judiciary has the monetary resources it needs to administer justice effectively, while also isolating the institution from politicization of the other branches of government. Still, it is not uncommon for actual allocations to the judiciary to fall short of these constitutional targets (Justice Studies Center of the Americas 2006–2007). Table 2.4 lists the per capita budget of the judicial branch in each country from 2000 through 2006. Overall, domestic funding for the justice system has increased during this time frame, although there are clear cross-national differences. Costa Rican spending per capita far dwarfs spending in the other nations; this is not surprising considering it is the wealthiest nation in the region. Perhaps more interesting are comparisons between countries with similar levels of economic growth. For example, spending per capita

TABLE 2.4 Domestic Funding of the Judicial Branch, per capita (in US dollars)

Country	2000	2001	2002	2003	2004	2005	2006
Guatemala	5.7	5.1	4.3	6.6	6.3	6.4	6.9
El Salvador	16.4	16.8	17.3	16.9	18.2	20.1	23.8
Honduras	n/a	n/a	4.9	5.3	6.2	7.6	8.1
Nicaragua	n/a	n/a	n/a	n/a	5.8	7.3	8.4
Costa Rica	31.2	35.7	39.1	45.5	42.0	44.5	45.9
Panama	13.4	13.4	13.2	13.1	13.4	12.6	14.0

Sources: Funding of the judicial branch is based upon country reports in the Report on Judicial Systems in the Americas, Third Edition (Justice Studies Center of the Americas 2006–2007).

in El Salvador is at least three times that of Guatemala, despite the fact that levels of GDP per capita are comparable.

International entities have also actively promoted justice reform. For example, the World Bank, United Nations, Organization of American States, US Agency for International Development, and the Inter-American Development Bank have all engaged in justice reform. In US foreign policy, rule of law reform features quite prominently given its integral role in democracy promotion and economic development. Under USAID, the US government invested approximately $30 million in rule of law reform in Central American countries from 1995 through 2005; during this same time frame, the Inter-American Development Bank invested more than $165 million, and the World Bank over $75 million (Malone 2010b). In 2008, the United States announced that it would provide more targeted funding under the Mérida Initiative, pledging $1.5 billion to Mexico, Central America, Haiti, and the Dominican Republic for counter narcotics and border security measures, as well as institution building.[10] The international community has considered rule of law reform to be a crucial part of the front line defense against international crime, particularly the trafficking in drugs, people, and weapons.

Despite the resources and attention justice reform has garnered from a variety of actors, the track record of reform has been mixed. There are several reasons why rule of law promotion has encountered problems. Sarles (2001) underscores the failure of foreign governments, international organizations, domestic governments and civil society groups to coordinate reform efforts. The multitude of actors, and ambitious scope of reforms, have meant that rule of law promotion efforts have sometimes been diluted, uncoordinated, and occasionally in conflict with the agendas of other actors (Dakolias 2001). Other critics argue that success remains elusive due to the practice of reforming just one institution at a time, instead of pursuing comprehensive or holistic reforms (Nagle 2009; Prillaman 2000). Additional criticism has emerged surrounding the emphasis of reforms, as well as their specific implementation. One of the most prominent experts on rule of law reform, Linn Hammergren, argues that there has been an "excessive emphasis" on the introduction of oral trials, which can lead to the neglect of other crucial areas of reform, such as prison reform (2007). Nagle (2009) critiques the whole scale replacement of code law with the adversarial model of common law systems, particularly since foreign reformers "often fail to acknowledge fallibility in the systems they are transplanting, and they forget to communicate to reform recipients that the institutions being modeled are also deficient and in a constant state of evolution toward better goals" (2009, 94). International advocacy has been a lightning rod for critics, as it raises the question of whether the reforms are designed to meet the needs of Central American countries themselves, or promote the agendas of the international community or foreign governments. For example, Mendéz points out that the international community has tended to prioritize reforms that target "fighting crimes of

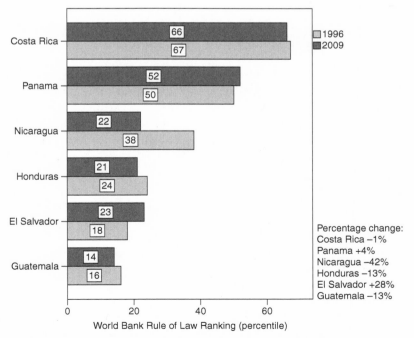

FIGURE 2.2 World Bank Rule of Law Rankings (1996 and 2009)

international interest and in expeditious resolution of investment disputes" (1999, 224). Finally, there is concern that reformers have not adequately recognized that rule of law promotion requires extensive cultural change as well (Belton 2005).

The World Bank's Rule of Law Rankings (a component of the widely used Governance Indicators) provide insight into the track record of reform in each Central American country over time.[11] Experts like Hammergren (2007) note the many problems inherent in measuring the quality of justice systems, advising that such rankings must be interpreted cautiously. Still, the World Bank rankings have the advantage of relying upon numerous sources in each country for each annual score, and do provide a valuable overview of overall trends in the rule of law (Kaufmann, Kraay, and Mastruzzi 2009).

Figure 2.2 depicts each country's world ranking in percentiles in 1996 and 2009. It is clear that the Costa Rican system performs far better than its regional counterparts, earning a spot in the top half of world rankings. Costa Rica's ranking in 2009 dipped by a rate of only 1 percent from that of 1996, but this comparison masks some problems in the early 2000s. As Figure 2.3 indicates, from 2003 through 2008 the quality of the rule of law deteriorated

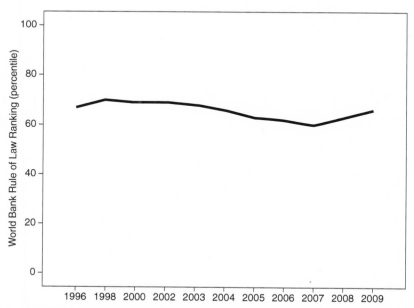

FIGURE 2.3 World Bank Rule of Law Rankings in Costa Rica (1996–2009)
Note: Prior to 2002, the World Bank compiled Governance Indicators only every two years.

slightly yet steadily before rebounding in 2009. Still, despite these fluctuations, the rule of law in Costa Rica far surpasses that of the other Central American countries.

The rule of law in Panama improved only slightly from 1996 to 2009, but still falls close on Costa Rica's heels, ranking in the middle of the global sample. Its performance has remained steady from the mid-1990s to the present, and is well above the remaining countries. Of these latter poor performing countries, only El Salvador has witnessed an improvement over the past two decades, registering a ranking in 2009 that was 28 percent higher than that of 1996. In the remaining countries, rule of law rankings deteriorated during the era of democratization instead of improving. In Guatemala and Honduras, the quality of the rule of law declined by a rate of 13 percent from 1996 through 2009, rendering their 2009 rankings the lowest in Central America. Nicaragua witnessed an even sharper deterioration, dropping at a rate of 42 percent during this same time period largely due to corruption and the manipulation of the law to facilitate the monopolization of power. Corruption has long been an endemic problem in the region, and remains acute in most countries. As Figure 2.4 indicates, Nicaragua and Honduras rank in the top third of corrupt countries in the world.[12]

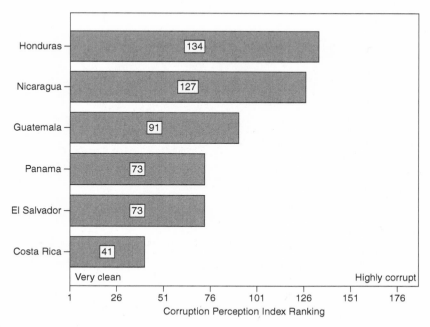

FIGURE 2.4 Transparency International Corruption Perception Index (CPI) Rankings 2010
Source: Transparency International (2010)

Despite so much effort, why have reforms languished in some cases? Some reforms stalled because they were not accompanied by other complimentary changes. In Guatemala, for example, the Peace Accords stipulated that justice reform would be accompanied by other transformational reforms, such as advancing the economic livelihood of the large indigenous population. As Booth and Seligson counter, "precious little progress has been made in this regard. Guatemalan elites have shown little commitment to democracy since the liberalization process began in 1985" (2010, 130).

Several scholars have attributed inertia to the incentives of elites. Nagel highlights the ability of institutions and actors to undermine the reform process, noting that "the very institutions upon which reform regimes are modeled are themselves susceptible to corruption, abuse, and political machinations" (2009, 93). According to Nagle:

> the rule of law is ineffective or has failed in many Latin states because the political leaders and the ruling class do not want the system to change; on the contrary, some leaders in the region want to maintain a system that serves their own ambitions and private interests as well as the personal interests of the constituents who put them in power. (2009, 81)

Finkel (2008) also finds that the incentives of political elites are a crucial factor explaining why some reforms are successful and others are not. Finkel argues that meaningful justice reform emerges when a ruling party fears its grip on power might slip. For example, if the ruling party fears that it could lose power in future elections, it might support judicial reform as an "insurance policy" and hope that a newly empowered judicial branch will check the power of future opposition governments. Thus, judicial reform acts as a kind of political insurance, allowing a waning party to strengthen the judiciary (to its liking) to provide protection from a rising opposition in the future. Thus, in systems with true electoral competition, there will be incentive to promote reforms that strengthen the rule of law. In political systems in which actors can either rig the electoral rules, or have no need to fear electoral losses, the incentive to engage in meaningful reform is absent. On the contrary, such actors might see incentives for just the opposite, and manipulate or undermine reform efforts in order to wield power unchecked.

Popkin (2000) and Call (2003) highlight an additional reason why reforms languished—they occurred against a backdrop of rising crime rates. In examining the transition to democracy in El Salvador, both Popkin (2000) and Call (2003) demonstrate that reform efforts swiftly faced criminal challenges. For example, one of the most welcomed components of the 1992 Peace Accords was the complete dismantling of the previous security apparatus and the creation of the National Civilian Police (PNC). In the wake of this complete overhaul, there was a security vacuum, as the old security system was dismantled before its replacement was in effect (Call 2003). The formation of a professionalized police force took time, as new recruits needed to pass entrance exams and undergo training before they could assume their posts. Unfortunately, reformers had little time. During this transition process, crime rates soared. Criminal actors, particularly gangs, took advantage of the security vacuum to entrench their criminal activities and undermine efforts to firmly establish the rule of law. The case of El Salvador clearly illustrates how the fate of the rule of law is tied not just to reform efforts, but also to crime.

Overview of Crime Crisis

In addition to the challenges posed by the need for extensive reform, rule of law promotion has been further hampered by the crime crisis. As most Latin American nations made the twin transitions to neoliberal economies and democratic forms of governance throughout the 1980s and 1990s, they were plagued with rising crime rates, particularly violent crimes like homicides. Rates of violent crime were among the highest in the world in the 1990s, tempering the initial optimism over democratization's potential to transform the region (UNDP 2009). Not only have crime rates themselves risen throughout the region, as measured by national homicide rates, but under new democratic regimes crimes feature prominently in media with less fear of censorship (Seligson and Azpuru 2001). For example, Krause (2009, 10) finds that in the Guatemalan media murder is treated as entertainment, and takes "advantage of the morbid and plays on the public's attraction to voyeurism." The profitability of sensationalist news coverage increases its appeal, thus creating "a lucrative business practice that has shifted both print and broadcast media towards more violent and sensationalist news reporting" (Krause 2009, 10).

These high rates of crime, coming on the heels of reform efforts, quickly led many observers to question whether the current crime crisis would erode the gains made under democratization. Relying upon national homicide rates, Figure 2.5 compares violent crime across the six countries.[13] As a point of comparison, the homicide rate in the United States tends to fluctuate between 5.5 and 6.0 per 100,000, and the rates of European countries tend to hover around 1 per 100,000.[14] As Figure 2.5 illustrates, Costa Rica, Nicaragua, and Panama have comparatively low homicide rates for the region, yet levels of violence are on the rise. This sharp surge is particularly prominent in Costa Rica and Panama, with homicide rate increases of 83 percent and 90 percent respectively. These countries are comparatively safe, but for citizens of these countries, the sudden and steep rise in violence is disturbing.

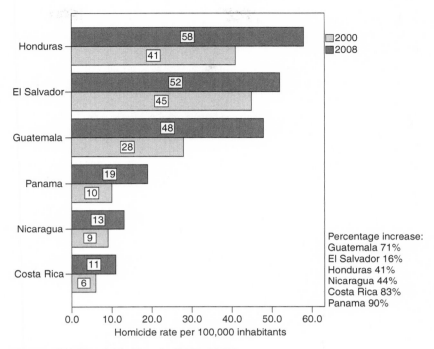

FIGURE 2.5 Homicide Trends (2000–2008)

Source: UNDP 2009

Note: All data are from the UNDP's 2009 report, *Informe sobre el Desarrollo Humano para América Central 2009–2010*, with the exception of the 2000 data for Honduras, which is from El Observatorio Centroamericano sobre Violencia (OCAVI), www.ocavi.com/ (last accessed May 22, 2011).

In Guatemala, El Salvador, and Honduras violent crime has soared, ranking these countries among the most violent in the world. In these latter countries, much of the violent crime has been related to gang activity (UNDP 2009). In Guatemala and El Salvador, the high murder rate is also attributable to the lingering effects of civil wars. As Millet (2009) notes:

> The end of civil conflicts frequently leaves thousands of former combatants, drawn from all sides, without jobs, land, or education and accustomed to a violent lifestyle. Efforts to incorporate these individuals into society are often inadequate and not sustained, providing ready recruits for criminal organizations. (Millet 2009, 252)

Incomplete disarmament exacerbates these problems, leaving a readily accessible supply of weapons behind. In the postwar countries of El Salvador, Guatemala, and Nicaragua, the potential was high for a sharp spike in rates of crime. In El Salvador and Guatemala, this potential became a very violent reality as gangs and organized crime capitalized on the transition process and became postwar fixtures. Honduras escaped civil war in the 1980s, but in the 1990s suffered from many of the same problems as the postwar countries (Booth et al. 2010). In the 1990s, Honduras found itself home to former combatants from the conflict in Nicaragua, many of whom were unable to assimilate into the workforce and retained access to weapons. US policy further exacerbated postwar problems, as the United States deported record numbers of Salvadoran gang members (particularly from Los Angeles) back to postwar El Salvador, where legitimate job prospects were dim (Nowalski 2006). These trends combined to create a particularly hospitable environment for gangs and organized crime to set up shop.[15]

Organized Crime

Guatemala, El Salvador, and Honduras have faced challenges from organized crime and gangs, thus the nature of their crime crisis is distinct. As Bailey and Taylor (2009) explain, there is an important distinction between organized and nonorganized crimes. While violent crime poses problems for governance, organized crime is an even more formidable opponent, as it tends to be a well-financed, well-organized counterpart with ready access to weapons and ammunition. In many cases, organized crime has been able to systematically challenge the state's monopolization of force, and consequently its legitimacy. This has certainly been the case in many Central American countries, as the Mexican antidrug offensive has pushed organized crime into Central America, particularly the Northern Triangle of Guatemala, Honduras, and El Salvador.

During the process of democratization, in many cases organized crime was able to take advantage of space created by the transition process. For example, a recent article in *The Economist* noted that in Guatemala:

> Free from prosecution, many veterans of the intelligence and security services who had run right-wing death squads regrouped into crime gangs with a lucrative kidnapping business, some of them continuing to serve in the police. Their profits were used to buy off witnesses, judges, and politicians. These networks, present in almost every government agency, joined forces with international drugs traffickers, giving them new funding and firepower. (*The Economist* 2011)

Pérez (2000) elaborates on this observation, identifying several characteristics that make countries susceptible to the infiltration of drug traffickers and practitioners of other illicit activities. According to Pérez, when state institutions are weak, they cannot "exercise control over many social and economic relationships" within the country (Pérez 2000, 139). Consequently, countries with weak institutions become ideal candidates for hosting illicit activities like drug trafficking. Public officials in such states seek to enrich themselves through illicit activities, eschewing their roles as "independent arbiters of social relations" in favor of using their positions to shield criminal activity (Pérez 2000, 139). Complicit officials will also bow to requests to tailor state policy (e.g., extradition, banking regulations, and tax codes) to meet the needs of illicit actors.

In addition to weak state institutions and corrupt officials, basic geography matters a great deal as well. Panama offers clear examples of how the proximity to strategically important trade routes, as well as to consumer markets for illicit goods, can attract drug traffickers (Pérez 2000). Honduras provides another illustration, as its northeastern coast "offers a remote, largely uninhabited rainforest that is perfect for the single-engine planes traffickers use, then hide or burn to destroy the evidence" (Archibold and Cave 2011, A1). Dense jungles and a long Caribbean coastline position Honduras as "the first corner of the triangle, leading into trade routes that eventually reach Mexico and the United States" (Shifter 2011, 51).

The policies of neighboring countries are also important. For example, when Mexico launched a militarized effort to crush drug cartels in 2006, the conflict eventually spilled over into Guatemala, El Salvador, and Honduras. In 2006, 23 percent of cocaine shipments moving north passed through Central America. By 2011, this amount had jumped to 84 percent, as the Mexican offensive pushed cartel activity south (Archibold and Cave 2011, A1). This southern extension of drug activity has even threatened Costa Rica, as drug trafficking boats have increased their activities on its Pacific coast. Pérez also notes that contemporary trends of liberalization and economic integration have rendered borders more porous, and provide "golden opportunities to illicit entrepreneurs to hide their profits among the licit flows" (Pérez 2000, 139).

When gangs and organized crime have taken advantage of political transitions, rates of violent crime have escalated exponentially, particularly when the transition takes place against a backdrop of demobilized soldiers and incomplete disarmament. Of the Central American countries, Guatemala, El Salvador, and Honduras have been most affected by gangs and organized crime. In Guatemala and El Salvador, criminal organizations capitalized on the legacy of civil war and political transitions. Millet (2009) estimates that the total number of gang members in Guatemala, El Salvador, and Honduras is over 60,000. El Salvador is the gang stronghold, and the prisons in particular serve as venues for training and recruiting gang members.

The presence of criminal organizations in Honduras, and the accompanying high rates of homicide, demonstrate that a legacy of civil war is not the only factor that can turn a democratizing country into a safe haven for crime. While Honduras did escape the direct violence of civil war in the 1970s and 1980s, "it experienced some of the same consequences, including a degree of militarization, tens of thousands of refugees, armed incursions across its borders, and a flood of weapons which became widely available" (Millet 2009, 255). Indeed, the situation in Honduras is one of the most dire in the Western Hemisphere, as gangs have opened fire on civilians in terrorist rampages, such as the 2004 execution of bus passengers and the more recent massacre on a soccer field (Reuters 2010). Additional tactics of drug cartels have exacerbated problems of public security in different ways. In the early 2000s, cartels began to pay drug dealers and their affiliates in drugs instead of cash. This caused a sharp rise in the domestic consumption of drugs, taking a heavy toll in poor neighborhoods in particular, where youth crime rates rose sharply (Millet 2009, 258).

Nicaragua is an important exception to this trend, as past experiences with civil war did not open the door to criminal organizations. Despite plenty of demobilized combatants and a disarmament process that generated criticism, criminal organizations have not penetrated Nicaraguan society. Small scale, neighborhood gangs do exist, but these small gangs (or *pandillas*) are territorial in nature, and do not have transnational contacts with other organized criminal elements or their corresponding drug activity (Sibaja et al. 2006). These pandillas are very different from the *maras*, the larger more organized street gangs, most of which originated in Los Angeles, CA in the 1980s, and were later deported to El Salvador, where they formed formidable criminal organizations like *Mara 18* (M18) and *Mara Salvatrucha* (MS) (Wolf 2011).[16] These maras are increasingly tied to even larger criminal organizations, such as the Mexican drug cartels that have violently confronted a government crackdown, and increasingly shifted their activities further south into Central America.

There are several reasons why maras and drug cartels have not gained a foothold in Nicaragua to date. First, the form of the Sandinista response to the Contra War seems to have impeded the ability of transnational criminal organizations to gain a foothold in Nicaragua in the 1980s, as they did elsewhere in Central America. Former Sandinista soldiers point out that their assignments in the war focused on securing the borders to block Contra attacks launched from Honduras. This emphasis on border security proved disruptive to organized crime, as the same border patrols that were tasked with confronting the Contras simultaneously blocked transnational gangs from entering Nicaragua in the first place.[17] Second, the police of Nicaragua have evolved quite differently from the other postconflict countries of Central America, making a complete break from the authoritarian and repressive past following the overthrow of the Somoza dynasty in 1979. The new constitution stipulated that the police would not be repressive, focusing instead on the prevention of crime. This has led Nicaragua to focus "most of its efforts on prevention and intervention, which have had important results in reducing criminality and youth violence" (Sibaja et al. 2006, 8). Even incarcerated populations have access to some rehabilitative measures, such as activities and job training. One of the major cities, León, has implemented a large-scale, holistic program of crime prevention, which relies extensively upon civil society. León has implemented an impressive computer tracking system to monitor potential crime zones, identify at risk youth, and target police resources where they can be most effective (Herrera and Espinoza 2008). This preventive and holistic model is also used to address related social problems, such as a high rate of suicide among youth (Herrera 2006). This model of crime prevention has blocked the easy recruitment of disaffected youth to work in the maras, although some do still join smaller scale neighborhood pandillas.

The structure of civil society has also prevented transnational organized groups from setting up shop in Nicaragua. Some "lingering socialist structures such as the neighborhood watch" as well as the impact of the Sandinistas' Committees for the Defense of the Sandinista Revolution have helped civil society to self-police their neighborhoods and keep more dangerous foreign gangs out (Sibaja et al. 2006, 5–6). This civil society organization is particularly valuable when matched with attempts like those of León, which aimed to promote police collaboration with civil society (Espinoza and Herrera 2009).

Finally, the economy of Nicaragua has also deterred violent crime by reducing the ability of organized criminal groups to operate. While the other postconflict countries are also poor, the Nicaraguan economy lacks basic opportunities for money-laundering, an essential need for organized crime.[18] Other Central American countries offer more appealing bases of operation for sophisticated crime networks.

Violence associated with criminal organizations has also been comparatively low in Panama, but for different reasons. Panama has historically had strong ties to the transport of illicit goods such as drugs, but it has traditionally served more as a hub facilitating the transfer of goods and services (Pérez 2000). In its role as conduit, Panama has felt the impact of organized crime to a far lesser extent, as drug traffickers tend to use Panama as a way station, rather than a permanent base of operations. To be sure, Panama has not escaped the wave of violence. As Figure 2.5 indicates, from 2000 through 2008, homicide rates rose 90 percent in Panama. While homicide rates in

Panama are approximately one-third those of the countries of the Northern Triangle, this does not mean homicide rates are low by any means. Panama has simply escaped the worst of the violence, but violence is still a problem.

Costa Rica has largely escaped organized crime's reach, although recent threats have emerged. Due to the crackdown on Mexican drug cartels, drug traffickers have seeped deeper into Central American countries, and there have been isolated reports of activity on the Pacific Coast. As Costa Rica does not have an army, it entered into an agreement with the United States to give permission to 46 warships and 7,000 troops to enter its jurisdiction should the need arise (Shifter 2011, 54). Despite these recent events, overall Costa Rica has maintained its image as a peaceful oasis in the region. Violent crime has risen, but is more comparable to incidents in major US cities rather than Central American ones. Still, Costa Rica has experienced extensive problems with less violent, common types of crime.

Common Crime

Homicide rates tend to be used most frequently in cross-national comparisons of crime rates, as despite their well-documented flaws, they do tend to be the most valid indicator of a phenomenon that is difficult to measure cross-nationally. Differences in definitions of crime, crime-reporting rates, and data collection make national reports on other types of crime difficult to compare country to country. Still, a strict reliance on homicide rates can mask problems with other types of crime, such as burglary, robbery, and assault. To examine levels of these forms of less violent crime, victimization surveys can be helpful. Of course, victimization surveys themselves can also be problematic, as respondents might self-report crimes outside the specified time range, or might dismiss crimes if they think of them as unimportant (Bergman 2006). In the context of Latin America, perhaps the most serious problem with victimization surveys is the fact that such measures "tend to over-report crimes against property and underreport violence," which can pose credibility problems for cross-sectional research (Bergman 2006, 221). Despite these recognized limitations, victimization surveys do provide valuable insight into respondents' self-reported experiences with less violent types of crime, provided such data are used to document general trends as opposed to absolute rates of victimization.

As Figure 2.6 illustrates, rates of self-reported victimization do not vary as dramatically across the Central American countries. Self-reported victimization rates also indicate that the countries considered "safe" according to national homicide rates have been plagued by other, less violent types of crime. For example, Costa Rica has the lowest homicide rate in Central

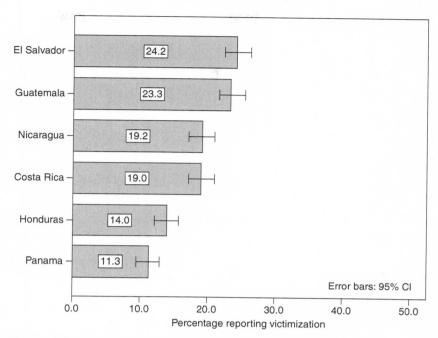

FIGURE 2.6 Self-Reported Victimization Rates (LAPOP 2010)

America, yet self-reported victimization rates are statistically no different from those of Nicaragua. When examining these rates, it is important to keep in mind Bergman's (2006) caution that victimization surveys tend to over-report property crimes. This largely explains Costa Rica's middle ranking in the region on these self-reported measures—its higher levels of wealth make property crime more likely, a type of crime that is more readily reported than those that do not involve property. Victimization surveys are more useful to gauge overall trends rather than absolute measures of the occurrence of crime. The victimization rates in Figure 2.6 should not be used to infer that victimization in Costa Rica is significantly higher than that of Panama, but rather that Costa Ricans have reported problems with crime that are not captured by national homicide rates. Self-reported victimization rates indicate that while some countries are considered safe due to low homicide rates, they still face challenges posed by less violent types of crime.

Table 2.5 breaks down self-reported victimization into its various offense categories. As Table 2.5 illustrates, the countries with the lowest homicide rates tend to have lower levels of victimization by other types of violent crime, such as robbery with physical aggression and armed robbery. In the two wealthiest countries, Costa Rica and Panama, robbery without physical

TABLE 2.5 Type of Victimization by Country (LAPOP 2010)

Country	Robbery without physical aggression (%)	Robbery with physical aggression (%)	Armed robbery (%)	Assault (%)	Property damage (%)	Home burglary (%)	Extortion (%)
Guatemala	16.3	7.8	54.0	3.0	2.0	5.5	7.6
El Salvador	26.4	9.3	32.5	1.6	1.6	4.5	18.1
Honduras	22.6	28.1	37.6	3.2	4.1	1.4	1.8
Nicaragua	23.1	16.9	28.5	3.7	6.1	12.9	2.0
Costa Rica	33.7	22.7	26.6	1.4	5.7	7.4	.7
Panama	34.1	18.5	25.4	5.8	4.6	7.5	.6

Note: For purposes of presentation, crimes with very small numbers of victims are not included in this table. These crimes and their corresponding percentages (for all countries) include: sexual assault (3); kidnapping (2); illegal retention of goods (4); persecution (1); car robbery (1); prosecution for a crime not committed (1); bicycle robbery (1); robbery of livestock (1).

aggression, which includes minor types of crime such as pick pocketing, is significantly higher than its prevalence in other countries, constituting roughly a third of all self-reported victimization. These countries also have virtually no problems with crimes like extortion, which tend to be linked to gangs and organized crime. Indeed, the highest rate of extortion victimization occurs in El Salvador, where the maras contribute to elevating this crime to the third most prevalent, with 18.1 percent of the victims self-reporting this type of crime.

State Responses to Crime

State responses to the crime epidemic vary substantially. Some of this variation is due to different national circumstances, but differences also emerge due to the ideology of the governing party, as well as the priorities and agenda of prominent national and international actors. If international organizations or foreign governments lend money to finance crime-fighting initiatives, they typically advocate public security measures that uphold their priorities, which could differ from those of the country. Frühling (2003) notes that the lack of public resources for crime-fighting agents like the police creates opportunities for private funds to influence security policy. This typically leads the police to direct more attention to the upper classes, who supply such funds.[19]

Tulchin and Golding (2003) provide a regional overview of citizen security in Latin America. They note the range of policy responses to crime, and their repercussions. On one extreme are mano dura approaches to fighting crime, which refer to tough, zero tolerance approaches to criminals. Such reforms frequently tout the benefits of "broken windows" policing, whereby any small infraction is dealt with swiftly and harshly, to deter the escalation of crimes. These tough crackdowns rely upon force or the threat of force, and are reactionary in nature. They do not aim to address the root causes of crime, but rather subject criminals (or suspected criminals) to harsh sanctions. Proposals for harsher sanctions range from longer jail terms to the reinstatement of the death penalty. In more extreme cases, mano dura approaches rely upon a militarized approach to fight criminals, sometimes even deploying the military despite peace accords to the contrary (Pérez 2003). Given the legacy of most Central American countries, such calls are problematic from a democratic standpoint, as they blur the line between civilian and military roles, and have the potential to return to a past of questionable human rights and civil liberties practices. Despite this potential, some politicians have found that tough on crime pledges resonate with violence-weary voters. In campaign ads, perennial Guatemalan presidential candidate Otto Perez Molina extols citizens to "vote with an iron fist," for example. While there are electoral payoffs to such pledges, there is not much empirical evidence that they succeed in reducing crime. Chevigny (2003) finds that there is no relation between mano dura tactics and reductions in crime rates. In addition to this empirical ambivalence, mano dura approaches also tend to focus on the short-term goal of apprehending criminals, rather than addressing the underlying social and economic problems that are conducive to criminality. Finally, mano dura approaches are more likely to result in violations of human rights or civil liberties, making them a liability particularly in countries with legacies of human rights abuses (Tulchin and Golding 2003).

Community policing has become a bit of a catch phrase in public security debates. Reformers tend to like this approach, as it aims to address public security concerns while simultaneously reducing the distance between social groups, as well as between society and the state (Tulchin and Golding 2003, 3). This approach has appeared most prominently in Costa Rica and in parts of Nicaragua (Chinchilla 2003, Espinosa and Herrera 2009). The potential to increase positive interactions between society and the state is particularly important in countries with legacies of human rights violations. Reformers have heralded community policing as an effective crime-fighting tactic that promotes interactions between the police and the community they protect; such collaborative efforts are regarded as more conducive for respecting basic human rights and civil liberties (Arias and Ungar 2009). Unfortunately, in some countries the legacy of past conflict is difficult to overcome, and closer interaction with police is not high on the list of many citizens. Community policing initiatives also run the risk of encouraging penal populism, whereby community groups use "the cloak of community policing to establish private security forces and to engage in what amounts to vigilantism" (Tulchin and Golding 2003, 3).

With the advent of democratization, fledgling institutions have struggled to rebuild themselves while simultaneously confronting skyrocketing crime rates (Frühling, Tulchin, and Golding 2003; Lafree and Tseloni 2006). The crime epidemic and the need for major justice reform create twin challenges for contemporary Central American democracies. The problem of crime compounds the problems of contemporary justice systems. Still, there are some important differences among countries. It is important to understand the distinct reality of each country, given trends in reform and crime, in order to understand citizens' political attitudes and behaviors. Such attitudes are not formed in a vacuum, and depend heavily on the status quo of reform and crime in each country, as well as temporal trends in reform and crime. This overview of both rule of law reform efforts and the accompanying crime wave is crucial for understanding citizen attitudes. To understand why citizens might adhere to the rule of law in some contexts yet not others, it is imperative to examine the respective realities they face.

Classifying Countries and Their Twin Challenges

Based upon this overview, the Central American countries can be classified into three groups. As Figure 2.7 illustrates, with low levels of violent crime and a justice system that performs far better than its neighbors, the Costa Rican system emerges as the success story of the region, trailed by Panama. According to World Bank estimates, when compared to other countries in the world, the rule of law in both Costa Rica and Panama ranks above the fiftieth percentile. In contrast, the justice system of Nicaragua ranks far below this threshold, but has not faced the stiff challenge of exceedingly high rates of violent crime. In the last category are the countries confronting the twin challenges of high homicide rates and poor performing justice institutions: Guatemala, El Salvador, and Honduras. In these latter countries, the problem is most severe, as these countries are facing a crime crisis and the justice system counters with only a very thin shield. Some have likened the situation to "fighting a war with a broken army" (Ellingwood 2008). To be sure, substantial resources and effort have been invested to fix these broken armies, but progress is frequently reversed by the crime epidemic in a negative reinforcing cycle.

As Figure 2.7 illustrates, the Central American countries can be grouped into three categories. First, there are two countries with World Bank

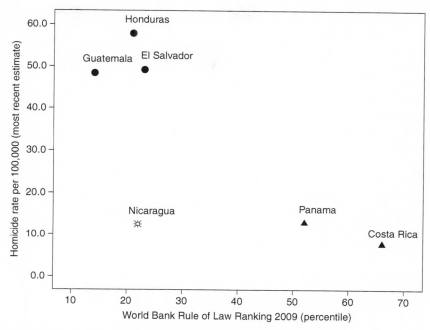

FIGURE 2.7 Country Groupings by Crime Rate and Rule of Law

rankings above the global average—Costa Rica and Panama. Costa Rica also boasts lower levels of violent crime, and while Panama's homicide rate is high globally, it is lower than the regional average. Nicaragua falls in a different category, as its rule of law ranking is below the global average, but its homicide rate is on par with that of Panama. Finally, there are three countries in which the situation is most critical: Guatemala, El Salvador, and Honduras. In this group of countries, high levels of violent crime coincide with a very low quality of the rule of law. This group faces the twin challenges of poor governance and high murder rates.

Figure 2.7 does not aim to provide a definitive score for individual Central American countries, but rather to group the countries loosely in terms of their problems with violent crime and justice system performance. By grouping countries according to these two dimensions, Figure 2.7 lays the groundwork for the empirical analysis, which will examine attitudes towards the law within each country. The classification of individual countries into these groups illuminates national level variations, and facilitates the examination of the effects of crime on support for the rule of law in three different types of national contexts.

Conclusion

This overview provides the necessary contextual information for understanding citizens' attitudes and behaviors toward the law. This context is vital
for understanding why citizens might favor one "escape" from the security
trap over another. O'Donnell has an anecdote that illuminates how context
shapes individual behavior. He contrasts the behavior of motorists in South
Bend (Indiana), Rio de Janeiro, and Buenos Aires, and notes that in some
Latin American cities:

> You have to be nuts (or a very naïve foreigner) to drive according to the
> formal rules of transit. In most parts of the city, and during the night in
> practically all of it, it is perfectly obvious that you should *not* stop at a red
> light, not to mention a yellow light or a stop sign. If you do this, you are
> subjecting yourself to serious risks. The first is being run over by the car
> behind you; *of course* the driver of this car does not expect you to stop. The
> second risk is that without, or before, or, even more, after the accident, you
> will be robbed. Everyone knows this, where *everyone* means all the actors
> involved in the relevant context of interaction. (O'Donnell 2006, 285)

O'Donnell contrasts the "incentives" for disobeying formal rules of transit
in this context with the incentives posed by a completely different scenario.
In most Latin American cities, and American ones for that matter, there are
times and areas where people do follow formal traffic laws—typically during
daytime hours in downtown sections, and in affluent neighborhoods. Failure
to do so has a high potential for incurring heavy fines and/or other sanctions.
Indeed, O'Donnell dryly notes that "Local fools and naïve foreigners risk both
serious accidents and heavy (formal and informal) fines" (2006, 286).

O'Donnell's point is very helpful for understanding the way in which context molds citizens' attitudes and behaviors toward not just transit laws, but
the rule of law more broadly. When citizens adhere to the rule of law, it is
typically with the expectation that doing so is the best way to address their
grievances or meet their goals, given their perceptions of how justice works
in their country. If the justice system is fundamentally flawed, there may be
little to be gained by respecting the rule of law. In such contexts, citizens
might disparage the law and seek out extralegal alternatives for resolving
disputes or protecting themselves from crime.

O'Donnell's anecdote illustrates another important point—while context
is important, people ultimately act on their *perceptions* of that context. It is
important to remember that these perceptions and expectations frequently
differ from macro level indicators. Two individuals might perceive the same

objective phenomena in entirely different ways, as the objective event is interpreted and filtered through citizens' expectations and personal experiences. Ultimately, policymakers respond to citizens' perceptions, not just macro level measures of a particular problem. Therefore, it is imperative to examine not just the macro level indicators of the rule of law and crime, but also citizens' perceptions of these problems and trends. When Central Americans look at the rule of law, justice institutions, and crime, how do they perceive it? These perceptions are crucial to understand, as ultimately, they drive political attitudes and behavior.

Notes

[1] Comments made during the 2010 Costa Rican presidential election campaign, as reported online by http://laura-chinchilla.com/laura-chinchillas-vision-as-costa-rica-president/. These remarks synthesize Chinchilla's empirical investigations on public security promotion, such as her 2002 book, *Citizen Security in Latin America: towards a Holistic Policy* (Rico and Chinchilla 2002).

[2] Comments made during the 2007 Guatemalan presidential debate between Álvaro Colom and Otto Pérez Molina, as reported on National Public Radio (www.npr.org/templates/story/story.php?storyId=14232839). Pérez Molina lost the 2007 elections, but has remained a popular candidate in the 2011 presidential elections.

[3] The US military never invaded Costa Rican territory, but it did engage in maneuvers off the coast to deter war between Costa Rica and Panama during a border dispute in 1921 (Grimmett 2004).

[4] The 1904 Panamanian constitution legally sanctioned the right of the United States to intervene militarily to maintain peace and order whenever it deemed it necessary (Pérez 2000).

[5] Fallout from the Iran Contra Affair also left the Contras without their main source of funding. American funding of the Contras became difficult after 1986, when the details of the Contras' funding arrangements were made public, and generated outrage due to the misappropriation of funds and numerous violations of international and US law.

[6] Democratization was the main impetus for rule of law reform, but trends toward privatization in the 1980s and 1990s also promoted reform efforts (Correa 1999). With the onset of the debt crisis in the 1980s, and the subsequent push for neoliberal reforms, rule of law reform became the mantra for international lending agencies, foreign donors, and domestic governments. Correa (1999) notes that as the state lessened its role in market regulation, government bureaucracies were no longer the primary venue for addressing disputes. Rather, due to privatization, many disputes were no longer between individuals and the state, but between private parties, and consequently phrased in legal terms rather than questions of state policy. As more disputes involved private parties, the arena for conflict resolution shifted to the

courtroom. Privatization also increased the amount of litigation (particularly in the areas of contract enforcement and property rights), which has in turn underscored the need for legal reform to process such litigation effectively and fairly (Finkel 2008).

[7] The exact text of these reforms is available through Georgetown University's Political Database of the Americas: http://pdba.georgetown.edu/Constitutions/ElSal/trans.html (last accessed May 6, 2011).

[8] See Hammergren (2007, 4–5) for a thorough yet concise overview of the many diverse components of the justice system targeted by reform efforts.

[9] For a practical example of this approach to reform, see the World Bank's (2002) *Legal and Judicial Sector Assessment Manual*, www.gsdrc.org/go/display/document/legacyid/1038 (last accessed May 12, 2011).

[10] As of 2011, however, less than 10 percent had been disbursed, and the US Congress expressed reservations over the release of the remaining allocated funds (Bailey 2011).

[11] While this chapter relies upon the World Bank's Governance Indicators, other databases also aim to assess the quality of the rule of law around the world. For example, the *Economic Freedom of the World* database (www.freetheworld.com/release.html) has a similar focus on the rule of law, and the World Bank's *Doing Business* report (www.doingbusiness.org/EconomyRankings/) also contains measures that can be valuable. Recently the Freedom House Organization began to publish its evaluations of specific components of democracy, such as the rule of law (http://freedomhouse.org/template.cfm?page=351&ana_page=341&year=2008) (all accessed September 7, 2009). Staats, Bowler, and Hiskey (2005) provide measures of judicial performance in Latin American countries through surveys sent to 147 prominent attorneys and law professors in seventeen countries.

[12] These rankings are based upon Transparency International's Corruption Perception Index, which in 2010 aimed to gauge the prevalence of corruption in 178 countries. For more information on the methodology of these measurements of corruption, the online report is available at www.transparency.org/policy_research/surveys_indices/cpi/2010/results (last accessed May 22, 2011).

[13] Given the difficulties of gathering reliable crime data, comparative scholars tend to rely upon homicide rates, as homicides tend not to have the same problem with underreporting and can be more easily compared cross-nationally than other crimes, where legal definitions may vary (Lafree and Tseloni 2006).

[14] For global data on homicide rates and trends, see the United Nations Surveys on Crime Trends and the Operations of Criminal Justice Systems (CTS), www.unodc.org/unodc/en/data-and-analysis/United-Nations-Surveys-on-Crime-Trends-and-the-Operations-of-Criminal-Justice-Systems.html (last accessed May 28, 2010).

[15] When discussing criminal groups in Latin America, typically observers distinguish between three types. The least organized of these groups are the pandillas, which are local groups of disaffected youth that typically engage in more localized and small scale crime. Next are the maras, gangs with a much

wider geographic span that engage in more violent and orchestrated crimes, such as extortion rackets. At the apex is organized crime like the Mexican drug cartels, which are international in scope and are capable of mounting armed assaults against government forces, such as the Mexican army.

[16] Mara is a diminutive of *marabunta*, the name of "a brutal ant that reproduces like the plague and is capable of destroying everything in its path" (Nowalski 2006, 12).

[17] Author interview, July 2010.

[18] Author interview with Francisco Bautista Lara, July 2010.

[19] A case study of São Paulo illustrates this process, as a business-oriented nongovernmental organization actively promoted police reform, which led subsequent reforms to privilege business interests (Mesquita Neto 2006).

3

Public Perceptions of Crime and Justice

In a seminal work on perceptions of the justice system in the United States, Peffley and Hurwitz (2010) provide striking examples of how individuals perceive the exact same events in starkly different terms. Highlighting prominent legal cases in the United States, such as those of Rodney King, O. J. Simpson, and the Jena Six, the authors point out that perceptions of justice vary tremendously according to race in the United States. In the 2007 case of the Jena Six, six black teenagers were charged with attempted murder after beating a white student, an incident that occurred shortly after nooses were found hanging from an oak tree where black students had eaten lunch during the school day.[1] Overwhelmingly, white residents of Jena (including the District Attorney) found it inconceivable that "race factored into any of the decisions pertaining to these incidents" (Peffley and Hurwitz 2010, 4). In contrast, most black residents and activists found it impossible to believe race was *not* involved, and launched a series of protests against what they viewed as persecution of the six black students (Peffley and Hurwitz 2010, 4). These different perceptions of justice extend beyond high profile and controversial cases, as the authors find that blacks are far more likely to view the American justice system as unfair, while whites overall consider it to be largely unbiased and legitimate. When asked whether there were serious problems of discrimination in police interactions, court sentencing, and police investigations, 70 percent of black respondents indicated that such problems existed and were serious, compared to only 18 percent of white respondents (Peffley and Hurwitz 2010, 43). These perceptions of fairness matter a great deal, as they shape crime control policy preferences on important issues like punishment, prevention, the death penalty, racial profiling, and juvenile justice. In a seminal work, Tyler (1990) addresses the crucial role of perceptions of fairness in creating legitimacy for the justice system and the law.

These examples from the United States highlight the importance of individual perceptions. Context is vital for understanding political attitudes and behaviors, but individuals interpret this context differently, based upon their own expectations, experiences, and values. In order to understand what leads citizens to respect the rule of law in some cases, and disparage it in others, it is imperative to examine not only macro level trends in crime and justice, but also public perceptions of these trends. Following the third wave of democratization, all of the citizens in Central America had the opportunity to have a voice in governance. To be sure, sometimes this voice was quite small in practice, and political leaders frequently did not listen to it. Nevertheless, for the first time citizens of every Central American country could have some type of input into their political systems. Public perceptions of politics, the economy, and society more broadly now have at least a small space in policy-making circles. Since citizen perceptions have a role in formulating policy, we need to examine not just macro-level indicators like institutional performance, horizontal accountability, and crime, but also citizens' perceptions of these phenomena. How do citizens view the performance of justice institutions, for example? How do they perceive the problem of crime? How do they evaluate their options for escaping from the security trap?

When examining citizens' perceptions of contemporary events and trends, not surprisingly, crime has emerged as a particularly salient issue. When a 2010 LAPOP poll asked respondents to identify the most serious problem facing their countries, respondents fingered crime in every country except Nicaragua.[2] As Table 3.1 explains, concern about crime even overshadowed economic issues in most cases.

This preoccupation with crime represents a large shift in priorities. When LAPOP posed this question in urban areas of Central America in 1990–1992, respondents overwhelmingly signaled that economic problems were of primary concern; in each country, the plurality of respondents stated that the economic crisis was the most serious problem facing the country. By

TABLE 3.1 Public Salience of Crime (2010)

Country	Most serious problem facing the country (response with highest frequency)	Percentage stating crime is the most serious problem (%)
Guatemala	Crime	31
El Salvador	Crime	54
Honduras	Crime	16
Nicaragua	Economic problems	2
Costa Rica	Crime	41
Panama	Crime	48

Source: Latin American Public Opinion Project (LAPOP)

2010, fear of crime had superseded economic worries in every country save
Nicaragua. In the aftermath of the global 2008 financial crisis, it is clear
that this shift in priorities is not attributable to a better economic situation.
Rather, it reflects the increasing salience of public insecurity as crime rates
surged.

Table 3.1 underscores another important point: at the national level, preoccupation with crime is not tied directly to the actual occurrence of crime,
as measured by national level indicators like homicide rates. If that were the
case, we would expect to see concern over crime highest in Honduras and
lowest in Costa Rica. LAPOP's survey results indicate that is not the case. In
both Honduras and Costa Rica respondents indicated that crime was the
most pressing national problem; however, only 16 percent gave this response
in Honduras, compared with 41 percent in Costa Rica. This discrepancy
emerges even in comparisons between two countries with similar levels
of crime and poverty, such as Guatemala and El Salvador. In El Salvador,
54 percent of respondents identified crime as the most pressing problem,
compared to 31 percent in Guatemala.

One explanation for the disjuncture between actual crime and people's
perceptions of criminality lies in individual expectations. Scholars have
noted that citizens' expectations can mitigate their evaluations of both
democratic governance and particular policies (Fuchs 1999; Rose, Shin,
and Munro 1999). For example, McAllister argues that citizens' evaluations
of democratic governance are mediated by their expectations, so that "a
major policy success when expectations are high will have less impact than
a more modest success, delivered when expectations are low" (McAllister
1999, 190). This reasoning gives insight into how people's expectations
might influence their perceptions of public security. In an interview in July
of 2010, Francisco Bautista Lara, one of the founders of the Nicaraguan
National Police, highlighted the importance of disparate expectations
to explain cross-national differences in public fear of crime. Batista Lara
pointed out that in Guatemala, El Salvador, and Honduras, it is not surprising that people worry a great deal about crime—their countries are
home to some of the highest homicide rates in the world. The reality of
the situation is one that commands fear. In contrast, in Costa Rica people
have high expectations and they are used to being safe from violent crime.
Any increase in violent crime is met with alarm, as the people are accustomed to low levels of violence and have higher expectations for public
security. Costa Ricans are not calmed by the fact that rates of violent crime
are the lowest in the region; they are alarmed that contemporary homicide rates are so much higher than those of the past. In contrast, Bautista
Lara quipped that Nicaragua has neither the reality of the high crimes to

its north, nor the high expectations of public security to the south, which explains why only 2 percent of LAPOP respondents in Nicaragua indicated that crime was the most pressing national problem.[3] Findings from other parts of Latin America confirm this trend. Cruz (2009) finds that Argentina and Chile, two of the safest countries in the region, register the highest levels of public insecurity. Dammert and Malone (2010) concur, identifying high levels of public insecurity in some of the safest countries of Latin America—Costa Rica, Chile, and Uruguay.[4]

Cross-national differences in perceptions of crime can also be traced to whether politicians politicize public security or not. As democratization ushered in a new era of political competition, most Central American countries began to follow a common electoral trend, as politicians tried to cultivate public support with tough anticrime measures that resonated with the public. Blumstein (2007) has found that such practices are quite common in democratic politics, as candidates frequently use crime in their electoral bids, politicizing crime control policy with the hope of increasing their share of the ballot box. In the United States as well as Europe, the political appeal of appearing tough on crime has led politicians to increase the punitive nature of convictions and sentencing. Blumstein (2007) traces the current politicization of crime in the United States, initiated in 1964 with Republican presidential candidate Barry Goldwater. He identifies the political gains associated with being "tough on crime," and how catchy crime-fighting slogans such as "three strikes' laws" can be used to boost one's poll numbers. Blumstein concludes, "As politicians in other democracies see the success of the 'tough on crime' rhetorical stance, it seems reasonable that they would be tempted to follow similar patterns" (2007, 12). This has clearly been the trend in Central America, as politicians have increasingly campaigned on crime-fighting platforms. Honduran President Ricardo Maduro (2002–2006) was a popular political candidate in part because voters thought his own tragic experiences with crime would lead him to decisively confront criminals, particularly the maras (Millet 2009). President Maduro's son was kidnapped and murdered in 1997, and Maduro indicated that this event galvanized him to run for the presidency. Once elected, Maduro ushered in a series of draconian laws that gave police and the courts wide latitude for arresting and convicting suspected gang members—measures that proved quite popular with the public, despite evidence of extrajudicial killings and an inability to actually lower the murder rate (Ungar 2009). Azpuru (2008) provides additional evidence of the politicization of crime in the 2007 Guatemalan presidential elections, where retired General Otto Pérez Molina campaigned on the slogan "*urge mano dura*" (insist on the iron fist), against

Álvaro Colom's motto "*la delincuencia se combate con inteligencia*" (fight crime with intelligence). Cruz (2006) argues that elites in El Salvador capitalized on crime to gain public support for measures that would allow them to resist the demilitarization of police forces called for by the Peace Accords. According to Cruz, "The elites did not commit violence, but they blamed criminal violence for the need to postpone changes in the policing system" (2006, 154). In Costa Rica, Laura Chinchilla's successful presidential bid in 2010 was due in no small part to her reputation as an expert in public security.

Media coverage can also politicize crime. Particularly under democracy, the media are free to publicize problems of violence, and in many cases, sensationalize it. In a content analysis of the media's crime coverage prior to the 2007 presidential elections in Guatemala, Krause (2009) identifies several ways in which newspapers politicize crime and help frame public security dialogue. One popular newspaper *Nuestro Diario* frequently features graphic images of crime (such as that of a convicted gang member holding the decapitated head of a rival gang member after a prison riot) followed by only brief news stories and captions. In addition to these sensationalist images, Krause (2009) notes that news coverage placed a disproportionate emphasis on murder, but very rarely included stories on the apprehension of suspects. In the 15 days leading up to the presidential elections, in *Nuestro Diario* the "majority of crimes reported were murders (76%) and the majority of these murders involve guns (80%). Only 7% include the capture of a criminal suspect" (Krause 2009, 13).[3] This formulation of news coverage can shape public attitudes about crime and increase support for punitive crime-fighting policies. The overemphasis on murder creates the impression that crime is almost always violent and murder is pervasive. The absence of stories on the apprehension and sanctioning of offenders emphasizes the inefficiency and failures of the police. Finally, the emphasis on victims of crime makes the news more personal and fosters the belief that crime can happen at any time, to anyone, with no warning and for no reason. Krause's analysis of news coverage explains how headlines like, "He Was on His Way to Work" or "They Were Eating Breakfast" intensifies public fear by portraying crime as unpredictable and random:

> These are not reports of gang-on-gang violence or wars between rival drug cartels; instead, they are news stories about regular people gunned down by unidentified *desconocidos* (strangers) or *sicarios* (assassins) while going about their normal lives. Readers are able to identify with the mundane tasks of going to work or eating breakfast and are encouraged to pictures themselves as victims of these cases. (Krause 2009, 13)

Empathy with victims cultivates the sensation that violent crime could happen to anyone at any time, and the failures of the police render citizens helpless in the face of rising criminality. Not surprisingly, such coverage has been linked to more support for iron fist policies to fight crime, as the police appear to be a hopeless cause and beyond reform, and people identifying with victims tend to favor punitive policies over those that address the underlying root causes of crime. The latter policies, focused on prevention, also lose appeal as they are portrayed as catering to criminals instead of confronting them decisively.

The sensationalism of crime is further promoted by many of the violent tactics gangs and cartels employ. Bailey and Taylor (2009) note that frequently criminal organizations deliberately orchestrate attacks that are designed to generate much media attention. For example, in January of 2011, a bomb detonated on a bus in Guatemala City, killing seven people. A member of Mara 18 was charged with the attack, which was linked to gang extortion of the public transport system (Shifter 2011). The use of bombs is designed to terrify civilian populations, and sends a frighteningly powerful message to bus drivers, who reportedly paid $1.5 million in extortion money in Guatemala in 2010 (Shifter 2011). In these tragic cases, the choice of tactics is purposeful, aimed to capitalize on sensationalism to instill fear in the population.

Frequently the media juxtapose these highly charged images of bus bombings with the incompetence or corruption of public security officials. While the media might place disproportionate emphasis on official corruption and inefficiency, in many cases this reputation is rightfully earned. If only 2.06 percent of homicides in Guatemala resulted in convictions in 2010, then such portrayals seem at least partially warranted (Hudson and Taylor 2010, 56). Still, there are consequences to the media's frequent pairing of crime and incompetence, as opposed to other frames of coverage that might contextualize crime more broadly. Millet contends that government failures to deal with crime generate a great deal of publicity, and "revelations of government corruption can reduce individual incentives to obey the law" (2009, 253).

Guatemala offers perhaps the most sobering example of this juxtaposition, in a bizarre case that garnered a great deal of attention domestically and internationally. In May of 2009, assassins shot Rodrigo Rosenberg, a Guatemalan lawyer. His murder sparked controversy with the revelation that he had made a video tape before his death, accusing the president of orchestrating his murder. In this videotape, Rosenberg began his statement by introducing himself, then calmly stating "regrettably, if you are currently watching or listening to this message, it is because I was murdered by President Álvaro Colom."

Rosenberg proceeded to list a series of co-conspirators, among them, Colom's wife, Sandra Torres, who harbored presidential aspirations. Internet technology ensured that this videotape spread rapidly, and this sparked outrage and demonstrations across Guatemala.[4] Investigations by the UN's CICIG did not completely quell this outrage, as CICIG concluded in January of 2010 that Rosenberg had staged his own murder. According to CICIG, Rosenberg was angry over the murder of his girlfriend, which he blamed on the government; he consequently staged his own murder as a catalyst to overhaul the political system (Seligson and Booth 2010). Later in 2010, LAPOP asked survey respondents how much they thought "the result of the Rodrigo Rosenberg assassination investigation was positive for the country." Respondents gave answers all over the spectrum (which ranged from one through seven). Thirteen percent responded that there was absolutely nothing positive about it (a value of one) and 16 percent stated that the resolution was absolutely very positive for the country (a value of seven), and similar percentages appeared at every place in between these two extremes. The legitimacy of CICIG bolstered the legitimacy of the investigation, and helped avert a full-scale political crisis, but many Guatemalans still expressed deep misgivings about the affair and its implications, although as Figure 3.1 illustrates, Colom

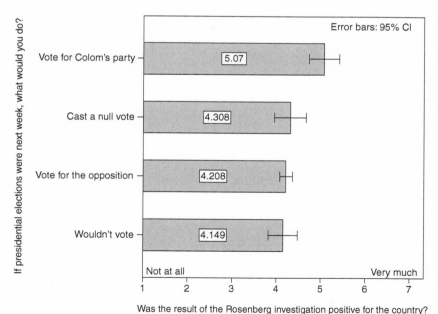

FIGURE 3.1 Attitudes toward Rosenberg Investigation (LAPOP 2010)

supporters registered opinions that were significantly more positive about the results of the investigation.[5]

For a variety of reasons – citizen expectations, political rhetoric, media coverage, or sensational cases – perceptions of crime and justice do not always match "objective" assessments. To understand citizens' attitudes toward the law, we must examine not just the historical and contemporary context of each country, but citizens' perceptions of that context as well. How do Central Americans view crime and justice? Are there major differences within countries? How have these perceptions changed over time?

Perceptions of the Rule of Law and Its Corresponding Institutions

LAPOP's survey data are extremely valuable for answering these questions, providing insight into how individuals perceive the trends of crime and justice around them. LAPOP is the only survey source that has posed identical questions in each of the Central American countries from the early 1990s to the present, providing the opportunity for some longitudinal analyses of attitudes toward justice, as well as cross-sectional comparisons of contemporary trends.

One question in particular is very useful for gauging perceptions of justice over time: "How much do you trust the courts in [country] to guarantee a fair trial?" Respondents could indicate their level of trust on a scale of one (no trust) to seven (high trust). This survey item taps into one of the key dimensions of the rule of law—do all citizens have equal access to justice? Figure 3.2 depicts respondents' answers to this question in the three postconflict countries: Guatemala, El Salvador, and Nicaragua. While the LAPOP data are very valuable in allowing for such temporal and cross-national comparisons, there is one caution for such examinations. The 1990–1992 wave of surveys was conducted only in urban areas, while the remaining surveys are national probability samples. This difference in sample design is important to keep in mind when comparing the 1990–1992 data to that of subsequent years.

As Figure 3.2 indicates, at the aggregate level public trust that the courts will guarantee a fair trial has not remained constant during the era of democratization in the three countries recovering from civil war. In El Salvador, citizens greeted initial reforms with approval, as trust in the fairness of trials improves steadily from 1991 through 2004. After 2004, public evaluations began to dip slightly, but still stayed above 1991 levels. Guatemala follows a similar pattern, as public evaluations improve from 1992 through 2006, but then drop sharply. In contrast to El Salvador, average levels of trust in 2010 were no different from those of 1990–1992. In Nicaragua the trajectory is

The Rule of Law in Central America

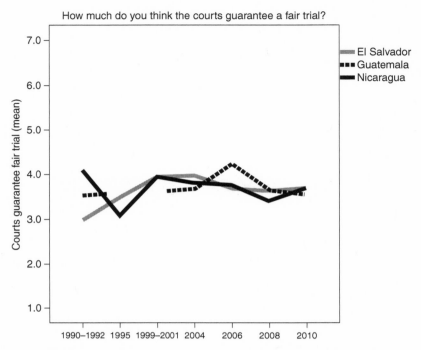

How much do you think the courts guarantee a fair trial?

FIGURE 3.2 Trust in Fairness of Trials in Postconflict Societies (LAPOP 1990–2010)

completely different, as public evaluations dipped sharply in the early years of democracy. This comparison between 1991 and 1995 is inhibited by the fact that the 1991 sample consisted of urban areas, and the 1995 sample was a national probability sample. Still, when one compares only the urban respondents of the 1991 and 1995 surveys, this same drop in public evaluations also appears. Despite a recovery at the end of the 1990s, by 2004, public evaluations once again began to slide, just as they did in the other postconflict societies. Overall, the past two decades of democratization witnessed a slight increase in judicial legitimacy in El Salvador, no change in Guatemala, and a decrease in Nicaragua.

Figure 3.3 depicts public confidence that the courts will guarantee a fair trial for Honduras and Panama—two countries that also transitioned to democracy in the 1990s. At the aggregate level, Panama is the clear success story, as evaluations in 2004 were much higher than in 1991, although once again this comparison is tentative as the 1991 survey included only urban respondents. Still, despite a dip in public trust in 2006, by 2008 public evaluations recovered and even improved. Honduras witnessed a slight but steady

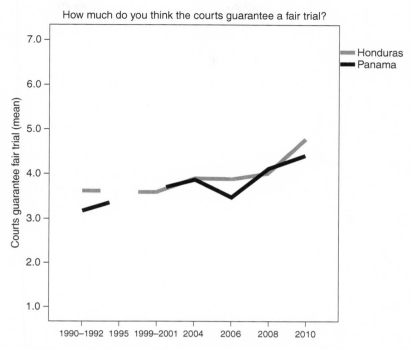

FIGURE 3.3 Trust in Fairness of Trials in Honduras and Panama (LAPOP 1990–2010)

increase in public support from 1991 through 2008, and then a sharp uptick in 2010. This was quite surprising, given Honduras experienced a military coup in 2009 and extensive problems with violence. However, on a much different level, citizens indicated that they felt trials were more equitable, perhaps a reflection of the success of more minor justice reforms.

As Figure 3.4 indicates, perceptions of the fairness of trials in Costa Rica were quite different. Aggregate evaluations of the Costa Rican justice system have been uneven, as public trust declined substantially in the late 1990s and again in 2006. The aggregate score for Costa Rica in 2010 was not that different from the 1990–1992 score, but still some scholars have watched the ebbs and flows of public confidence with concern, arguing that these fluctuations indicate that Costa Rica is experiencing a crisis of trust in its justice system (Walker 2009).

In more recent surveys, LAPOP added a series of questions to measure public attitudes toward a variety of justice institutions, included in a battery of items designed to gauge dimensions of support for various political institutions. This battery of questions was preceded by the following introduction:

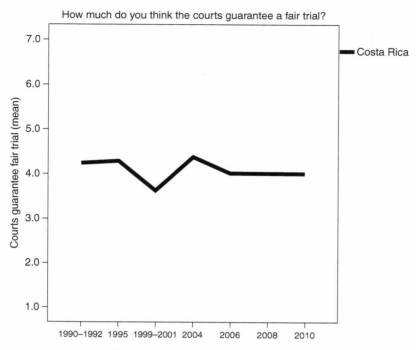

FIGURE 3.4 Trust in Fairness of Trials in Costa Rica (LAPOP 1990–2010)

Now we are going to use a card. This card has a scale of seven points; each one indicates a range that goes from one (that means none) through seven (much). For example, if I were to ask you how much you trusted the news on television, if you did not trust it at all you would choose the number one. If on the contrary you trusted it a lot, you would choose number seven. If your opinion was between none at all and a lot, you would select an intermediate point.

Respondents then answered a series of follow-up questions in a similar format. In addition to the prior question measuring perceptions of the fairness of trials, these questions included items gauging trust in the system of justice, trust in the police, and trust in the Supreme Court. Figure 3.5 provides a cross-sectional look at national levels of trust in each of these institutions, and indicates that overall, Central Americans rate their justice institutions with only average or slightly below average scores.

An additional item measuring trust in the human rights ombudsmen was also posed in every country except Honduras. As Table 3.2 indicates, average levels of trust in the human rights ombudsmen were overall quite high.

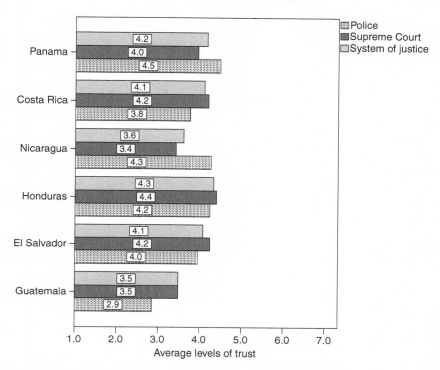

FIGURE 3.5 Average Trust in Justice Institutions (LAPOP 2010)

In Guatemala, El Salvador, Honduras, and Costa Rica, respondents rated the human rights ombudsmen with the highest scores. In Nicaragua and Panama, the police earned slightly higher public evaluations, but the human rights ombudsmen still ranked ahead of the judicial institutions.

In their illustrations of public trust in judicial institutions, Figure 3.5 and Table 3.2 offer some intriguing insights. Perhaps most interesting is that public perceptions of justice institutions do not directly conform to the objective measures discussed in Chapter 2. Given the evaluations of Costa Rica's justice institutions by international organizations, one would expect to see Costa Rica earn top marks from its citizenry. As Figure 3.5 and Table 3.2 indicate, this is not the case for the justice system as a whole, or for the judiciary and the police. Only in the case of the human rights ombudsmen do Costa Ricans express higher levels of trust than their neighbors. This finding most likely underscores the importance of expectations. Costa Ricans expect their justice institutions to perform to high standards, and are not comforted by the thought that international observers rank their justice system better than the others of the region. Instead, Costa Ricans register disappointment that

TABLE 3.2 Trust in Human Rights Ombudsmen (2010)

Country	Average level of trust
Guatemala	4.3
El Salvador	4.9
Honduras	n/a
Nicaragua	3.8
Costa Rica	5.1
Panama	4.2

Source: Latin American Public Opinion Project (LAPOP)

institutions do not perform better, particularly in reigning in the current crime wave and official malfeasance.

Measuring Perceptions of Institutional Performance

In addition to these estimates of diffuse trust in the justice system, which measure, a durable, generalized attachment to political objects, it is also important to examine public perceptions of justice in particular policy areas (Easton 1975). As Table 3.1 demonstrated, for most citizens of Central America, the most important policy area is crime control. When citizens look at their justice systems, how well do they evaluate performance in the policy area that is widely considered to be the most important?

To answer this question, LAPOP included several items to assess whether citizens thought their justice systems were up to the task of confronting escalating crime rates. Questions evaluated perceptions of the justice system's ability to sanction criminals, personal experiences with justice institutions, as well as incidents of corruption. Together, these questions allow for the examination of public perceptions of the performance of the justice system in areas that citizens deem most vital.

To measure evaluations of institutional capacity to apprehend and punish criminals, LAPOP asked: "If you were the victim of a robbery or assault, how much would you trust the judicial system to punish the guilty party? (1) not at all; (2) very little; (3) somewhat; (4) very much." Figure 3.6 compares average national responses to this question, with some surprising findings. Once again, Costa Rica ranks at the bottom of the list. When asked whether the justice system was capable of punishing the guilty party, Costa Rican responses were statistically identical to those of Guatemalans. Despite myriad problems with both crime and justice, Hondurans registered significantly more trust that their justice systems would sanction the guilty parties. This finding underscores an important point—Costa Ricans do not compare their situation favorably with that of the other countries of the isthmus.

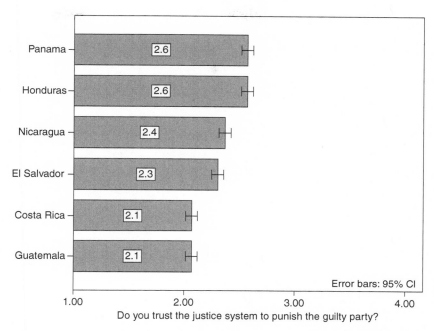

FIGURE 3.6 Trust that the Justice System Can Sanction Criminals (LAPOP 2010)

Rather, to understand Costa Rican attitudes, it is imperative to consider the percentage increase in violent crime over time within the country, instead of comparing the country to its neighbors.

In addition to this measure of perceptions, LAPOP also included two items that gauged respondents' interactions with the police and judiciary. First, the survey included a question to identify those respondents who had personal experiences with the courts: "In the past twelve months, did you have any contact with the courts?" Responses were coded as (1) yes (0) no.[6] Next, the survey asked respondents about the problem of police corruption: "Did a police officer ask you for a bribe in the past twelve months?" Responses were again coded dichotomously, (1) yes (0) no. While it would be helpful to have a wider array of questions probing interactions with justice institutions, these questions offer a good starting point. These items can be used to assess whether respondents with personal experience in the courts will register higher levels of support for democracy and its norms, while controlling for the effects of crime. The more specific questions pertaining to police corruption and abuse can be used to determine whether negative experiences with police officials will reduce support for the rule of law in subsequent data analysis.

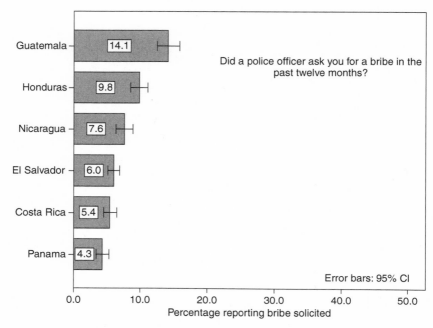

Figure 3.7 Police Solicitation of Bribes (LAPOP 2010)

As Figure 3.7 illustrates, police bribery is quite common in some Central American countries. Particularly in Guatemala and Honduras, sizeable percentages of respondents report that police asked for a bribe within the past 12 months. Since the police are the most visible face of the justice system, and the actor with whom citizens are most likely to have contact, these levels of corruption are problematic. If Millet is correct, and "government corruption can reduce individual incentives to obey the law," the prevalence of police corruption does not bode well for citizens' willingness to respect the rule of law in other areas of life (2009, 253).

A much smaller number of respondents had interactions with the courts, but of these 590 respondents (6.4 percent of the sample), 12 percent reported that they paid a bribe. As Figure 3.8 indicates, statistically it is difficult to make inferences given the small number of observations within each country. Still, Figure 3.8 does offer some interesting observations. Despite its higher levels of trust in the ability of the justice system to sanction criminals, Panama does appear to have problems with the solicitation of bribes in its courts. In contrast, Costa Rica performs far better on this measure, as it did in the case of police corruption as well. Furthermore, lower levels of corruption in some

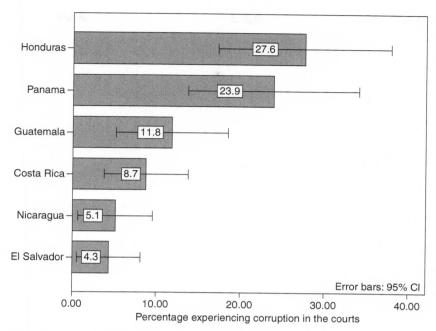

FIGURE 3.8 Corruption in the Court System (LAPOP 2010)

areas of the justice system do not mean that there are not problems in other areas. For example, Panama reported the lowest average incidence of police corruption, yet one of the highest levels of corruption in the courts.

This examination of personal interactions with justice institutions is very important given recent studies in other global regions. In particular, in an examination of US attitudes toward the justice system, Peffley and Hurwitz (2010) point out that individual experiences can matter a great deal in molding public trust in justice institutions, as well as attitudes toward crime control policy and the law more broadly. In the context of the United States, Peffley and Hurwitz (2010) argue that personal experiences with law enforcement can influence perceptions about whether the justice system is fair. When different groups, such as black and white Americans, have such dramatically different experiences with law enforcement, it leads the two groups to appraise the justice system in sharply different terms. The two groups might share some concerns, such as the potential to be victimized by crime personally, but their different views of the justice system will lead them to address these common concerns in very different ways. These findings are quite sobering when applied to the cases of Central America. Despite ongoing reform efforts, personal experiences with the police and justice authorities run the risk of not producing positive outcomes.

Perceptions of Crime

Given the salience of crime in public discourse, perceptions of justice are irrevocably intertwined with perceptions of crime. As Bautista Lara (2008) notes, security is an inseparable combination of facts—facts that include not just the act of delinquency itself, but also institutional responses to delinquency and perceptions of institutional capability. Attitudes toward the rule of law are linked not just to institutional performance, but also to perceptions of crime. In the last decade, fear of crime has increased steadily throughout Latin America, dominating public discourse and social interactions (Bailey and Dammert 2006). This rise in fear of crime is driven in part by obvious trends—if people live in one of the most violent countries in the world, one would expect them to be fearful. However, levels of public fear of crime cannot be completely explained by the actual occurrence of crime. In addition to the national level factors discussed earlier in this chapter, scholars have long noted that fear of crime is strongly conditioned by several individual level factors as well. Fear of crime is somewhat related to victimization and objective crime rates, but is also heavily influenced by socioeconomic status, trust in law enforcement, media exposure, and economic and political insecurities (Pain 2000; Walklate 2001; Dammert and Malone 2006). Women and the wealthy tend to be more fearful of crime, yet men and the poor are actually most frequently victimized. Overall, fear of crime, especially in terms of personal vulnerability to violence, tends to be greater than an objective assessment would justify (Bailey 2009).

Sociotropic and Pocketbook Perceptions

The trends of crime and violence in Central America highlight the need to think carefully about perceptions of crime. If citizen perceptions influence public policy, or if perceptions make people more (or less) likely to endorse officials' policy recommendations (such as mano dura campaigns), it is important to include perceptions in analyses of public security. To understand the role perceptions of crime play in politics, insights from the vast literature on economic voting are particularly helpful. The economic voting literature has devoted much time and attention to identifying different types of economic perceptions, most importantly, distinguishing between pocketbook voting (voting on the basis of one's own economic situation) and sociotropic voting (voting on the basis of perceptions of the national economy). These distinctions can help to delineate different types of fear of crime, as it is reasonable to suppose that perceptions of public security would fall into similar categories. When evaluating public security, people most likely make similar distinctions between their own personal safety and the problem of crime in the country as a whole. People might respond differently if they perceive a threat to their own personal security situation, versus what they perceive is happening in the country as a whole. For example, the gruesome violence of the drug war might steal the headlines, but in reality most people do not have first-hand experiences with these types of crimes. This does not mean that the violence of the drug trade will not affect political attitudes and behaviors, however. Indeed, the ample literature on economic voting has shown that in the realm of economic performance, evaluations of the national economy tend to exert a larger impact on public policy preferences. In many cases, citizens hold the national government, and sometimes the regime itself, accountable for poor economic performance. It is reasonable to hypothesize that people would do the same for performance in other salient policy areas, like crime control.

However, evaluations of personal safety also matter. In the economic voting literature, many scholars have observed that "individuals suffering economic setbacks . . . seldom connect their personal financial misfortunes to more systemic forces, like the national economy or failed economic policies" (Peffley and Hurwitz 2010, 54).[7] Still, there is reason to suspect that the relationship between the personal and the political is stronger in the arena of public security. Security provision is the fundamental task of any government, thus it is likely that citizens will hold their government directly responsible if it fails to uphold its primary responsibility. If citizens fear for their personal safety, a likely candidate to blame would be governmental actors, particularly the justice institutions of the courts and police.

While scholars have long linked government performance to citizen evaluations, this relationship is not necessarily straightforward. In a comprehensive review of the literature, Anderson (2007) points out that the effects of economic performance on public preferences have proven inconsistent over time and place. Anderson argues that these inconsistencies demonstrate that the impact of economic performance is highly contingent upon institutional factors, which can "allow representatives to escape attention and shift blame" (Anderson 2007, 281). This emphasis on institutions is important for applying the lessons of the economic performance literature to the study of crime and the rule of law. It is difficult for governments to completely dodge the blame for high crime rates, as it is the primary responsibility of the government to provide public security. Still, institutions might mitigate the impact of crime on public support for democracy and its norms. For example, crime victims might not register support for undemocratic alternatives if they found the police to be responsive to their reports, and successful in apprehending suspects. If the courts and police are able to apprehend and prosecute the perpetrators of crime, this efficacy might temper the effects of crime. Once again, we see that the impact of crime is coupled with that of institutional performance. Thus, in addition to variables measuring experiences with and perceptions of crime, scholars must also examine the efficacy of formal crime-fighting institutions. The two factors are intertwined.

Measuring Victimization and Fear of Crime

To distinguish among these various dimensions of crime, the economic voting literature signals the need to think in terms of personal experiences with crime (victimization), perceptions of crime in one's own immediate environment, and perceptions of crime in the country as a whole. These three dimensions distinguish between personal experiences with crime and perceptions, and further divide the latter into local and national levels.

To measure personal victimization, this analysis relies upon respondents' self-reporting on the following survey item: "Now, changing the subject, have you been a victim of any type of crime in the past twelve months? That is, have you been a victim of robbery, burglary, assault, fraud, blackmail, extortion, violent threats or any other type of crime in the past twelve months?" Respondents were coded as (1) yes and (0) no. This question aims to gauge respondents' self-reported experiences with crime, but there are some limitations associated with this measure.[8] Respondents' definitions of an incident might not be the same as the legal definition of a crime, for example. Respondents tend to over-report crimes against property and under-report crimes of violence (Bergman 2006). This makes cross-national comparisons particularly difficult, and can explain the relatively high rates of self-reported victimization in Costa Rica. Furthermore, sometimes respondents report crimes that occurred outside the given scope (in this case in the past 12 months). While it is important to note these limitations, such survey measures of victimization are considered to be the best indicators available of a phenomenon that can be difficult to measure.

In addition to measuring self-reported victimization, it is also important to examine other types of victimization that hit close to home. To this end, LAPOP included a question to gauge whether other people in the respondent's home were victimized: "Was somebody in your house victimized by some type of criminal act in the past twelve months?" Once again, responses were coded dichotomously, where (1) yes and (0) no. This measure of vicarious victimization is important, as it indicates whether the respondent experienced stories of victimization second hand from someone close. Vicarious victimization can shape perceptions of crime and calculations of personal risk—if someone close by has been victimized, respondents likely feel more vulnerable themselves. Figure 3.9 compares the percentages of respondents who indicated they were crime victims themselves, compared to the rates of vicarious victimization. In each country, there is no significant difference between national rates of self-reported victimization and vicarious victimization.

To assess public perceptions of crime, this chapter employs two measures. Just as the literature on economic voting distinguishes between pocketbook evaluations and sociotropic ones, this analysis examines the impact of respondents' assessments of personal security in their neighborhoods, as well as their perceptions of crime in the country as a whole. To measure

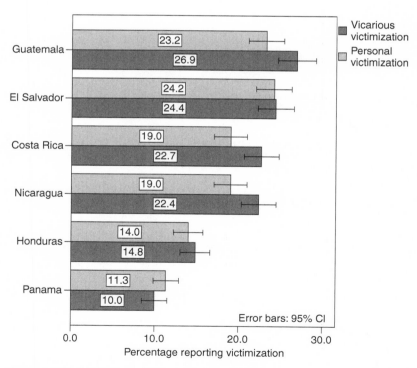

FIGURE 3.9 Self-Reported Victimization Rates of Respondents and Family Members (LAPOP 2010)

sociotropic evaluations of crime in the country, the survey asked respondents, "And speaking of the country in general, how much do you think that the level of crime we have now represents a threat to our future well-being?" Responses included: (1) not at all; (2) very little; (3) somewhat; (4) a great deal. This question focuses on the national context, gauging fear of crime in more general terms. This item is an affective measure of fear of crime as it gauges emotive evaluations of crime in the country as a whole. It is also prospective, asking respondents to evaluate the impact of crime in the future, not assess the efficacy of crime policy in the past.

To estimate respondents' evaluations of their own personal security, the survey posed the following question: "Speaking of the neighborhood where you live and thinking of the possibility of being assaulted or robbed, do you feel (1) very safe; (2) somewhat safe; (3) somewhat unsafe; (4) very unsafe?" This question is a cognitive measure of fear of crime, as it determines respondents' own risk assessments of the chances of personal victimization by specific crimes in their immediate environment. This cognitive measure asks

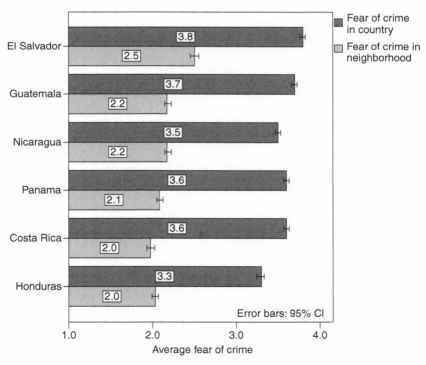

FIGURE 3.10 Fear of Crime in Central America (LAPOP 2010)

respondents to indicate their fear of victimization by more "commonplace" crimes, as opposed to those sensationalized drug-related crimes that feature so prominently in the media.

Figure 3.10 illustrates current levels of fear of crime in Central America, and at the aggregate level, provides further evidence that fear of crime is not entirely related to the actual occurrence of crime. Despite their widely divergent rates of homicide and other types of victimization, the sociotropic measure of fear of crime in the country is comparable across the cases. Again, the findings from Costa Rica stand out most prominently. Costa Rica has one of the lowest rates of violent crime in Latin America, yet levels of fear of crime are significantly higher than those of Honduras, one of the most violent countries in the world.

Figure 3.10 indicates that overall, respondents are less likely to fear victimization in their own neighborhoods than in the country as a whole. Still, an examination of fear of crime in one's own neighborhood was surprising, as once again, Honduras registered the lowest levels of fear. In contrast, El Salvador and Guatemala ranked at the top of the list on both measures of fear of crime, a finding that matches their high levels of crime.

As Table 3.3 demonstrates, Pearson correlations indicate that there is some overlap among these four measures of crime. Not surprisingly, the strongest correlations occur between vicarious and personal victimization (r=.225; p<.01) and personal victimization and fear of crime in the neighborhood (r=.189; p<.01). People who live in the same dwelling, and thus share a variety of socioeconomic traits as well, are likely to have overlapping experiences with victimization. It is also intuitive to expect respondents who have been victimized in the past 12 months to consider it likely they will be victimized again in their neighborhoods. While significant, the correlations between

TABLE 3.3 Pearson's Correlations among Fear of Crime Measures

	Another member of household victimized	Fear of crime in neighborhood	Fear of crime in country
Victim	.225** (N=9148)	.189** (N=9164)	.084** (N=9094)
Fear of crime in neighborhood	.142** (N=9139)	—	.061** (N=9096)
Fear of crime in the country	.098** (N=9072)	—	—

** p <.01

victimization and fear of crime in the country are weaker in magnitude. The correlation between the two different measures of fear of crime is also significant, but of an even smaller magnitude (r=.061; p<.01). Thus, while these four measures of crime are related, they do tap into different aspects of crime.[9] By distinguishing among these different components of crime, the subsequent analyses aim to specify exactly how crime might undermine the rule of law.

The Impact of Public Perceptions on the Rule of Law

In order to understand why citizens respect the rule of law in some cases and dismiss it in others, many observers point to the performance of justice institutions and the problem of crime. If justice institutions perform poorly, either by failing to protect citizens' safety and property, or by engaging in corruption, citizens will have few incentives to respect the rule of law. Why should citizens uphold the law, if the primary justice institutions fail to do so? In a similar vein, citizens' disregard for the rule of law has also been tied to experiences with and perceptions of crime – fearful citizens can be driven to desperate measures, such as vigilante justice. In connecting institutional performance to public attitudes toward the law, however, one must remember that actual institutional performance may differ from individual perceptions of it. Individual perceptions of institutional performance vary considerably, both cross-nationally as well as across individuals. The same pattern emerges when examining the linkage between the actual occurrence of crime and public fear of crime. Through a basic examination of descriptive statistics, this chapter illustrates that people's perceptions of crime and justice are not straightforward manifestations of their countries' rule of law rankings or rates of violent crime. Rather, these perceptions are filtered through what respondents expect, and what they perceive they have received. These expectations and evaluations are further influenced by other actors, such as the media and political candidates.

How do perceptions of crime and justice affect citizens' political attitudes and behavior? What impact do these perceptions have on the rule of law, particularly at the micro level? To answer these questions, the next chapter examines how these perceptions affect citizens' support for the rule of law within each country. Chapter 4 aims to unpack the ways in which perceptions of crime and institutional performance encourage citizens to abide by the rule of law, or disregard it altogether. To understand citizens' orientations toward the rule of law, it is imperative to develop the theoretical underpinnings of the effects of crime and justice. How exactly does crime affect democracy? Is it the personal experience of crime, or the perception of crime? Is it the perception of local crime that is the main problem? Or is it the perception of crime at the national level? That is, does fear that a criminal will steal from one's home have the same effect as fear of the growing power of armed drug cartels far from home? Under what conditions will citizens hold their governments accountable for crime?

The answers to these questions have large implications for the rule of law in the Central America. When citizens clamor for the state to address deficiencies in public security and the justice system, they may be acting on their own personal experiences with crime or police, their perceptions that crime has soared beyond what is manageable, or their perceptions that the justice system is not capable of addressing the problems at hand. Consequently, an understanding of the mechanisms by which crime and justice affect citizens' attitudes toward the law is vital for formulating good policy, particularly since officials must take both objective measures and public perceptions of crime and justice into account when constructing public security policies.

The answers to these questions are also important for understanding how citizens react to being caught in the security trap. When Bailey (2009) described the security trap, he indicated that it was a state of negative equilibrium, whereby citizens respond to poor state performance with a set of suboptimal survival skills, which allow them to get by in day-to-day life, but do not actually challenge the status quo. Rather, these survival skills actually reinforce the negative equilibrium, as "notions of law and norms of behavior in civil society differ markedly from formal law, the citizenry tolerates or promotes formally illegal exchanges, and state and regime themselves act as principal engines of crime, violence, and corruption" (Bailey 2009, 256). To understand how to escape from the security trap, it is necessary to identify the factors that lead citizens to reinforce the negative equilibrium rather than challenge it.

Notes

[1] The principal of the school recommended expulsion for the white students found responsible for hanging the nooses, but the school district overturned his decision and gave the students short suspensions from school instead.

[2] The exact text of this survey item read: "In your opinion, what is the most serious problem faced by the country?" Responses were transcribed and later coded to fall into one of 38 categories. Responses that evaded classification were coded as "other."

[3] According to Bautista Lara, the basic hierarchy of needs has kept economic issues at the forefront of national attention in Nicaragua. At its present levels, crime will not surpass economic concerns until the economic situation improves.

⁴ For in-depth accounts of how exactly people relate to crime in their own lives or in their country as a whole, see Huhn (2008, 2009) and Moodie (2008).

⁵ Krause does point out that the type of news coverage varies by news source. In the rival newspaper *Prensa Libre*, "63% of crimes reported were murders, 73% of which involved guns" (2009, 13).

⁶ Rosenberg's videotape, with English subtitles, is available at: www.youtube.com/watch?v=mC_ODpxMA10 (last accessed May 24, 2011).

⁷ Identification with Colom, represented on the Y axis, was measured by respondents' answers to the following question: "If the next presidential elections were held next week, what would you do"?

⁸ A follow-up question concerning bribery was then posed to respondents who had contact with the courts. Given the small number of respondents who had contact with the courts, the number of people who were asked to pay bribes was too small to include in later statistical analyses.

⁹ In a comprehensive review of the literature, Anderson (2007) does point out that in cross-national studies of economic voting behavior some scholars do report linkages between pocketbook evaluations and voting behavior.

¹⁰ Table 2.5 and Figure 2.6 describe the prevalence of different types of crime and cross-national victimization rates respectively.

¹¹ In a study of the relationship between crime and democracy in a select group of Latin American countries, Ceobanu, Wood, and Ribeiro (2011) report similar findings.

4

Support for Extralegal Justice

District Attorney: Where the hell does it say that you've got a right to kick down doors, torture suspects, deny medical attention and legal counsel? Where have you been? Does Escobedo ring a bell? Miranda? I mean, you must have heard of the Fourth Amendment. What I'm saying is that man had rights.

Detective Harry Callahan (aka Dirty Harry): Well, I'm all broken up over that man's rights.

Scene from Dirty Harry, *1971*

As the popularity of the legendary movie *Dirty Harry* indicates, extralegal justice has a mixed reputation in many different parts of the world. There are plenty of examples in which extralegal justice is celebrated in popular culture. In the United States, it is easy to find signs, t-shirts, and bumper stickers proudly proclaiming support for vigilantism with sayings like "We don't call 911." Vigilante heroes feature prominently in movies, books, and comic series ranging from Batman to Zorro. This celebration rests uneasily, however, given the darker sides of extralegal justice. Extralegal justice is only considered to be "justice" when people agree with its ends. When doubt surrounds the goals of extralegal justice, it has fewer champions. For example, the Dirty Harry movies idolize a police officer who stands up for victims, and does not hesitate to abridge suspects' legal rights to mete out his own brand of justice. When people do not approve of such a police officer's brand of justice, however, the officer is said to have "gone rogue." The morality of extralegal justice is very much in the eye of the beholder.

The same ambivalence surrounds extralegal justice in contemporary Central America. When one looks at the state of crime and justice in much of the region it is easy to see why extralegal justice might be appealing. Many citizens feel as if they are stuck between a rock and a hard place. Bailey and Dammert argue that the public appears "willing to allow the police to bend or break the law if doing so helps combat violent crime," as the public perceives violent criminals pose "more of a human-rights problem than do aggressive police" (2006, 254). In the high crime/low rule of law countries of Guatemala, El Salvador, and Honduras, the situation is most critical. Long standing problems with justice institutions exacerbate the contemporary crime crisis, which "has become so pervasive that many citizens look back on the days when violence was mostly political almost with nostalgia" (Seligson and Booth 2010, 124). Cruz (2003) argues that the crime crisis might be particularly problematic for people who have lived under military governance, as military leaders emphasized the importance of public order. Some people might look to the past with rose-colored glasses, forgetting the massive human rights abuses, and becoming even more radicalized by the failure of democratic governance to keep order. Particularly in Guatemala and Honduras, rampant impunity, corruption, and even official collusion with organized crime combine to make the justice system an even less attractive option for redressing grievances and solving problems. As Diamond cautioned more than a decade ago:

> In the context of weak states and inefficient, poorly disciplined police, crime may inspire drastic, illegal, unconstitutional, and grotesquely sadistic responses to try to control it. These responses can take various forms, including popular vigilante squads that mete out instant justice to suspected perpetrators, police torture and killing of prisoners and suspects, and police-led extermination squads. (1999, 91)

The situation is not as critical in the low-crime countries, but still far from ideal. Crime is still a problem, especially in Panama and Nicaragua, and citizens of these countries might not be consoled by the fact that at least their situation is not as bad as that of Guatemala, particularly if they have been victimized by a crime. Citizens of these countries are likely to show frustration if they cannot turn to the authorities to redress grievances and solve problems. The case of Costa Rica demonstrates that frustration can also grow when contemporary performance dips from that of the past—citizens might be more willing to turn to extralegal justice if they see contemporary institutions failing to perform up to their past reputations.

Against this backdrop, it is easy to see why many citizens would reject the rule of law rather than respect it. In countries engulfed by violent crime, what options do citizens see for themselves? Do people in the low crime countries perceive that they have more options? How do citizens translate their experiences and perceptions of crime into action, given the state of their respective justice systems? Do citizens' responses provide a way to escape from what Bailey (2009) referred to as a negative equilibrium? Or do their responses reinforce the security trap?

Answering these questions is crucial for understanding the relationships among crime, institutional performance, and support for extralegal justice. Currently, the dynamics of these relationships are unclear. Observers have linked support for extralegal justice to both the experience of crime, as well as the failure of justice institutions to address criminality and garner legitimacy in the eyes of the citizenry (Bailey and Dammert 2006; Cruz 2006). Still, the nuances of this relationship are not clearly understood, and exceptions remain. In a comparative analysis of the postconflict Central American countries, Cruz (2003) finds that in Guatemala and El Salvador, crime significantly influenced citizens' attitudes and behavior, but this was not the case in Nicaragua. Malone (2010a) provides additional evidence that the effects of crime can be nuanced, rendering citizens more willing to allow authorities to circumvent the law in some Central American countries, but not others. In addition, while some scholars have linked crime to reduced public participation in politics and civil society (Smulovtiz 2003), others have identified alternative scenarios, arguing that it is possible that citizens could respond to crime in ways that strengthen the rule of law and consequently democracy. Following this reasoning, crime could possibly "contribute to pro-democratic behavior as civil society organizes itself in positive ways to contribute to rule-bound law enforcement" (Bailey and Flores-Macías 2007, 18). For example, large, legal protest demonstrations have been organized in Mexico City to confront rising crime rates and kidnappings (Briscoe 2006; Llana 2008). Hinton (2006) links mass participation in demonstrations to police reform in Argentina. Similar to "take back the streets" groups organized in high crime areas in the United States, this type of citizen action could have the potential to strengthen democracy, channeling discontent into measures that strengthen civil society. In an analysis of Latin American survey data, Bateson (2009) lends empirical evidence to this theory, finding that at the micro level, crime victimization is associated with increased civic participation.

These alternative scenarios indicate that extralegal justice might not be the only response to high crime and lackluster justice institutions. To understand exactly how crime and institutional performance are related to extralegal justice, it is important to examine this relationship carefully. This chapter takes a close look at both crime and justice, tracing the impact of both personal experiences and perceptions of crime and justice institutions on attitudes toward two types of extralegal justice: officials acting on the margins of the law and popular vigilante justice. These two types of extralegal justice both manifest a rejection of the rule of law; however, they are distinct in important ways. When people give authorities license to act on the margins of the law, they are empowering official actors against suspected criminals. Typically, the "suspected" label is disregarded, and people endorsing such extralegal action assume that the suspects are in fact guilty of the charges in question. This does not give citizens additional power, but rather, strengthens the discretionary power of public officials. While such extralegal action circumvents the law, it does not necessarily bypass state institutions completely. Police might act on the margins of the law to extract a confession from a suspect, and then turn the suspect and confession over to the court and penal systems.

Vigilante justice also disregards the rule of law, but such action empowers private citizens to take the law into their own hands; it does not give additional power to state actors like the police. Under vigilante justice, typically citizens directly sanction suspected criminals, completely avoiding the state apparatus. For Cruz, vigilantism poses the primary threat for the rule of law, as it indicates that citizens have come to view their institutions as completely useless, and will not rely upon them to solve problems. Instead, citizens will ignore political institutions and solve problems themselves or apply laws on their own (Cruz 2003, 51).

Extralegal Justice in Central America

The Central American countries have varied markedly in terms of their incidents of extralegal justice. Extralegal justice has featured most prominently in the three high crime countries of the Northern Triangle. In El Salvador and Honduras, this extralegal justice has been primarily in the form of officials abusing their powers to act against suspected criminals. Popular forms of vigilante justice have been more common in Guatemala, as groups of citizens have banded together to sanction those they consider to be criminals.

Around the world extralegal justice invokes ambivalent responses, as support for extralegal justice depends heavily upon whether the ultimate goal is deemed worthy. In the case of contemporary Central America, however, extralegal justice has become particularly salient in debates over crime control policy. Extralegal justice has become politicized, primarily because it maintains a de facto link to mano dura policies. Under mano dura, the justice system cracks down on crime, issuing heavy sanctions on even petty crimes, as these petty crimes can culminate into more serious types of criminal behavior. Such policies are credited with a sharp drop in violent crime in New York City under Mayor Giuliani in the 1990s, and Giuliani and his police chief during that time, William Bratton, have gone on to provide consulting services to Latin American police forces hoping to emulate New York City's record. As in many other areas of justice reform, however, the transplantation of models from the United States to Central America is problematic. Most importantly, in the United States there is a fairly well-developed infrastructure for protecting civil rights, with explicit guarantees granted to those accused of committing a crime. Even with these guarantees, however, crackdowns on crime are frequently accompanied by charges of police abuse and excessive force. Much praise is heaped on the dramatic decline of homicide rates in New York City in the 1990s; however, there were complaints of abuse during this time as well. In one of the most inflammatory cases, a New York City police officer beat and tortured Abner Louima, a Haitian immigrant, with the help of three other police officers (Chevigny 2003). Since such abuse can take place even with an extensive framework for protecting the rights of the accused, the potential for abuse is even greater when this framework is not firmly in place. Ungar clearly outlines how mano dura and extralegal justice are intertwined in practice; he notes that to be effective while still respecting civil rights, mano dura:

> requires solid training for police officers, consistent oversight over their practices, coordination with social services to resolve the problems that lead to public disorder, and more effective courts to process detainees. But in Latin America, zero tolerance is applied without such supports or outside controls, so that the mano dura is often just a continuation of predemocratic practices and a justification for the dividing line drawn by many officials between "public order," associated with a strong state, and "human rights," associated with delinquency. (2009, 95)

As crime control policy is increasingly politicized, it becomes difficult to have actual debates about the challenges of mano dura policing without adequate resources and safeguards. In a highly charged political atmosphere, crime control policy is frequently presented in black and white terms, with mano dura politicians claiming to stand firmly with the victims, and labeling their reformist opponents as soft on crime and consequently siding with the criminals (Appialoza and Dammert 2011)

Honduras illustrates how this process unfolds. In 1996, just as the civilian government was consolidating its control over the country and sidelining the military from governance, constitutional reforms created a civilian police force, followed a year later by new police laws and penal process codes in 1997. These reforms became the target of mano dura politicians, particularly President Ricardo Maduro (2002–2006), whose son had been killed in a botched kidnapping. Once elected, Maduro deemed the new reforms to be too soft on crime. Ungar reports that Maduro's Minister of Security argued that the new penal code embodied "the garantista approach of rights protection," which privileged the rights of criminals over the needs of victims and society (2009, 98). Maduro's government distanced itself from the new reforms, opting instead for penal codes that would fight crime decisively by targeting gang members, such as Provision 332. Provision 332, an amendment to the penal code, punished gang membership with mandatory prison terms of 9 to 12 years. Other laws went even further. The Law of Police and Social Coexistence increased the discretionary powers of police by allowing them "to detain arbitrarily 'vagabounds'—people who have no honest means to earn a living or are suspected of intending to engage in criminal activities" (Ungar 2009, 98). Such measures have swelled the prison population, leading to riots and subsequent prison massacres in 2002 and 2004. Even in the absence of riots, overcrowded prisons serve as a base of operations for gangs, as well as recruitment and training grounds for new members (Arana 2005).

Both Provision 332 and the Law of Police and Social Coexistence widened the discretionary powers of police without providing additional training or resources to fight crime, essentially relegating police back to their roles as "border guards" between social classes. In addition to augmenting the powers of the police, Honduras also joined a regional trend in deploying the military to fight crime. Under *Operación Guerra Contra la Delincuencia* (Operation War against Crime), Maduro dispatched approximately 10,000 officers to patrol the streets under the leadership of a military official (Booth et al. 2010, 173). Ungar reports that the mano dura measures of the Maduro administration "encouraged the increased use of mass raids, extended preventative detention, forced confessions, and extrajudicial killings of suspected *mareros* (gang members)" (Ungar 2009, 98). From a human rights standpoint, these extrajudicial killings were the most sobering consequence of these trends in crime and punishment. Booth et al. document that between 1998 and 2002, "more than 1,500 youths were murdered, most of them males under the age of eighteen" (2010, 173). In the face of harsh criticism from organizations like Amnesty International and the United Nations, the government investigated the extrajudicial killings and acknowledged that police and security forces had played a role. This acknowledgment did not lead to convictions, however, as the Chief of the Internal Affairs Unit who implicated the police officers and security forces began to receive death threats shortly after she made her report public.

As Figure 4.1 demonstrates, the initial crackdown did coincide with a dramatic plunge in murder rates at the national level. According to some estimates, mano dura resulted in "an 80% decline in kidnapping and a 60% decline in youth violence" (Ribando 2005). However, by 2004 the murder rate again began to rise steadily, particularly as maras regrouped and responded to government crackdowns with harsh reprisals of their own, opening fire on

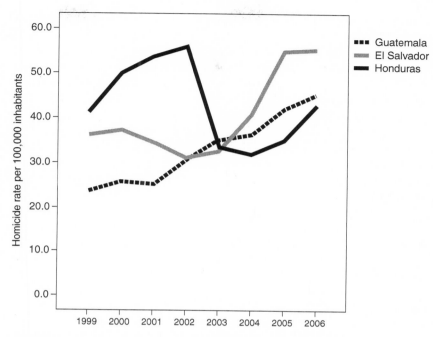

FIGURE 4.1 Homicide Rates in Northern Triangle (1999–2006)

Source: El Observatorio Centroamericano sobre Violencia (The Central American Observatory of Violence, OCAVI) 2006

crowded buses and parks, particularly in the high crime area of San Pedro Sula. Leading politicians argued that the only way to change these trends was to be harsher. In the 2005 elections, presidential candidate Porfirio Lobo campaigned on promises to reinstate the death penalty. He lost narrowly to José Manuel Zelaya, but after Zelaya's ouster, he won the 2009 presidential elections and assumed office in 2010.

Honduras did not rely solely on mano dura, however. In 2002, the Maduro government also launched a national community policing program, *Comunidad Más Segura* (Safer Community), which focuses on preventive strategies like fixing street lights and regularly meeting with the community to address local security concerns (Ungar 2009). Some communities have reported success under these programs, measured by drops in local homicide rates. Still, this community-based policing model has also been plagued by violence. Ungar relates that the "head of community policing of one district was arrested in connection with police killing youths, for example, and a member of the citizen policing group in LaCeiba said that they used it to attack suspected delinquents" (2009, 100). This example serves as a reminder that citizen participation does not automatically translate into more respect for human rights. Citizens themselves can use such forums to call (and in this case engage in) extralegal action that undermines the rule of law.

Mano dura has been accompanied by extralegal justice in other countries as well. El Salvador's police reform and crime control policy had a very different starting point from Honduras, but these two paths began to converge as both employed mano dura tactics and militarized their policing policies. Violent crime has persisted in both countries.

Policing was highly salient in El Salvador even before crime began its rise under democracy. As Chapter 2 highlighted, the 1992 Peace Accords focused extensively on the proper role of the military and the creation of a new civilian police force. The politicization of public security shaped the implementation of these accords, however, as some politicians used rising crime rates as a justification for resisting the demilitarization of domestic policing (Cruz 2006). Despite resistance, El Salvador introduced a new Criminal Code and Criminal Procedures Code in 1998, which opponents lambasted as being too soft on crime. With this cue, these reforms to the criminal justice system quickly became the scapegoat for public anger over crime. Amaya argues that in the late 1990s, politicization of criminal justice reform transformed public attitudes toward crime and punishment:

> At the beginning of the postwar period, the public had blamed structural factors, such as socioeconomic conditions or institutional weakness, for the increase in crime rates. After 1998, the public began to think that the new legislation was a factor in the growth of ordinary crime, and that perception led to a major shift in public support for authoritarian postures. (2006, 136–7)

Crime control policy continued to be politicized throughout the late 1990s and early 2000s, and this politicization ultimately increased El Salvador's reliance on mano dura policies. To be sure, El Salvador did incorporate other policing tactics into its arsenal, improving efficiency with computer tracking programs and incorporating the community through initiatives like the *Patrullas de Intervención Policial Comunitarias* (Community Police Patrolling). Also, while the military was not completely banished from domestic security matters, the Peace Accords did succeed in transforming policing practices. The level of demilitarization of crime control might not have met the standards of the Peace Accords, but it was a dramatic improvement from the past. Still, policymakers emphasized the need for quick results in the fight against crime, which meant that large numbers of arrests were prioritized over long-term, holistic responses to reducing crime by addressing its underlying causes. Just as in the case of Honduras, the prison population swelled, leading to a different set of conflicts (Wolf 2011).

Overall, the late 1990s ushered in a trend of increasingly harsh anti-crime measures. According to human rights activists and many members of the judiciary, these measures limited citizens' rights in the name of fighting crime. The 1992 Peace Accords, and the vision of domestic security they entailed, represented a compromise between left and right political actors. Until 2009, however, the right was victorious in every presidential election, and it used this political leverage to chip away at provisions that restrained state action—provisions the right never truly wanted in the first place (Cruz 2006). The first decade of the twenty-first century witnessed the enactment of more than 300 reforms of criminal law, leading one judge to conclude that "it is hard to identify the original draft law" (Gutiérrez 2008). Supreme Court lawyer Jaime Martínez labels this trend a "counter-reform" and argues that these modifications "have tended to curb the protections enjoyed by citizens against the power of the state," particularly the guarantees of due process (Gutiérrez 2008, 1). For example, before the counter-reform movement, people subject to arrest had to be shown a warrant; this provision was scrapped, and the PNC now have no obligation to do so.

Under President Flores (1999–2004), El Salvador embraced mano dura more closely, launching *Plan Mano Dura* in 2003 (eight months prior to presidential elections). Included in this plan was the controversial measure that allowed police to arrest suspected gang members on the basis of their physical appearance (Amnesty International 2003). *Plan Mano Dura* proved very popular with the public, despite its inability to actually reduce rates of violent crime. As Figure 4.1 illustrates, homicide rates in El Salvador dipped from 2000 through 2002, but then continued to climb at the end of Flores's term, just like in the other countries of the Northern Triangle.

In light of the failure of *Plan Mano Dura* to curb rising homicide rates, Flores's successor, President Saca (2004–2009), unveiled his plan to fight crime—*Plan Super Mano Dura* (Wolf 2011). Like its predecessor, *Plan Super Mano Dura* proved very popular with a public weary of so much crime and violence. Its provisions included increasing the penalties for gang membership to up to 5 years of incarceration and allowing the conviction of minors under the age of twelve (Ribando 2005). In 1 year, *Plan Super Mano Dura* led to the arrests of approximately 11,000 alleged gang members (Booth et al. 2010). Also like its predecessor, *Plan Super Mano Dura* failed to curb crime. In designing his crime-fighting strategy, Saca did respond to critics and incorporated preventive and rehabilitative measures into the program; however the emphasis was on suppression (Wolf 2011). As in the case of Honduras, gang members adapted to the new playing field and employed more violent tactics. When President Funes took office in 2009, his electoral victory marked the first time that the left had succeeded in capturing the presidency. This shift in ruling party did not lead to a major change in crime control policy, however. Funes faced a gang problem that experts considered intractable; in response, Funes announced a "comprehensive crime policy comprising social prevention, law enforcement, rehabilitation, victim support, and institutional and legal reforms" (Wolf 2011, 1). Lack of funding has led Funes to put the prevention part of his program on the backburner, but at least the police have stopped the practice of mass raids, and steps have been made to strengthen the police's ability to investigate crimes. Some justice officials have welcomed these small steps, noting that criminals tend to fear effective investigations and trials more than the length of the sentences stipulated by the penal code. Still, Funes has continued the policies of his predecessors, and even dispatched the military to patrol the streets in efforts to curb the power of gangs.

Against this backdrop, in El Salvador extralegal violence has increased in the name of sanctioning criminals. The media prominently featured high-profile incidents of police misconduct, such as the involvement of police in a 2000 kidnapping. In addition to problems of police misconduct and abuse, there have been some reports of extrajudicial killings. While the level of extrajudicial killings never rose to the level of that of Honduras during this time, some high-profile incidents called attention to the problem. For example, in 1998, the *Sombra Negra* (Dark Shadow) case grabbed the attention of the public for its blanket use of extrajudicial killings against marginalized groups. Members of this paramilitary group included police officers as well as higher level officials and even a departmental governor (Cruz 2006). While the *Sombra Negra* was disbanded and prosecuted, political pressure led to the release of its members. The human rights ombudsman in El Salvador did help monitor police performance and address misuses of power, but the reports generated did not always lead to the sanction of individuals or change the behavior of police forces more broadly.

Guatemala has followed a slightly different pattern, as incidents of extralegal justice have been endemic even without mano dura legislation. Throughout the transition to democracy, Guatemala has suffered from problems of gang violence as well as organized crime. Also, clandestine security organizations that perpetrated human rights violations during the civil war were never completely dismantled, and resumed operations under democracy. Extralegal killings have been extremely problematic, and the victims have been wider in scope. In addition to targeting the youth of marginalized groups who fit the stereotype of gang members, extralegal killings in Guatemala include assassinations of a more political nature, as victims include human rights activists, unionists, journalists, and protestors; many have been tortured prior to their executions (Booth et al. 2010, 151; Briscoe 2007). In one high-profile case that garnered a great deal of international attention, four Guatemalan police officers were charged in the murder of three Salvadoran representatives to the Central American Parliament, but these officers were found murdered in their maximum security prison before they could be questioned. Booth et al. note that "death squads appeared within the Interior Ministry and National police" and used extralegal killings as a means of "so-called social cleansing" (2010, 151). As Chapter 1 explained, a deeply ingrained culture of impunity, facilitated by the infiltration of organized crime and paramilitary groups into government and state agencies, has led international organizations to intercede and work with domestic reformers to try to bring some semblance of the rule of law to Guatemala. The UN's Comisón Internacional contra la Impunidad en Guatemla (CICIG) is the most prominent of these efforts.

Political violence accelerated greatly with the lead up to the 2007 elections, as "more than fifty congressmen, candidates, and activists were killed in pre-election violence" (Booth et al. 2010, 153). Álvaro Colom, with his slogan "fight crime with intelligence," emerged victorious over General Otto Pérez Molina's iron fist. As Figure 4.1 indicates, homicide rates continued to rise steadily. Colom did not employ the strict anti-mara laws of El Salvador and Honduras; maras were not the most pressing security problem, when compared to the power of organized crime that had entrenched itself in the state.[1] During his first year in office, the legislature passed laws to address rampant violence against women, as well as limit ready access to weaponry.[2] While strict anti-maras laws are not in place, the police have engaged in periodic raids to round up suspected gang members (Ribando Seelke 2011). Guatemala has also signed agreements with its neighbors for joint patrols along the borders to discourage transnational gang activity.

In addition to the extralegal killings perpetrated by police and clandestine security forces, the rule of law in Guatemala has been further compromised by vigilante justice. Guatemala has been the scene of the most publicized incidents of vigilante justice, where *linchamientos* (lynchings) began during the early 1990s, accelerating after the signing of the 1996 Peace Accords (Godoy 2002). Many attacks can be linked to former paramilitary leaders, but the public has also engaged in the violence as well (Godoy 2002). Representing the dark side of social capital, citizens have banded together to sanction suspected criminals extrajudicially. Public support for vigilantism has been on the rise, as average support rose in both urban and rural areas from 2004 through 2006 (Azpuru 2006).

Such episodes represent a complete rejection of the rule of law—rather than rely upon hopeless legal avenues to address crime-related grievances, citizens instead are turning to mob justice. Rosenberg (2007) relates interviews with self-proclaimed vigilantes in desperately poor areas like Villa Nueva (on the edge of Guatemala City), who describe themselves as private citizens who turn to murder suspected gang members as a means of survival. While this type of vigilantism tends to grab the headlines, Godoy (2006) provides a thorough examination of the complexities of lynching through a series of narratives of people who have witnessed such violence. Very rarely is vigilantism a simple, knee-jerk reaction to crime and institutional failure. Rather, acts of vigilantism are tied to longstanding tensions and disputes. Often targeted criminals are members of marginalized ethnic/racial groups and classes, raising the alarm that vigilante justice is a new way to abuse minority rights. Godoy (2002) notes that in Guatemala, labeling an individual as a criminal, and thus a potential target for vigilantes, is a means of redressing past abuses occurring during the nations' 36-year civil war.

Fernández (2004) also takes a close look at the dynamics of lynching, arguing that this form of extralegal justice is part of the violent legacy of Guatemala's civil war. The civil war unleashed horrific amounts of violence on the countryside, especially indigenous communities. This excessive violence left an imprint on local communities, and contemporary lynching frequently relies upon the same tactics to execute criminals as state forces had used against suspected guerrillas. The civil war also left an institutional legacy as well. Fernández (2004) explains how before the war, indigenous communities relied upon established common laws to empower village elders to resolve conflicts. During the war, the military usurped these community institutions, killed many village leaders, and assumed authority in their stead. Fernández notes that:

> After the war it was not possible to re-build the traditional justice system, as the fabric of society had been irreparably torn. Nor has the official system of justice been able to fill this vacuum—it frequently fails to respond to the interests and needs of this sector of the population. The majority of Guatemalans has no access to the official system of justice. Furthermore, when access to the system is reached, it often produces social and cultural shocks that only create tension and frustration. (2004, 3)

According to Fernández, this power vacuum in conflict resolution has precipitated a rise in vigilante justice during the era of democratization. The concentration of lynchings in indigenous communities is not tied to indigenous common law or culture, rather it is tied to a legacy of violence and an institutional void. Officials entrusted with protecting indigenous rights concur, declaring firmly that "These acts do not have anything to do with indigenous law" (*Prensa Libre* 2011).

Mendoza (2006) echoes many of these findings, arguing that the rise in lynching in Guatemala is linked to two main structural factors—the state's failure to provide justice and adequate protection to its citizens, and the solidarity of ethnic groups. According to Mendoza, these ties of ethnic solidarity remove impediments to collective action, thus facilitating the coordination among citizens necessary to engage in vigilante justice. This does not mean that lynching is part of indigenous common law or custom, however. Rather, it is simply an indication that a shared ethnic identify can facilitate all types of collective action, even violent ones. Mendoza (2006) contends that the current wave of lynchings in Guatemala is partially due to an historical legacy, as the state has long failed to provide the most basic goods and services to its indigenous population, so the indigenous have developed a "cultural repertoire" for providing these goods and services for themselves. These historical patterns of collective action facilitate contemporary efforts of collaboration, even collaborations with violent ends like lynching. To test his argument, Mendoza compares incidents of lynching to the ratio of courts per 100,000 inhabitants. He finds that when this ratio is low, more lynchings occur; a weak or nonexistent judicial infrastructure leaves citizens seeking other alternatives for justice. According to Mendoza (2006), when weak infrastructure combines with ties of solidarity, lynching can be the unfortunate outcome.

Nicaragua, Panama, and Costa Rica have largely escaped these trends of extralegal justice. Cases of extralegal justice might emerge, particularly in the area of police misconduct. In Nicaragua, there have been reports of police overstepping their constitutionally proscribed roles and using excessive force, for example (Ribando Seelke 2011). However, these cases tend to be isolated and/or of less severity. There are several reasons for these divergent trends. Most obviously, all three countries have far lower rates of violent crime, and have escaped widespread infiltration of maras and organized crime. With its long democratic history and emphasis on human rights, Costa Rican police have a long institutional tradition of adhering to the law (Eijkman 2006). In Nicaragua, the constitution also restrains the police, limiting them to a strictly preventive role, although some scholars have noted that there is a disconnect between official rhetoric and individual police action at the street level (Ribando Seelke 2011).

These three countries have also employed different methods to fight crime and rejected mano dura approaches; however, these alternatives to mano dura have also not succeeded in reducing homicide rates at the national level (OCAVI 2006). Still, this rejection creates less space for authorities to engage in extralegal action. In Panama, President Martin Torrijos (2004–2009) steered crime control policy in the opposite direction, extending the *Mano Amiga* (Friendly Hand) to fight crime. The *Mano Amiga* revolved around crime prevention, offering alternatives for at-risk youth to dissuade them from joining maras. With the help of domestic and international non-governmental organizations, *Mano Amiga* provides access to extracurricular activities like theatre and sports to approximately 10,000 Panamanian youth, as well as rehabilitation for former gang members (Ribando Seelke 2005).

Nicaragua has also adopted a very different strategy from the other post-conflict countries. While the potential for rampant violence was present in the 1990s, Nicaragua avoided such pitfalls in part due to its policing strategies. Nicaragua has employed a holistic crime fighting policy, targeting at-risk youth and engaging the police in "preventive and rehabilitative efforts" that focus on "family, school, and community interventions" (Ribando Seelke 2011, 11). León has pioneered the use of GPS tracking and other technology to identify at-risk areas and individuals, and target preventive measures accordingly (Espinoza and Herrera 2009). When asked why Nicaragua focused on prevention instead of mano dura suppression, officials explained their motivations quite simply: "Mano dura just does not work. It just sets up cycles of repression and counter-violence. Prevention works."[3]

Costa Rica has also centered on preventive and rehabilitative measures. Given President Chinchilla's own academic and professional background in community-oriented policing policies, not surprisingly these tactics have dominated political discourse. Despite Costa Rica's focus on prevention and rehabilitation, Chinchilla cautions that crime's erosion of the justice system's legitimacy can make repressive measures more popular, despite the fact that they show "little effectiveness in containing the problem" (Chinchilla 2002, 23). To counter such trends, Chinchilla argues that community security and community policing are well-suited to address the complexity of public insecurity, as such programs:

> . . . emphasize the citizen as beneficiary of and participant in the design, implementation, and control of security policies. From this perspective both the objective behavior of crime and citizens' fear of crime are matters of concern, and balanced actions are proposed not only with respect to the offenders but also with respect to the victims. (Chinchilla 2002, 17)

Such innovations offer insights into the ways in which the rule of law can coexist with effective responses to insecurity (Chinchilla 2003). However, will they prevail, particularly if crime has the potential to erode the legitimacy of the justice system even in countries with strong democratic traditions like Costa Rica? Will the public support such innovations given trends of violence, especially the extreme violence of the Northern Triangle? To answer these questions, this chapter turns to examine citizen support for extralegal justice, grounding this examination in the contextual realities of each country's trends in crime and justice.

Should Authorities Always Uphold the Law? Examining Public Views

This overview of extralegal justice in each country provides an important context for understanding political attitudes. When surveys ask respondents if they support authorities acting on the margins of the law in Honduras, this is very different from asking the same question in Nicaragua. In the context of Honduras, respondents are indicating whether they would support authorities acting on the margins of the law, despite a highly publicized record of extrajudicial killings. Of course, given the desperation many citizens feel when facing violence on such a scale, such an option might still have appeal. In Nicaragua, when people are asked if they support authorities acting on the margins of the law, the authorities in question have a much better track record in terms of respecting human rights, and the scope of the crime crisis is more modest. This analysis begins by examining public support for one type of extralegal justice—support for authorities acting on the margins of the law (aka, the Dirty Harry solution) in each country. It then examines the linkages between crime and justice to support for this extralegal alternative.

Measuring Attitudes toward Officials Acting on the Margins of the Law

The 2010 LAPOP survey asked respondents, "To capture criminals, do you think that the authorities should always respect the laws, or do you think that sometimes they can act on the margins of the law?" Responses were coded (1) they should always respect the laws and (0) sometimes they can act on the margins of the law. Figure 4.2 depicts the percentage of respondents in each country who thought that occasionally authorities should act on the margins to capture criminals.

As Figure 4.2 illustrates, in every case but El Salvador, more than half of the citizenry indicated that the authorities should always uphold the law. It is not that the current crime wave and frustration with justice institutions has unilaterally led citizens to give authorities free reign to enforce the law

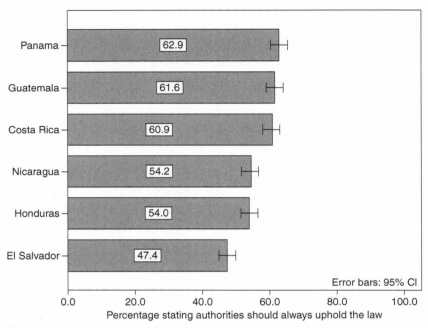

FIGURE 4.2 Attitudes toward Authorities' Adherence to the Law

as they see fit. Rather, most people still want to see authorities uphold the law while pursuing suspected criminals. Even in Guatemala, a country with one of the highest homicide rates in the world, 62 percent of citizens want to see authorities uphold the law. This percentage is the second highest in the sample, on par with Costa Rica and significantly higher than the other high crime countries of Honduras and El Salvador. As a point of comparison, when this question was posed in the United States in 2010, 69 percent of respondents stated that authorities should always uphold the law.[4]

It is important to note, however, that this question was asked in distinct national contexts. As the World Bank rankings depicted in Figure 2.2 illustrated, when citizens contemplate giving authorities more discretionary power, they are talking about very different authorities. In Costa Rica, said authorities have a long tradition of upholding the law, respecting human rights, and treating citizens equally. Costa Ricans might interpret "acting on the margins of the law" as not involving "serious" limitations on civil liberties. In contrast, as this chapter has demonstrated, in Guatemala the authorities in question are infamous for corruption and violations of civil liberties and human rights. Indeed, a 2008 LAPOP survey of Guatemala contained a question that asked, "Some people say that the police in this neighborhood protect the people from criminals, while others say that the police themselves are involved in crime. What do you think?" Responses were quite dismal. In Guatemala, 66 percent of respondents thought that police themselves were involved in crime, which might explain the high number of people who stated that they thought authorities should always uphold the law. Given officials' involvement in crime, and the impunity they typically receive, many Guatemalans prefer authorities to uphold the law for a change, even if crime rates continue to soar. Thus, it is important to keep in mind that when citizens indicate willingness to allow authorities to circumvent the law, their responses might have different connotations.

Data Analysis: Should Authorities Always Uphold the Law?

To examine the impact of crime and institutional performance on this measure of public support for the rule of law, this analysis employs the variables measuring experiences with and perceptions of crime and institutional performance discussed in Chapter 3. Chapter 3 distinguished between objective measures of crime and justice, and people's perceptions of crime and justice. It explained the various reasons why there is frequently a disjuncture between perceptions and objective measures—that there are a variety of mechanisms (people's expectations, experiences, media coverage, politicization) that help shape citizens' perceptions.

To understand why some citizens insist that authorities should always uphold the law, while others are willing to grant authorities leeway to act on the margins, this analysis examines the impact of both crime and justice on people's views toward this form of extralegal justice. Table 4.1 provides a summary of the measures of crime and justice discussed in the review of the literature in Chapter 3, and their corresponding hypotheses. Following the examples in the literature, the analysis expects that both personal experience with crime (in the form of victimization) and perceptions of crime (fear of crime in one's neighborhood and in the country at large) will lead respondents to be more willing to support authorities acting on the margins of the law. In contrast, this analysis expects that public perceptions that the justice system can punish criminals will lead respondents to register more support for the law, and disapprove of actions on the margins. According to the literature, support for extralegal action occurs when the justice system appears to be broken, or when the laws are perceived to be too soft on criminals. If institutions are perceived as doing a good job, then why act on the margins? The procedures and laws in place should be sufficient.

Just as crime is measured through personal experience and perception, so is institutional performance. To measure personal experiences with the justice system, this analysis relies upon the item measuring experiences with police corruption. If respondents have experienced police corruption first hand, in the form of soliciting a bribe, then the analysis expects that they will be less supportive of authorities acting on the margin. If personal experience with authorities is negative, it seems logical to surmise that people would be unwilling to give the same authorities discretion to act on the margins of the law. Unfortunately it is only practical to examine respondents' interactions with police, as only a small fraction of respondents have contact with the court system or other parts of the justice system in a given year. Police are the officials with whom respondents tend to have the most contact, so it is possible to see if these interactions shape attitudes toward the law more broadly. The number of people who interact with other components of the justice system, such as the courts, is too small to engage in meaningful statistical analysis.

As Table 4.1 details, this analysis follows common practice in public opinion analyses and takes individual attributes into account as well. In order to determine the impact of crime and justice institutions, it is imperative to control for individual-level attributes that might also explain the dependent variable. In particular, scholars note the importance of socioeconomic characteristics in explaining political attitudes and behaviors. To take these characteristics into account, this analysis follows the conventions of survey research and incorporates variables measuring sex (men=1, women=0), age (measured in years), and education (measured as the number of years of formal schooling respondents completed). It also contained a variable measuring the size of respondents' hometowns,[5] and measured income according to the number of household possessions owned by respondents.[6] Given Guatemala's large indigenous population, in the analyses of Guatemala an additional variable was included to measure ethnicity. This dummy variable was coded as follows: (1) self-identifies as indigenous; (0) self-identifies as ladino or other.[7]

To test these hypotheses and explore the linkages between crime, justice institutions, and the rule of law, this analysis relies upon binomial logistic regression. Binomial logistic regression is the most appropriate statistical tool for examining the dichotomous dependent variable, which is coded as (1) authorities should always uphold the law and (0) authorities can sometimes act on the margins. Table 4.2 reports the first set of regression results for the high crime/low rule of law countries.

The results reported in Table 4.2 demonstrate that crime can lead citizens to endorse extralegal justice, but its effects are nuanced. In the two postconflict countries of Guatemala and El Salvador, people's immediate environments were most important in shaping attitudes toward extralegal justice. In both

TABLE 4.1 Variables and Hypotheses for Understanding Public Attitudes toward Extralegal Action

	Independent variables	Hypotheses
Crime	Victimization	Victims will be less likely to constrain authorities to the law than nonvictims.
	Fear of crime in the neighborhood	As fear of crime in the neighborhood increases, support for limiting authorities to the law will decrease.
	Fear of crime in the country	As fear of crime in the country increases, support for limiting authorities to the law will decrease.
Institutional performance	Ability to punish criminals	As people's trust that the justice system will punish criminals increases, support for limiting authorities to the law will also increase.
	Experience with police corruption	People who have experienced police corruption will be more likely to support limiting authorities to the law.
Individual attributes	Gender	Women will be more supportive of limiting authorities to the law than men.
	Age	Older respondents will be more supportive of limiting authorities to the law than younger respondents.
	Income	As income increases, support for limiting authorities to the law decreases.
	Education	As education increases, support for limiting authorities to the law increases.
	Size of municipality	As the size of the municipality increases, support for limiting authorities to the law will decrease.
	Indigenous dummy variable (Guatemala only)	In Guatemala, indigenous respondents will be more likely to support limiting authorities to the law than ladinos.

The Rule of Law in Central America

TABLE 4.2 Should Authorities Always Uphold the Law? Logistic Regression Results (High Crime/Low Rule of Law Countries)

	Independent variables	Guatemala	El Salvador	Honduras
Crime variables	Victimization	−.267[a] (.142)	−.146 (.129)	−.426** (.154)
	Fear of crime in the neighborhood	−.156* (.065)	−.172** (.053)	−.106 (.068)
	Fear of crime in the country	.083 (.088)	−.096 (.093)	.225*** (.062)
Institutional performance	Ability to punish criminals	.124* (.061)	.168** (.049)	.033 (.057)
	Experience with police corruption	−.318 (.167)	.062 (.233)	.201 (.186)
Individual attributes	Gender	−.284* (.120)	−.101 (.107)	−.020 (.106)
	Age	.060** (.021)	.079*** (.018)	−.019 (.019)
	Income	−.112 (.310)	−.159 (.336)	−.492 (.289)
	Education	−.016 (.054)	.059 (.060)	−.058 (.076)
	Size of municipality	−.217*** (.044)	−.041 (.039)	.030 (.043)
	Indigenous dummy variable (Guatemala only)	.500*** (.141)		
	Nagelkerke pseudo *R* Squared	.123	.051	.032
	N	1332	1524	1519

* *p*<.05; ** *p*<.01; *** *p*<.001

Note: Binomial logistic regression coefficients with standard errors in parentheses.
[a] This variable was close to attaining statistical significance (*p*<.06) but multicollinearity prevented it from falling below the *p*<.05 threshold.

cases, respondents' fear that they would be victimized by crime in their own neighborhoods significantly reduced their support for the law. The results of this analysis indicate that as fear of crime in the neighborhood increased, respondents were significantly less likely to state that authorities should always obey the law. In Guatemala, personal experience with crime also reduced support for the law; this variable was not significant according to the conventional statistical threshold of p<.05, but this is due to problems of multicollinearity, or a high degree of overlap between personal victimization and fear of crime in the neighborhood.[8] In El Salvador, personal victimization did not significantly reduce support for the law, and this was not due to multicollinearity. To probe the relationship between victimization and support for the law further, the analysis distinguished between violent and nonviolent victimization. Even with this distinction, there was no relationship between victimization and support for the law. Victims of violent crime were not more likely to sanction extralegal justice than victims of nonviolent crime or people who had not experienced any victimization at all in the past year. While victimization had different effects on attitudes toward the law in these countries, in both cases the results demonstrate that perceptions of crime are more powerful than the actual experience of it.

In Guatemala and El Salvador, perceptions of justice institutions were also significant. Respondents who thought the justice system could sanction criminals were significantly more supportive of the law than those who perceived the justice system as ineffective. Personal experiences with police corruption were not significant, however. Overall, these results indicate that perceptions shaped attitudes more than personal experiences.

In Guatemala and El Salvador, the individual attributes variables performed unevenly. Age was significantly linked to support for the law, and older respondents were more likely to say that authorities should always uphold the law. None of the other individual attributes were significant in El Salvador; while gender and size of municipality were significant in Guatemala. In Guatemala, the indigenous registered more support for the law than their ladino counterparts, as the indigenous were 65 percent more likely to say that authorities should always support the law.[9] This is probably attributable to the legacy of the civil war in Guatemala, where the indigenous bore the brunt of the extralegal action that resulted in massive human rights violations.

Honduras followed a very different pattern—only the crime-related variables were significant. Institutional performance and individual attributes did not affect citizens' willingness to allow authorities to act on the margins of the law. Instead, personal victimization by crime significantly lowered respondents' support for the law, as crime victims were more likely to let authorities bend the law. In contrast to Guatemala and El Salvador, fear of crime in the neighborhood was not significant, but fear of crime in the country was significant yet *positive*. In contrast to the theoretical expectations articulated in Table 4.1, as citizens of Honduras expressed more fear of crime in their country, they were significantly *more* likely to state that authorities should always respect the law. This finding indicates that as fear of crime at the national level rises, respondents are *more likely* to respect the law. This counterintuitive result makes more sense when interpreted in the context of Honduras, where authorities have engaged in high-profile crimes such as extrajudicial killings. The perception that the police are committing their fair share of crime, and/or colluding with criminal organizations, might lead respondents to react to crime at the national level with a desire to strengthen the rule of law, and thus reduce the occurrence of extralegal and corrupt acts.

These same variables were examined in a second set of logistic regression analyses in the low crime countries of Nicaragua, Costa Rica, and Panama. While these three countries have far lower rates of violent crime than in the Northern Triangle, as Figure 2.7 demonstrated, Nicaragua and Panama still have homicide rates that are substantially higher than Costa Rica. These countries also vary considerably according to the rule of law. The quality of the rule of law in Costa Rica has long been regarded to be among the highest in Latin America. According to the World Bank, the rule of law in Panama is slightly better than the global average, but Nicaragua's score ranks among the bottom third in the world. How do crime and institutional performance affect citizens' willingness to allow authorities leeway to bend the law in these contexts? Table 4.3 reports the results by country.

The results of Table 4.3 provide a great deal of insight into how crime and institutional performance influence attitudes toward the law. Most striking is that in Costa Rica, all of the crime-related variables significantly affect citizens' willingness to grant authorities discretion to act on the margins of the law. Personal victimization, fear of crime in the country, and fear of crime in the neighborhood all emerged as significant predictors of citizens' support for the law (although the impact of fear of crime in the neighborhood was muted due to problems of multicollinearity). People who experienced crime first hand were significantly more likely to give authorities discretion to act on the margins of the law. In a similar vein, as fear of crime in the neighborhood increased, people were less likely to state that authorities should always uphold the law. These findings are consistent with the hypotheses stipulated in Table 4.1. However, the findings concerning fear of crime in

TABLE 4.3 Should Authorities Always Uphold the Law? Logistic Regression Results (Lower Crime Countries with Varying Levels of Rule of Law)

	Independent variables	Costa Rica	Nicaragua	Panama
Crime variables	Victimization	−.395** (.147)	−.171 (.139)	.040 (.179)
	Fear of crime in the neighborhood	−.122ᵃ (.066)	.024 (.058)	−.125 (.073)
	Fear of crime in the country	.366*** (.077)	.027 (.071)	−.198* (.088)
Institutional performance	Ability to punish criminals	.235*** (.055)	.128* (.053)	.046 (.060)
	Experience with police corruption	−.452 (.254)	−.348 (.205)	.998** (.335)
Individual attributes	Gender	−.218 (.116)	−.207 (.109)	−.135 (.109)
	Age	.056** (.020)	.029 (.020)	.045* (.020)
	Income	.022 (.357)	.343 (.334)	.223 (.302)
	Education	.080 (.066)	−.061 (.061)	−.037 (.061)
	Size of municipality	−.091* (.036)	.037 (.038)	.031 (.040)
	Nagelkerke pseudo R Squared	.085	.020	.026
	N	1369	1462	1464

* $p<.05$; ** $p<.01$; *** $p<.001$

Note: Binomial logistic regression coefficients with standard errors in parentheses.
ᵃ This variable was close to attaining statistical significance ($p<.07$) but multicollinearity prevented it from falling below the $p<.05$ threshold.

the country went against theoretical expectations, just as they did in the case of Honduras. According to Table 4.3, as fear of crime in the country increased, respondents were more likely to say that authorities should always uphold the law. Again, it appears that fear of crime at the national level is mixed with concern about extralegal actions more broadly.

Institutional performance was also significant in Costa Rica. As respondents perceived the justice system to be more capable of punishing criminals, they were more supportive of the law and less tolerant of authorities acting on the margins of the law. This is consistent with theoretical expectations—if the system is working well enough to punish criminals, there is little need to turn to extralegal justice. Personal experiences with police corruption were not significant, however, and the variables measuring socioeconomic status performed inconsistently.

In contrast to the strong impact of the crime-related variables on public support for the law in Costa Rica, in Nicaragua none of these variables are significant. Neither personal experiences nor perceptions of crime influenced citizens' attitudes toward this form of extralegal justice. Once again, additional regressions were run to see if victims of violent crime were more willing to allow authorities to bend the law, but this variable was also insignificant. Neither violent nor nonviolent crime victims registered significantly lower support for the rule of law. These findings reflect the lack of politicization of crime in Nicaragua. Economic problems are more salient than crime to the public, and politicians have not campaigned as heavily on anti-crime platforms. Crime is not politicized, and has no effect on citizens' attitudes in this analysis.

In Nicaragua, perceptions of justice institutions do matter, however. Similar to the findings in Costa Rica, people who perceive the justice system to be capable of sanctioning criminals are more supportive of the rule of law, and less likely to allow authorities to act on the margins of the law. None of the individual attributes were significant.

Crime had slightly more of an impact in Panama, where personal victimization and fear of crime in the neighborhood were not significant, but fear of crime at the national level was significant. This sociotropic measure of fear of crime shaped people's attitudes toward the law, but in the opposite direction of Costa Rica and Honduras. In Panama, this variable performed consistent with the hypothesis—as fear of crime in the country increased, people were less likely to state that authorities should always uphold the law. As citizens perceived crime to be more of a threat to their country's future, they were more willing to allow authorities to circumvent the law to capture criminals. These cross-national differences are important, as they indicate that people perceive the problem of crime at the national level quite differently. In Honduras and Costa Rica (an unusual match to find commonalities), sociotropic perceptions of crime appear tied to citizens' concerns about authorities' extralegal actions. In contrast, in Panama sociotropic perceptions of crime appear to focus on suspected criminals, and thus citizens aim to give authorities latitude to go against these suspects.

Experiences with justice institutions also mattered in Panama, as people who experienced police corruption were significantly less likely to give these same authorities more power to apprehend criminals. The magnitude of this effect was quite large—people who reported paying bribes to police were 107 percent more likely to say that authorities should always follow the law.[10] This finding indicates that official corruption is still a problem in Panama and it can affect attitudes toward the law; however, it does not appear that this problem is conflated with the broader problem of crime at the national level. Individual attributes also performed inconsistently in Panama, with only age registering statistical significance; older respondents were more likely to support the rule of law.

Now that this analysis has examined the relationships among crime, institutional performance, and support for official extralegal justice, the next section turns to examine citizen support for a very different type of extralegal justice—vigilantism. While vigilantism is also a type of extralegal justice, it takes a very different form. Rather than granting officials more power to sanction suspected criminals, vigilantism bypasses the justice system entirely to grant more power to citizens.

Public Support for Vigilante Justice

To understand public support for authorities' extralegal actions, the analysis relied primarily upon two factors—crime and institutional performance. Support for vigilantism involves a third dimension—attitudes toward fellow citizens. Under vigilantism, citizens band together and engage in collective action to sanction those they suspect of criminal activity. Thus, to explain support for vigilante justice, it is imperative to include a measure of attitudes toward fellow citizens, particularly views about what role citizens should play in politics and society. In order for the perceived failure of the justice system to translate into collective action, citizens would need to have some sense of solidarity with the other members of their communities, and view citizen action as a viable means for achieving their goals. People would need to view citizen action as an appropriate vehicle for addressing crime, as opposed to granting more discretionary power to officials or supporting harsh crackdowns. In order to understand public support for vigilantism, additional variables measuring these attitudes toward fellow citizens need to be included in the analysis. This section examines public support for vigilante justice, and then discusses the various hypotheses that can explain this support (including measures of attitudes toward fellow citizens). These hypotheses set the stage for an empirical examination of survey data, followed by a discussion of the results.

Measuring Support for Vigilante Justice

The LAPOP measure of support for vigilantism is part of a larger battery of survey items measuring support for a series of illegal behaviors. The survey asked respondents: "I am going to read a list of actions and things that people sometimes rely upon to meet their goals and political objectives. Could you tell me to what degree you approve or disapprove of people doing the following things?" Respondents were shown a card that ranged from (1) strongly disapprove and (10) strongly approve.[11] Included in this battery of questions were items measuring support for:

- People blocking or closing streets or highways
- People invading private property or land
- People participating in a group that wants to overthrow the elected government through violent means
- People taking justice into their own hands when the state does not punish criminals.

Figure 4.3 depicts respondents' average levels of support for people taking justice into their own hands. On a range of one through ten, respondents in

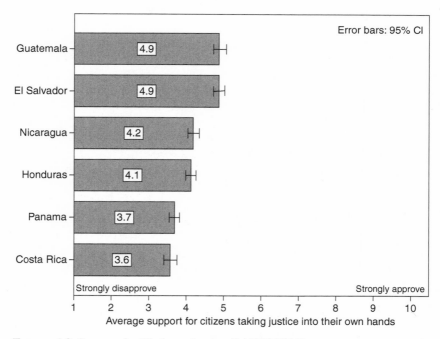

FIGURE 4.3 Support for Vigilante Justice (LAPOP 2010)

Guatemala, El Salvador, Nicaragua, and Honduras fell close to the middle of the distribution.[12] Figure 4.3 reveals some interesting patterns. Average support for vigilantism is lowest in the two countries with the highest World Bank rule of law rankings—Panama and Costa Rica. That is, in the countries where the rule of law performs better than the global average, people register less support on average for turning the crime control reins over to their fellow citizens.

Figure 4.3 illustrates support for vigilante justice at the macro level; however these country means hide important individual-level variations. When one examines support for vigilante justice within each country, some interesting findings emerge. Most striking is that within each country, the modal response category was (1) strongly disapprove. A plurality of citizens clustered at the extreme end of the distribution, indicating their strong disapproval of vigilantism.

Table 4.4 compares support for vigilantism with the other illegal behaviors included in the survey, and reveals that for each of these illegal behaviors, a plurality of respondents indicated their strong disapproval for the illegal activities at hand. The crucial difference among countries is the percentage of the population grouped at the extreme left of the distribution. In every case, Costa Rica, with its democratic head start, has the highest percentage of respondents strongly disapproving of the illegal actions. At the other extreme, on each item Honduras had the smallest percentage registering very strong disapproval.

While a plurality in each country registered very strong disapproval for the illegal activities at hand, this disapproval was tempered when it came to the question of vigilante justice. For example, in El Salvador, 58 percent of respondents were adamantly opposed to violently overthrowing the government, 52 percent to property invasions, and 41percent to blocking streets. However, when it came to vigilante justice, the percentage dwindled to 25 percent. This pattern repeats itself in Guatemala and Honduras, and to

TABLE 4.4 Percentage Strongly Disapproving of Illegal Activities

	Guatemala (%)	El Salvador (%)	Honduras (%)	Nicaragua (%)	Costa Rica (%)	Panama (%)
Blocking streets	43	41	30	46	**56**	**38**
Property invasions	52	52	38	68	71	52
Overthrowing the government	47	58	39	63	75	49
Taking justice into their own hands	**28**	**25**	**23**	**41**	**56**	**39**

a lesser extent in Nicaragua. In Costa Rica and Panama, support for vigilante justice was on par with support for blocking streets, but these two items ranked far below property invasions and overthrowing the government. Overall, the trend is that respondents proved willing to suspend some of their disapproval when it came to vigilantism (and in some cases, also blocking streets). Table 4.4 indicates that while substantial numbers of respondents register strong disapproval for citizens engaging in many unlawful activities, this disapproval does not always carry over to the question of vigilante justice.[13]

Measuring Attitudes toward Fellow Citizens

Given the collective nature of vigilante justice, in order to understand public support for vigilantism, it is imperative to gauge respondents' views of their fellow citizens, particularly their role in politics. To create such a measure, this analysis turned to the items included in the previous battery of questions, which asked respondents if they approved of a series of protest actions that were illegal: blocking streets, property invasions, and overthrowing the government. While a factor analysis revealed that support for vigilantism tapped into a different phenomenon than these other types of illegal behaviors, still there is reason to suspect that there would be a linkage. That is, people who are reluctant to support citizens engaging in *any* type of illegal protest behavior might be predisposed to voice trepidation when it comes to vigilante justice.

To measure attitudes toward citizens' illegal forms of protest, this analysis relies upon an additive index, which calculated respondents' mean level of support for these three behaviors. Respondents were included as long as they provided valid responses for three of the four behaviors listed. The Chronbach's alpha for this scale is .744. Table 4.5 articulates the hypothesis for this variable, as well as the other variables pertaining to crime, institutional performance, and individual attributes.

Data Analysis: Support for Vigilante Justice

Since the dependent variable, support for vigilante justice, is an ordinal scale ranging from one through ten, the statistical analysis relies upon ordinal logistic regression. This analysis aims to determine how crime and institutional performance shape support for this citizen-oriented form of extralegal justice, and whether there are variations between support for official and citizen extralegal justice. Table 4.6 reports the results for the high crime/low rule of law countries.

TABLE 4.5 Variables and Hypotheses for Understanding Public Attitudes toward Vigilante Justice

	Independent variables	Hypotheses
Crime	Victimization	Victims will be more supportive of vigilante justice than nonvictims.
	Fear of crime in the neighborhood	As fear of crime in the neighborhood increases, support for vigilante justice will also increase.
	Fear of crime in the country	As fear of crime in the country increases, support for vigilante justice will also increase.
Institutional performance	Ability to punish criminals	As people's trust that the justice system will punish criminals increases, support for vigilante justice will decrease.
	Experience with police corruption	People who have experienced police corruption will be more supportive of vigilante justice than those who have not.
Attitudes toward citizens' illegal protest	Approval of citizens' illegal protest action	As approval for citizens' illegal protest actions increases, support for vigilantism will also increase.
Individual attributes	Gender	Men will be more supportive of vigilante justice than women.
	Age	Younger respondents will be more supportive of vigilante justice than older respondents.
	Income	As income increases, support for vigilante justice decreases.
	Education	As education increases, support for vigilante justice decreases.
	Size of municipality	As the size of the municipality increases, support for vigilante justice will decrease.
	Indigenous dummy variable (Guatemala only)	In Guatemala, indigenous respondents will be more supportive of vigilante justice than ladinos.

TABLE 4.6 Ordinal Logistic Regression Results for Support for Vigilante Justice (High Crime/Low Rule of Law Countries)

	Independent variables	Guatemala	El Salvador	Honduras
Crime variables	Victimization	−.004 (.120)	**.233*** **(.111)**	.204 (.136)
	Fear of crime in the neighborhood	**.193*** **(.054)**	**.139** **(.046)**	**−.163** **(.060)**
	Fear of crime in the country	**.176*** **(.075)**	−.053 (.080)	**.209*** **(.056)**
Institutional performance	Ability to punish criminals	**−.181*** **(.051)**	−.030 (.042)	−.088 (.051)
	Experience with police corruption	**.274**[a] **(.141)**	**.857*** **(.200)**	**.593*** **(.163)**
Attitudes toward citizen collective action	Support for illegal protest action	**.373*** **(.028)**	**.252*** **(.026)**	**.553*** **(.026)**
Individual attributes	Gender	.072 (.099)	**.243** **(.092)**	−.031 (.093)
	Age	−.018 (.018)	**−.049** **(.016)**	−.027 (.017)
	Income	−.389 (.261)	.176 (.288)	**.692** **(.256)**
	Education	−.041 (.045)	**−.105*** **(.051)**	−.017 (.068)
	Size of municipality	**.082*** **(.037)**	.030 (.033)	**−.149*** **(.038)**
	Indigenous dummy variable (Guatemala only)	−.085 (.115)		
	Nagelkerke pseudo *R* Squared	.175	.105	.289
	N	1328	1533	1502

* $p<.05$; ** $p<.01$; *** $p<.001$

Note: Ordinal logistic regression coefficients with standard errors in parentheses.
[a] This variable was very close to attaining statistical significance ($p<.055$), but multicollinearity prevented it from falling below the p<.05 threshold.

Table 4.6 indicates that the dynamics of support for citizen-driven extralegal justice are slightly different from those of official extralegal justice. Overall, perceptions of crime were more important than actual victimization. In El Salvador victimization was significant, and increased the likelihood that people would support vigilante justice, but personal victimization was insignificant in the other countries. In contrast, perceptions of crime were important in all of the countries. In Guatemala and El Salvador, as people grew more fearful of crime in their neighborhoods, they were more likely to support vigilante justice. In Honduras this relationship was puzzlingly negative, however. This negative result could perhaps be tied to respondents' fear of vigilante justice potentially increasing the level of violence in their own neighborhoods. It is clear that this result is not attributable to a broader fear of vigilante justice, however, as fear of crime at the level of the country was significantly linked to *more* support for vigilante justice. This same relationship also emerged in Guatemala, where increases in fear of crime at the national level rendered respondents more likely to support vigilante justice.

Personal experiences with police corruption mattered far more in the vigilante model than in the models predicting support for officials' extralegal justice. In all three cases, respondents who reported that police had solicited a bribe from them were significantly more likely to support vigilante justice (although in Guatemala multicollinearity problems hindered this variable from meeting the conventional .05 standard of statistical significance). In the case of Guatemala, perceptions of institutional performance were important as well. This conforms to the theoretical expectations of the hypotheses, as well as earlier findings reported in Table 4.2; the perception that institutions are not capable of sanctioning criminals increases the likelihood that citizens will support extralegal justice in Guatemala.

Attitudes toward other citizen protest activities were significant across the three models, indicating that in order to understand public support for vigilantism, it is imperative to control for levels of support for other types of illegal collective action. The socioeconomic variables performed inconsistently, but it is interesting to note that the indigenous dummy variable was insignificant in Guatemala. Vigilante justice, especially lynching, might be more prevalent in rural, indigenous areas, but overall the indigenous do not register significantly more support for the practice than ladinos.

To examine the dynamics of these relationships in other contexts, these same regressions were conducted in the comparatively lower crime countries. Table 4.7 displays these results. As Table 4.7 indicates, the best predictor of support for vigilante justice is support for citizens' illegal protests more broadly. This variable significantly increases the likelihood of supporting vigilante justice across all three cases. In Panama, this is the only significant

TABLE 4.7 Ordinal Logistic Regression Results for Support for Vigilante Justice (Lower Crime Countries with Varying Degrees of the Rule of Law)

	Independent variables	Costa Rica	Nicaragua	Panama
Crime variables	Victimization	.075 (.140)	.106 (.126)	−.054 (.161)
	Fear of crime in the neighborhood	**.124*** **(.062)**	**.113*** **(.052)**	.024 (.066)
	Fear of crime in the country	**.265**** **(.079)**	.057 (.066)	.057 (.077)
Institutional performance	Ability to punish criminals	**−.248***** **(.053)**	−.088 (.048)	−.076 (.054)
	Experience with police corruption	**.451*** **(.227)**	−.008 (.186)	.012 (.253)
Attitudes toward citizen collective action	Support for illegal protest action	**.338***** **(.026)**	**.338***** **(.027)**	**.578***** **(.028)**
Individual attributes	Gender	.100 (.112)	**.218*** **(.099)**	.126 (.098)
	Age	**−.080***** **(.020)**	−.008 (.018)	−.032 (.018)
	Income	.489 (.343)	−.325 (.305)	−.532 (.273)
	Education	**−.160*** **(.064)**	−.030 (.056)	.085 (.054)
	Size of municipality	.056 (.035)	−.029 (.035)	.001 (.036)
	Nagelkerke pseudo R squared	.230	.124	.303
	N	1395	1462	1444

* $p<.05$; ** $p<.01$; *** $p<.001$

Note: Ordinal logistic regression coefficients with standard errors in parentheses.

variable. In contrast to the results of Table 4.3, Panamanians were more wary of this type of extralegal justice, and proved reticent to allow citizens to address problems of crime and poor institutional performance. There was also not a strong connection between vigilante justice and crime and institutional performance in Nicaragua. While fear of crime in the neighborhood significantly increased the likelihood of supporting vigilante justice, no other crime or institutional variable attained statistical significance. In contrast, the results of Costa Rica indicated that support for vigilantism was very much tied to perceptions of crime and punishment. While victimization did not predict support for vigilantism, fear of crime in the neighborhood and in the country as a whole clearly did. In both cases, increased levels of fear of crime translated into more support for vigilantism. Institutions mattered a great deal too. Perceptions that institutions could not punish criminals rendered respondents more likely to support vigilantism, as did experiences with police corruption. These findings underscore the fact that a long tradition of institutional legitimacy is not necessarily enough to ward off the appeal of extralegal action, particularly when crime is a salient and politicized issue in public discourse.

Conclusion

In the context of contemporary Central America, this analysis has good news and bad news. The bad news is that crime and poor institutional performance do have the potential to reduce public support for the rule of law by sanctioning extralegal justice. It is not just the personal experience with crime and justice institutions that has this potential, but also perceptions. The effects of crime and institutional performance are not limited to the high crime/low rule of law countries, where the situation is most critical. Even a long tradition of democracy, which has prioritized the law, does not make countries immune to the pernicious effects of crime and lackluster institutional performance, as the case of Costa Rica illustrates. Still, there is good news, as the effects of crime and institutional performance are not uniform. For example, in Nicaragua crime had no impact on attitudes toward authorities acting on the margins of the law; in Panama, there was no linkage between crime and support for vigilantism. Such findings can potentially shed light on ways in which countries might shield themselves from crime's pernicious effects. It is striking that crime has been far less politicized in Nicaragua and Panama than in most of the other countries, for example.

When contemplating ways in which to escape from the security trap, citizens do not necessarily have a knee-jerk reaction to supporting extralegal options. This analysis brings up an interesting follow-up question: How do victims of crime react to their experiences? Chapter 5 looks more closely at victimization and victims' responses to their experiences. It aims to identify the conditions under which citizens turn to the law to address problems, as well as the circumstances that lead them to turn to extralegal sources, or no one at all. An examination of crime reporting can shed some light on why victims might perceive this as a viable response, as well as the cases in which the option is dismissed altogether.

Notes

[1] Anti-mara legislation, similar to that of El Salvador and Honduras, was proposed in 2003 but failed to pass the legislature (Ribando Seelke 2011).

[2] Violence against women has been particularly disturbing during the transition
     to democracy; most tragically, over 1,183 young women were found murdered
     between January 2002 and June 2004; many had faced rape and torture prior
     to their deaths (Booth et al. 2010, 151).

[3] Author interview with Andrés Herrera, July 2010.

[4] In 2010, LAPOP carried out a shortened version of its survey by telephone in
     the United States.

[5] The variable measuring the size of respondents' town or city was coded as:
     (1) rural area; (2) small city; (3) medium city; (4) large city; (5) capital city.

[6] The income scale was calculated based upon answers to the following survey
     items: Do you or any member of your household have any of the following
     possessions? TV; car; refrigerator; telephone; cell phone; computer; micro-
     wave oven; washing machine; drinking water; sewage system. Responses were
     coded as (1) yes and (0) no. I created an index of personal income using a
     means formula that included a case if there were valid responses to at least
     eight of the ten items. The Cronbach's alpha for this scale is .837.

[7] Some scholars have also highlighted the role of ideology in predicting sup-
     port for the rule of law, arguing that people who identify with the right of
     the ideological spectrum are "law and order types" who prioritize the main-
     tenance of public order. Despite this potential importance of ideology, these
     analyses do not include measures of ideology because the survey questions
     measuring ideology contained large numbers of missing respondents. Some
     research indicates this might be due to the fact that the significance of tradi-
     tional right/left labels has diminished in the eyes of the public (González and
     Quierolo 2009).

[8] As one indication of this overlap, or shared variance, the correlation between
     fear of crime in the neighborhood and victimization was $r=.256$; this correla-
     tion was highly significant ($p<.001$).

[9] To interpret the logistic regression coefficient, it is helpful to examine the
     exponentiated B coefficient, which for the indigenous dummy variable was
     1.649, indicating that the indigenous were 65 percent more likely to say that
     authorities should always uphold the law compared to ladinos, holding all
     other independent variables constant.

[10] This interpretation is based upon the exponentiated B coefficient, 2.713.

[11] It is important to note that this item measures support for vigilantism, not
     actual participation in vigilantism. The actual participation in vigilantism
     is influenced by additional factors, such as the ways in which a group of
     aggrieved persons overcomes collective action problems and actually engages
     in vigilante justice. Mendoza (2006) provides an interesting account of how
     theories of social mobilization and collective action explain the occurrence of
     lynchings in Guatemala.

[12] As a point of comparison, support for this item averaged 3.3 in the United
     States in the 2010 LAPOP survey.

[13] A factor analysis confirmed this observation. A factor analysis of these five
     items indicated that four of the questions (blocking streets, property invasions,
     occupying buildings, overthrowing the government) loaded on one dimen-
     sion, but the question pertaining to vigilante justice loaded on another.

5

Reacting to Victimization

To understand citizen respect for the rule of law, it is imperative to examine not just attitudes, but also behaviors. This chapter relies upon a behavioral measure of respect for the law: reporting crime. It is one thing to talk of crime as a problem facing Central American countries, but in these abstract discussions it is easy to forget that crime is a problem that hits close to home and affects citizens on a personal level. When victimized by a crime, citizens must decide to turn to the law, or to extralegal institutions, or to no one at all. Reporting crime indicates that people accept, at least begrudgingly, the legal system and its authorities as the legitimate arbiters of justice. Rather than pursuing extralegal means to address crime, or seek personal vengeance or retribution, citizens turn to legal authorities to address the problem through the rule of law. If citizens are to address their crime-related grievances through legal means, reporting the crime is the first step. Crime reporting rates can indicate whether lackluster institutional performance has lead citizens to disregard legal venues, and conclude that they are "on their own" in confronting criminality. Crime reporting goes beyond merely complying with the law, as it indicates that citizens will rely upon the law to address victimization.

The study of crime reporting is important to understand how citizens navigate personal issues like victimization, particularly if they live in a country that is caught in a security trap. The results in Chapter 4 indicate that extralegal justice is not an immediate reaction to crime, as personal experiences with crime had disparate outcomes. Victimization significantly increased support for vigilante justice in El Salvador, for example, but not in the other countries. This chapter aims to examine this relationship further and focus on how people translate their experience with crime into action. First, this chapter looks at how victims react to crime. What leads them to report the crime, the first step of relying upon the law, instead of extralegal justice? What leads them to turn to other venues? The LAPOP surveys offer an opportunity to answer these questions, as the 2008 wave of surveys asked a variety of questions about experiences with different types of victimization, the decision to go to authorities, and interactions with these authorities. In 2010, these same items were included in Panama, the Central American country with the highest rates of crime reporting according to the LAPOP data. The 2010 survey of Panama also asked respondents an extensive series of questions about their interactions and perceptions of the police, providing additional insight into police-society relationships. This chapter relies upon these survey data to examine citizens' responses to personal experiences with crime, once again taking care to contextualize these reactions in their appropriate national settings. It also examines police-society relationships in Panama in greater depth, to see what lessons might be gleaned for other countries in the region.

Reporting Crime

Prior research examining cross-national trends in crime reporting has found that crime reporting rates are overall quite low in Latin America. One of the most expansive surveys of victimization and crime reporting internationally is the International Crime Victim Surveys (ICVS), conducted under the auspices of the Dutch Ministry of Justice.[1] The ICVS compares personal experiences with victimization, as well as victims' responses, in countries around the world, including Eastern and Western Europe, Latin America, Scandinavia, and the common law countries (Canada, the United Kingdom, and the United States). When compared to these other global regions, Latin America had the highest rates of victimization, but the lowest rates of reporting crime (Malone 2004). When Latin American respondents did report crimes, the most frequent rationale they gave was to recover property. In contrast, in Eastern Europe and Scandinavia, respondents stated that they reported crime so that the offender would be caught. In Western Europe, victims indicated that they reported crime because of insurance reasons, in addition to their feelings that crime "should be reported." This latter response was the most common rationale given in the common law countries. This response underscores respondents' sense of civic duty, as well as the degree to which justice institutions garner a sense of legitimacy from the citizenry. This sense of civic duty and institutional legitimacy are intertwined. In order to be effective, justice institutions often rely upon citizens to bring crimes to their attention. Reporting crime alerts officials to the prevalence of criminal behavior and creates the opportunity for justice institutions (particularly the police) to respond. In addition to allowing the justice system the chance to address the immediate crime at hand, crime reporting also provides

valuable information for crime control efforts in a broader sense, inform-
ing officials of the prevalence and location of certain types of crime, for
example. If citizens do not report crime, it is frequently not possible for
justice institutions to react and earn legitimacy from the people. On average, in the ICVS Latin American respondents indicated that they reported
a crime simply because "crime should be reported," less than half the time
of respondents from other global regions (Malone 2004). According to
the ICVS, in Latin America loss of property was the primary motivation for
reporting crime. In contrast, in other global regions property concerns
were important, but they tended to be on par or even overshadowed by
other rationales for reporting crime, such as a sense of civic duty or the
belief that the police would apprehend the perpetrator.

These global differences highlight different strategies for coping with the
reality of justice in each country. Similar to O'Donnell's (2006) driver, who
adjusts to the various informal rules of transit in different cities, different
parts of the same city, and different times of day, citizens adjust their behavior to fit the realities of their environments. When Bailey (2009) applied this
logic to the justice system, he differentiated between a positive and negative equilibrium. In a positive equilibrium, the state adheres to the rule of
law and operates mostly legally to address problems of public security. To
be sure, some officials might engage in corruption, violate civil liberties, or
abuse the law in some other way. However, such incidents tend to be on a
small scale and do not jeopardize the overall ability of the state to correct
problems originating in society, such as crime. In contrast, under a negative
equilibrium or a security trap, both elected and appointed officials engage
in unethical behavior and commit crimes, and take advantage of civil society to "extract resources or command obedience outside the formal law"
(Bailey 2009, 256). As noted earlier, negative and positive equilibriums are
drawn in stark contrast here to illustrate the different justice environments;
however, in reality the negative and positive equilibrium points create more
of a spectrum, and countries tend to find themselves closer to one end than
the other.

These differences between positive and negative equilibriums are important for understanding citizens' motivations in reporting crime. At first,
reporting crime seems like it is driven by self-interest. If citizens wish to
redress their victimization using legal channels, they must first report the
incident to legally sanctioned authorities. However, if citizens are caught in
a country with a negative equilibrium (or in a security trap), this self-interest
is less clear. What incentive do citizens have to report crime if there is little
expectation the crime will be solved, on top of the possibility that the police
might take advantage of the incident to solicit a bribe? For example, Hudson

and Taylor (2010) found that in the case of homicides, the most serious of crimes, Guatemala had a conviction rate of 2.06 percent. According to the 2010 LAPOP survey, police corruption in Guatemala was the highest in Central America, with 14 percent of respondents indicating that a police officer had solicited a bribe from them in the past year. Under such conditions, what incentive do people have to report crime?

There are three main reasons that can explain why people might report crime even when caught in the security trap. First, the seriousness of the crime may create incentives for reporting it, even if there is little chance of apprehending the perpetrator. This is most certainly the case for homicides, as the gravity of the crime leads people to report it immediately, rendering homicides the most widely reported crimes cross-nationally. Second, crime reporting can also be driven by practical considerations. Some crimes, by their very nature, require official police reports before any additional steps can be taken. For example, in the case of stolen property, before pursuing an insurance claim individuals typically need to document the incident by way of an official police report. In this case, people might not think that the police are going to solve the case, but before their insurance company can replace the stolen goods in question, official documentation of the theft is required. Practicality also promotes crime reporting in other scenarios. Occasionally it is in people's best interest to go on the record and declare that a particular item has been stolen and is no longer in their possession. If a person finds that her or his car is stolen, for example, there is strong reason to report the incident in case the stolen vehicle in question is found linked to another crime in the future.

Finally, people might also report crimes because quite simply there are few other viable options. In Costa Rica, which despite its current problems comes closer to a positive equilibrium, reporting crime might not mean that the justice system will necessarily succeed in solving the case and holding the perpetrator accountable, but there is a chance at least that reporting crime could have a positive outcome. In countries that are more clearly caught in the security trap, like Honduras, the potential for success is more dubious. However, citizens might feel as if they had few other alternatives. Under a basic cost-benefits analysis, reporting crime might not be a good option, but it could be the only option.

To understand what leads citizens to turn to the law to solve the problems caused by victimization, this chapter turns to the 2008 LAPOP surveys. In 2008, LAPOP posed an extensive battery of questions to examine crime in Central America. Most importantly for this analysis, it contained a series of items to measure the type of victimization, willingness to report the crime to the police, and attitudes toward crime reporting more broadly.

Measuring Crime Reporting

After assessing respondents' personal experience with victimization, LAPOP added a follow-up question to determine how victims responded to the incident: "Did you report the crime to any institution?"[2] Respondents were coded as (1) reported the crime; (0) did not report the crime. Figure 5.1 displays the percentage of crime victims in each country who indicated that they reported the crime. Panama registered the highest rates of crime reporting, with more than half of crime victims stating that they reported the crime. Surprisingly, Guatemala and Nicaragua followed, technically in a statistical tie with Panama. In this regional comparison, Costa Rica ranked lower than expected, with crime reporting rates significantly lower than those of Panama, and statistically on par with Guatemala, Nicaragua, Honduras, and El Salvador—all countries with strikingly weaker justice systems. Still, given the smaller number of respondents in this subset, such cross-national comparisons must be made tentatively due to the larger confidence intervals associated with these national averages.

This unusual result for Costa Rica raises an additional question—why are national rates of reporting crime so low in the country? To examine these results in greater depth, Figure 5.2 compares crime reporting rates in 2008 with those of 2004, the first time LAPOP posed the same question concerning crime reporting in each Central American country. As Figure 5.2

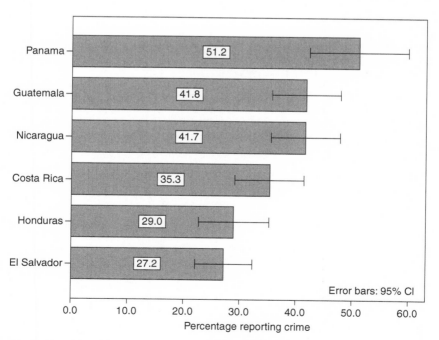

FIGURE 5.1 Reporting Crime by Country (LAPOP 2008)

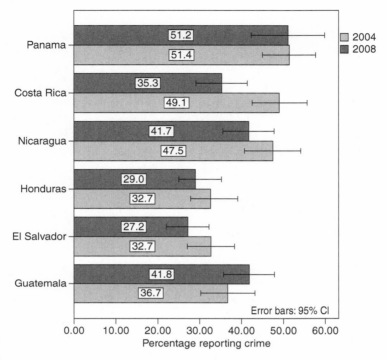

FIGURE 5.2 Percentage Reporting Crime over Time (LAPOP 2004 and 2008)

indicates, the rates of reporting crime appear to be quite stable between 2004 and 2008 except in Costa Rica. In 2004, nearly half of the victims indicated that they reported the crime. By 2008, this percentage had declined at a rate of 28 percent, with only about one-third of the victims reporting the crime. This is another indicator of the strain that crime has put on the contemporary Costa Rican justice system, a strain both in terms of stretching institutional capacity as well as garnering citizen legitimacy.

In addition to measuring crime reporting rates, LAPOP also included a follow-up question for individuals who stated that they did not report the crime: "Why did you not report the crime?" Responses were transcribed and later grouped into six categories:

- it would not do any good;
- it is dangerous/afraid of retaliation;
- did not have any proof;
- it was not that serious;
- did not know where to report;
- other reason.

As Table 5.1 indicates, some cross-national differences emerge when one examines the reasons given for not reporting crime, but there are commonalities as well. In all countries, the most common response was that reporting the crime wouldn't accomplish anything. In Costa Rica, an overwhelming 62 percent of nonreporting victims gave this rationale. This response indicates that victims sensed a futility in engaging with the justice system for the particular crime at hand. However, it is not clear why this futility emerged. The exact reason could encompass anything from police incompetence in solving crime to the improbability of finding stolen goods. Despite this common theme, important cross-national differences emerged when examining the second most frequent response in each country. In Guatemala, El Salvador and Honduras, countries noted for problems with gang violence, fear of reprisals was the second most common reason cited. In contrast, in Costa Rica and Nicaragua the second most cited reason was that the victim did not have proof, while in Panama it was that the crime was not considered serious. While fear of reprisals ranked much lower in Nicaragua than in the countries of the Northern Triangle, the percentage of victims stating that they feared reprisals was not small—16 percent.

As Table 5.1 indicates, the modal response people gave for not reporting crime was that "it wouldn't accomplish anything." However, it is not clear exactly why respondents think it would not do any good to report a crime. On one hand, this could be a reflection of institutional performance, that it would be an exercise in futility to report a crime to institutions that would not be able to solve the case. This perception could be attributable to inefficiency or corruption, for example. On the other hand, this modal response could indicate that the crime in question would be difficult to solve due to the nature of the crime. For example, pickpocket incidents at a crowded

TABLE 5.1 Reasons for Not Reporting Crime (LAPOP 2008)

Reason	Guatemala (*N*=142) (%)	El Salvador (*N*=213) (%)	Honduras (*N*=147) (%)	Nicaragua (*N*=147) (%)	Costa Rica (*N*=150) (%)	Panama (*N*=61) (%)
It wouldn't accomplish anything	45.1	41.8	53.1	45.6	62.0	31.1
It is dangerous and I feared reprisals	22.5	24.4	19.7	16.3	4.7	11.5
I did not have proof	12.7	9.9	8.8	17.0	17.3	26.2
It was not serious	4.9	16.4	13.6	12.2	10.0	27.9
I did not know where to go to report it	2.1	0	2.7	1.4	2.0	3.3
Other	12.7	7.5	2.0	7.5	4.0	0

market have a very low likelihood of being solved even with the best police officers on the case, given the nature of the crime. To understand why some victims report crimes and others do not, it is important to probe this response more at the individual level of analysis.

Data Analysis: Examining Why Some Citizens Report Crime and Others Do Not

To understand differences in reporting crime, this analysis relies upon binomial logistic regression analysis. Crime reporting is the dichotomous dependent variable, where (1) the victim reported crime and (0) the victim did not report crime. As only victims are included in this analysis, robust statistical tests were inhibited by the small sample size of victims in each country. Given these small sample sizes, it was necessary to pool the data to conduct meaningful statistical analysis. However, the analysis still aimed to embed the decision to report a crime or not into the appropriate national context. Thus, responses for the three high crime/low rule of law countries of the Northern Triangle were pooled in one analysis, and the data from the three low crime countries were pooled in a second analysis. In each case, country dummy variables were included to control for country-level effects.

Table 5.2 articulates a series of hypotheses for understanding why victims would report crime. The hypotheses of Table 5.2 build upon those that aimed to predict support for extralegal justice in Chapter 4, as the institutional performance variables in particular should matter for reporting crime as well. Theoretically, there is reason to suspect that a willingness to report crime is tied to the perception that justice institutions will be able to do something about it, and sanction the perpetrators of the crime. Experiences with police corruption should also factor into the decision to report crime, as people who have experience with corrupt police might not be willing to turn to them when victimized by crime. This analysis also follows the standard survey practice of controlling for the effects of individual attributes, namely gender, age, income, education, and size of respondents' municipality.

The main way in which this analysis of crime reporting differs from that of extralegal justice is that it breaks down victimization into three categories: violent crime involving property, nonviolent property crime, and violent crime without property. As part of its extensive coverage of crime in Central America in 2008, LAPOP asked respondents about their experiences with several different types of crimes, including: armed robbery, home robbery, home vandalism, theft of vehicle, theft from vehicle, stabbing, death threats, assault, maltreatment by police, sexual assault, extortion, as well as injuries caused by gunfire or other weapons. In addition to asking about personal victimization

TABLE 5.2 Variables and Hypotheses for Understanding Crime Reporting Behavior

	Independent variables	Hypotheses
Victimization	Violent crime involving property	Crimes involving both violence and property will be more likely to be reported than nonviolent property crimes or crimes involving only violence.
	Nonviolent property crime	Nonviolent property crimes will be less likely to be reported than violent property crimes.
	Violent crime without involving property	Violent crimes not involving property will be less likely to be reported than violent property crimes.
Institutional performance	Ability to punish criminals	As people's trust that the justice system will punish criminals increases, they will be more likely to report crime.
	Experience with police corruption	People who have experienced police corruption will be less likely to report crime.
Individual attributes	Gender	Women will be more likely to report crime than men.
	Age	Older respondents will be more likely to report crime than younger respondents.
	Income	As income increases, the likelihood of reporting crime increases.
	Education	As education increases, the likelihood of reporting crime increases.
	Size of municipality	As the size of the municipality increases, the likelihood of reporting crime increases.

by a wide range of crimes, LAPOP also asked respondents if violence was used in the perpetration of crime: "Did the criminal or criminals use violence against you?" This question concerning violence is useful to determine the exact nature of the crime at hand. Together, these specific questions about victimization allowed the analysis to distinguish whether crimes involved violence and/or the theft of property. Respondents were coded as "one" if they experienced that particular type of crime, and "zero" if they did not. By grouping crime into three discrete categories (violent crime involving property, non-violent property crime, and violent crime without property) the analysis can examine victims' reactions to different types of crimes.

Intuitively, the nature of the crime should be important, as it should influence what type of action victims decide to take. Previous work has found that in Latin America more broadly, property concerns motivate people to report crime (Malone 2004). If violence is also used to perpetrate a property crime, the seriousness of the crime is intensified. All other things equal, a victim of armed robbery should have more incentive to report the crime than the victim of a pickpocket on a bus. Thus, the statistical models aim to

TABLE 5.3 Logistic Regression Results for Reporting Crime (High Crime/Low Rule of Law Countries)

	Independent variables	Full model	Trimmed model
Crime variables (Reference category is violent crime without property)	Nonviolent property crime	−.397 (.227)	−.376 (.226)
	Violent property crime	.635** (.205)	.652** (.204)
Institutional performance	Ability to punish criminals	.242** (.087)	.232** (.087)
	Experience with police corruption	.500* (.199)	
Individual attributes	Gender	.101 (.173)	.167 (.170)
	Age	.054 (.032)	.053 (.032)
	Income	.859[a] (.455)	.997* (.449)
	Education	.018 (.022)	.018 (.022)
	Size of municipality	−.068 (.063)	−.059 (.063)
Country dummy variables (Reference category is Honduras)	Guatemala dummy variable	.569** (.218)	.581** (.217)
	El Salvador dummy variable	−.147 (.223)	−.187 (.221)
	Nagelkerke pseudo R squared	.130	.121
	N	735	736

* $p<.05$; ** $p<.01$; *** $p<.001$

Note: Binomial logistic regression coefficients with standard errors in parentheses.
[a] This variable was close to attaining statistical significance ($p<.06$) but multicollinearity prevented it from falling below the $p<.05$ threshold.

distinguish among these three broad categories of crime, as well as disentangle the impact of experience with law enforcement, and the perceptions of the efficacy of justice institutions.

Table 5.3 reports the results for Guatemala, El Salvador, and Honduras. As these results indicate, in this group of countries caught in the security trap, perceptions of the justice system were very important in determining whether victims will turn to the law to solve crime-related problems. As perceptions that the justice system could punish criminals increased, victims were significantly more likely to report the crime. These results demonstrate that victims will turn to the law if they perceive that the justice system is capable of sanctioning criminals. Unfortunately, in this group of countries the number of victims who fell into this category was small—only 31 percent stated that they trusted the justice system at least somewhat to punish criminals.

Table 5.3 also indicates that crime reporting is strongly tied to the type of crime experienced in this group of countries. As the type of crime was measured using three dummy variables, statistical analysis requires that one of these dummy variables (or categories of crime) serve as the reference category. In Table 5.3, the reference category was violent crime that did not involve property. Thus, the results concerning the other two types of crime need to be interpreted vis-à-vis this reference category. As Table 5.3 demonstrates, when predicting the likelihood that victims will turn to the law and report crime, there is no significant difference between people victimized by nonviolent property crimes and people victimized only by violence (the reference category). The likelihood of reporting crime is the same for both. However, when comparing the reactions of victims of violent property crimes and the victims of only violent crimes, there is a significant difference. Victims of violent property crimes are significantly more likely to report crime than those who suffer from only violence. Crimes that combine violence and property give two potential incentives for citizens to report them—citizens might need to report the crime to receive compensation for the stolen good, and the violence involved increases the seriousness of the incident.

One unanticipated finding was the positive and significant relationship between police corruption and reporting crime. Further examination of this result found that in addition to being positively related to reporting crime, police corruption was significantly correlated with the variables property crime and income. Table 5.4 lists these significant correlations. As Table 5.4 highlights, in this group of countries people who report crime are more likely to experience police corruption, particularly when the crime in question is a property crime. Taken together, these variables suggest that experience with police corruption probably occurs at the time of crime reporting, as

TABLE 5.4 Police Corruption and Its Relationship to Other Variables (High Crime/Low Rule of Law Countries)

Variable	Pearson correlation with police corruption
Victimization by property crime	.094**
Income	.197**
Reporting crime	.124**

** $p<.01$

wealthier victims reporting a property crime might pay bribes to encourage the police to investigate and recover the stolen property. The data cannot state this definitively, as the survey did not ask respondents explicitly if their experience with police corruption occurred when they reported a crime to police. However, the significance and direction of these correlations most certainly suggests that this is a strong possibility. In the trimmed model, the variable police corruption was removed to ensure that these correlations did not pose a problem for the other variables in the model. When police corruption was removed from the model, income became a significant predictor of reporting crime at the .05 level. The other variables retained their original interpretations. With the exception of income, the other individual attributes were not significant predictors of reporting crime. The country dummy variables indicate that there is no significant difference between the willingness of victims in El Salvador and Honduras (the reference category) to report crime; however, victims in Guatemala were significantly more likely to report crime than those in Honduras.

To compare these findings with those from the comparatively low crime countries, Table 5.5 reports the results for this same logistic regression analysis conducted in this different context. Once again, as the analysis included only crime victims, the small sample size necessitated the pooling of the data of Costa Rican, Nicaraguan, and Panamanian respondents. The incorporation of country dummy variables aimed to take into account country fixed effects. The Costa Rica dummy variable served as the reference category.

Table 5.5 reveals a slightly different pattern than that of the high crime/low rule of law countries. In this context, the type of crime was the most important factor in predicting the willingness to report crime. Respondents were significantly more likely to report property crimes (both violent and nonviolent) than crimes involving only violence. In contrast, perceptions of the justice system's ability to punish criminals were not significant. In these countries, victims did not connect their personal experiences with crime to their perceptions of institutional performance. Rather, victims responded

TABLE 5.5 Logistic Regression Results for Reporting Crime (Lower Crime Countries with Varying Degrees of the Rule of Law)

	Independent variables	Full model	Trimmed model
Crime variables (Reference category is violent crime without property)	Nonviolent property crime	.396[a] (.217)	.425* (.216)
	Violent property crime	.572* (.221)	.602** (.220)
Institutional performance	Ability to punish criminals	.038 (.091)	.034 (.091)
	Experience with police corruption	.305 (.251)	
Individual attributes	Gender	−.138 (.177)	−.117 (.176)
	Age	.063* (.032)	.062[a] (.032)
	Income	−.164 (.498)	−.114 (.496)
	Education	.033 (.025)	.036 (.025)
	Size of municipality	−.122* (.054)	-.124* (.054)
Country dummy variables (Reference category is Costa Rica)	Nicaragua dummy variable	.378 (.240)	.393 (.239)
	Panama dummy variable	.696** (.254)	.684** (.254)
	Nagelkerke pseudo R squared	.069	.066
	N	579	580

* $p<.05$; ** $p<.01$; *** $p<.001$

Note: Binomial logistic regression coefficients with standard errors in parentheses.
[a] This variable was close to attaining statistical significance ($p<.07$) but multicollinearity prevented it from falling below the $p<.05$ threshold

to the immediate problem at hand, and were more likely to report crimes when property was at stake. This practical motivation was intensified when the property crime grew more serious and violence was employed during its commission. Once again, only approximately 30 percent of respondents indicated that they had at least some trust that the justice system could punish criminals. The difference is that in this context, perceptions of the justice system were not crucial in predicting crime reporting. Victims reported the crime based upon the nature of the offense, and practical considerations appeared to factor into the cost/benefit analysis for reporting crime. Perceptions of institutional performance did not factor into the equation.

TABLE 5.6 Police Corruption and Its Relationship to Other Variables (Lower Crime Countries with Varying Degrees of Rule of Law)

Variable	Pearson correlation with police corruption
Victimization by property crime	.106[**]
Income	.088[**]

[**] $p<.01$

The law, however imperfect, was viewed as a viable outlet (or at least a viable first step) to address victimization.

While experience with police corruption did not significantly affect crime reporting, once again police corruption did share significant correlations with other independent variables. Most importantly, as Table 5.6 details, experiences with police corruption were significantly and positively associated with income and victimization by nonviolent property crimes. Again, this raises the possibility that property crimes create opportunities for bribe solicitation. When police corruption is trimmed from the model, victimization by nonviolent property crime attains significance at the traditional .05 threshold.

Overall, individual attributes did not affect victims' willingness to report crime, with the exception of age and size of town. Older respondents were more likely to report crimes, holding all other variables constant. Respondents who lived in larger cities were less likely to report crime than those living in smaller towns or rural communities. In terms of country-level differences, these results conform to those identified in the bivariate analysis of Figure 5.1: victims in Panama were significantly more likely to report crimes than victims in Costa Rica and Nicaragua. There was no statistical difference in reporting rates between victims in Costa Rica and Nicaragua, holding all other factors constant.

Police-Society Relationships in Panama

The results from the comparatively lower crime countries (Table 5.5) raise several additional questions. Why did perceptions of institutional performance more broadly not affect individual decisions to report crime? Why was there a disconnect between victims' broader perceptions of crime and justice, and their reactions to their personal experiences with crime? A closer examination of Panama provides some answers to these questions. In

2010, LAPOP explored police-society relationships extensively in Panama, asking respondents about their personal interactions with police officers, their views of police-society collaborations, and their perceptions of crime and justice in their immediate environments. As Panama has the highest rate of reporting crime in the LAPOP surveys of Central America, it is an excellent case to probe in greater depth.[3] These survey questions allow for a closer examination of individual interactions with police in a variety of settings, and how these interactions foster a greater willingness to work with police on crime-related issues.

Panamanian policing has witnessed major transformations under the transition to democracy. After the United States deposed General Noriega in 1989, one of the first priorities (after apprehending Noriega) was to dismantle the apparatus that had enabled Noriega to seize power in the first place—the Panamanian Defense Forces (PDF). The PDF had combined the police, presidential guard, and military under one centralized command; there was no real institutional separation between domestic policing and national defense (Caumartin 2007). Following the demise of the PDF, recruitment began for a new domestic police force, as well as more specialized security details like the Technical Judicial Police (PTJ), to maintain order and stop the looting that emerged in the wake of the US invasion. The dismantling of the PDF was not followed by the creation of another standing army. For internal security, Panama created a new police force, the National Police of Panama (PNP).[4]

At its inception, the PNP did not stray far from Panama's militarized tradition, utilizing what Gosselin (2006) refers to as a paramilitary framework. Paramilitary styles of policing rely upon a military system of management, in contrast to civilian-based policing, "rooted in the British 'watch and ward' system that uses civilian officers to solve social problems" (Gosselin 2006, 15). During the transition to democracy, however, Panama shifted its focus from these paramilitary roots to policy models based upon civilian, problem-oriented strategies. Caumartin (2007) describes this evolution as comprising three interrelated components: demilitarization, professionalization, and depoliticization. In addition to making the shift from a military framework to a civilian one, the police also embarked on a series of reforms to modernize and train officials for the realities of policing under democracy, where the maintenance of internal security should be balanced with the protection of rights and guarantees of due process (ABA ROLI 2011). Finally, reformers aimed to depoliticize the PNP, rendering it an apolitical actor interested in upholding public order, rather than furthering the interests of specific political actors. In a particularly detailed analysis, Caumartin identifies the many difficulties encountered during this reform process, noting that "There was no mapping out of reform, or clear sense of how to achieve it, and some measures were poorly designed. Both ICITAP and the Endara Government were novices, with limited staff and knowledge and no experience of such undertakings" (2007, 132). Ultimately, Panama's police reform emerged as a success story only when domestic political actors reached consensus that a demilitarized, professional, and apolitical police force was in the best interests of both major political parties.

This consensus reached by the major political actors has extolled the benefits of the police's collaboration with the community. Panama's policing evolution stands in stark contrast to the zero tolerance approach advocated by admirers of the New York City crime control model (Bratton and Andrews 2001). As Chapter 4 explained, when transplanted to Latin America, the zero tolerance model tends to become mano dura, and encourages the militarization of internal security and occasionally the actual deployment of the military internally. Instead, Panama evolved away from its paramilitary inception and began to adopt civilian-oriented models. Interestingly enough, one consultant noted that Panama's policing shift was inspired by the problems of paramilitary policing in major US cities, particularly when enforcing drug laws. Based upon his work with the Boston Police Department (BPD) in the 1980s, Gosselin (a US Law Enforcement Development Advisor to Panama in 2004) noted that:

> the work of the BPD, particularly in regards to drug law enforcement, became decidedly paramilitary in nature during the 1980s despite the civilian, problem-solving roots of the American policing system. The problems experienced using this type of paramilitary strategy in the United States helped inform the work of the Panamanian National Security Planning Workshop in 2004 [which helped lead] the PNP away from a paramilitary crime control response in Panama and toward a problem-solving approach rooted in the principles of a civilian police force. (2006, 15)

Under a civilian-oriented model, Panama introduced a *mano amiga* (friendly hand) model of crime control, as opposed to the mano dura approach popular in the Northern Triangle. The shift to civilian, problem-solving tactics also included infrastructure upgrades, a national crime statistics and mapping database, and a public relations campaign.[5] The public relations campaign stressed the need for outreach to citizens, a tactic made clear on the PNP's webpage, which is replete with references to community-police cooperation:

- *Vecinos vigilantes: ¡Cuidado! Estámos observando* (Vigilant Neighbors: Careful! We're Watching!)
- *Buscando una cultura de seguridad ciudadana* (Building a culture of citizen security)
- *La seguridad ciudadana es un compromiso de todos "proteger y servir"* (Citizen security is a promise of everyone to "protect and serve")
- *Denuncia el delito—sé parte de la solución del problema* (Report crime—be part of the solution to the problem)[6]

This last slogan helps to explain why crime reporting was significantly higher in Panama than in other parts of the region, and not necessarily connected to perceptions of the efficacy of justice institutions—Panama has stressed the importance of reporting crime as part of citizens' collaboration with the police against delinquency. In addition to these slogans, the homepage contains a tab dedicated to the community, with a plethora of additional programs inspired by domestic and international advocates: *Vecinos Vigilantes* (Vigilante Neighbors), *Comercios Vigilantes* (Vigilant Businesses), Drug Abuse Resistance Education (DARE), *Jovenes Contra El Delito* (Youth Against Crime), and *Niños Seguros* (Safe Children).[7]

In addition to actively courting citizens to collaborate with police, the PNP's outreach has targeted other important actors, such as journalists. With the help of the American Bar Association's Rule of Law Initiative (ABA ROLI), the PNP has hosted seminars to train journalists on Panama's new Criminal Procedure Code and its shift to an oral, adversarial legal system. These activities included socialization measures such as workshops to provide "journalists with the necessary knowledge to report accurately on the country's transition to this system and with an improved understanding of their role—and of the roles of various justice sector actors—under the system" (ABA ROLI 2011).

Public Perceptions of Reform Efforts

The 2010 LAPOP surveys provide insight into how citizens have regarded these initiatives. It is one matter for the Panamanian state to launch programs to include citizens into public security policies, it is quite another for citizens to respond positively to these gestures. Survey questions specifically targeting citizens' interactions with police, and evaluations of police action in their own neighborhoods, can illuminate whether the Panamanian style of policing has affected citizens' attitudes and behaviors toward the law in their daily lives.

Analysis of the LAPOP data indicates that when asked specific questions about their interactions with the police, respondents by and large had favorable impressions. When asked how safe they felt when a police officer was near, 82 percent of respondents replied that they felt very safe or at least

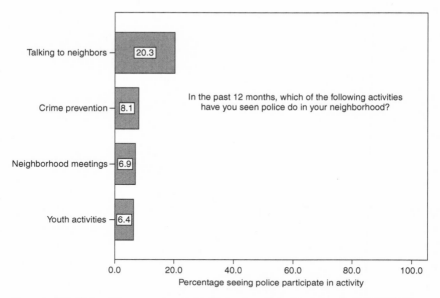

FIGURE 5.3 Police Engagement in Neighborhoods in Panama (LAPOP 2010)

somewhat safe. Of the small percentage that reported feeling unsafe, the most frequent rationale was because police were corrupt (37 percent).[8]

Many respondents reported that the police were active and visible in their neighborhoods. Fifty-five percent of respondents indicated that they knew police officers patrolling their neighborhoods by name, face, or both. Furthermore, 76 percent of respondents stated that they saw the police patrolling their neighborhoods at least once a week, and 19 percent reported having a casual conversation with a police officer in their neighborhoods in the past year. Still, much of the police presence is less structured, manifesting itself through patrols or talks with neighbors. When asked whether police participated in more organized or structured activities, such as prevention programs for youth, as Figure 5.3 reports, the percentages were much smaller.

As respondents perceived the police as being more active in their neighborhoods, they registered more positive opinions for police action in their neighborhoods, as well as closer ties between the community and police. To measure evaluations of police action in respondents' own neighborhoods, LAPOP posed three questions:

● How would you rate the work the national police is doing with people in this neighborhood to solve the problems of this neighborhood? Would you say that the work they are doing is (1) very bad, (2) bad, (3) neither good nor bad, (4) good, (5) very good? (Respondents who spontaneously responded that the police were not doing anything at all were coded as zero).

- In general, would you say you are (4) very satisfied, (3) satisfied, (2) unsatisfied, (1) very unsatisfied with the quality of police services in this neighborhood? (Once again, respondents who spontaneously responded that the police were not doing anything at all were coded as zero).

- How would you rate the work the national police are doing to prevent crime in this neighborhood or community? Do you think the work that the police are doing to prevent crime is (5) very good, (4) good, (3) neither good nor bad, (2) bad, (1) very bad. (Similar to the previous two questions, respondents who spontaneously responded that the police were not doing anything at all were coded as zero).

When necessary, these items were recoded so that higher values corresponded to more positive evaluations. These three separate items were then combined into an additive index, which computed respondents' average answers across these three items, provided respondents answered at least two of the questions.[9] This new variable was a composite measure of local police evaluations. This variable differs from traditional measures of attitudes toward the police, which tend to focus on public legitimacy or trust in the institution of the police as a whole, or the ability of police to effectively respond to crime. In contrast, this index focuses on how people rate the police's work in their own neighborhoods. People are asked to categorize the work they see the police do firsthand in their own neighborhoods, rather than discuss the ability of the police in general to respond to crime or garner legitimacy. This measure of local evaluations is a particularly valuable counterpart to broader, more diffuse measures of legitimacy and perceived efficacy.

As Table 5.7 demonstrates, the more respondents interacted with the national police in their own neighborhoods and communities, the more positive their evaluations of police performance in their immediate environments. The same relationship also held when respondents were asked to describe the relationship between the police and the community. To measure police relationships with local communities, LAPOP asked respondents: "To what extent would you say that the people of this neighborhood get along well with the police?" Responses ranged from (1) not at all through (7) very much. As the Pearson's correlations demonstrate in Table 5.7, familiarity breeds support. The more respondents interacted with police, the better they thought the relationship was between police and the neighborhood. On a variety of indicators, when respondents described their interactions with police, they tended to be frequent and positive. As reported in Figure 3.7, in Panama respondents reported far less instances of police corruption than in the other Central American countries, with only 4 percent of respondents

TABLE 5.7 Impact of Local Police Activities on Local Evaluations in Panama (LAPOP 2010)

Local police activity	Pearson's correlation with local police evaluations	Pearson's correlations with neighborhood-police relationship
Talking to police	.112**	.135**
Recognizing police	.152**	.121**
Frequency of police patrols	.261**	.111**

** *p*<.01

stating that police had solicited a bribe, compared to the regional high of 14 percent in Guatemala.

Most importantly, these positive evaluations of local-level police activity appear to have fostered more respect for the rule of law. Earlier analyses found that people in Panama were tepid in their endorsement for extralegal justice, on average registering low levels of support for vigilante justice as well as for authorities' circumvention of the law (Chapter 4). This chapter has found very high levels of reporting crime in Panama. An additional survey item, asked only in Panama, provides more evidence that citizens are willing to turn to the law to solve problems.

This survey question asked respondents what level of police involvement they would like to see in the future: "What do you prefer? (1) that the national police get more involved in the resolution of problems in your neighborhood; (2) that the national police get less involved with the resolution of problems in your neighborhood; (3) that things stay the same." An overwhelming 91 percent of respondents indicated that they would like to see the national police get more involved in resolving problems in their neighborhood, indicating a willingness to rely upon the law to solve problems.

Insights from Panama

If rule of law reform efforts have taught one thing, it is to be very cautious when generalizing the reform records of one country to another. Still, the example of Panama does illustrate that crime does not necessarily erode citizens' respect for the law. Respondents in Panama indicate that they are worried about crime, but this fear does not translate into strong support for measures that undermine the rule of law. Crime is a problem, but its potential solutions have not been extensively politicized to date. Policymakers have been pragmatic in their crime-fighting proposals and have aimed to combine their current focus on reducing crime with the prior trajectory of demilitarizing, professionalizing, and depoliticizing the police. Crime control has emphasized prevention and collaboration with communities rather than repression. It is important to remember that this emphasis on prevention and collaboration is not a result of more favorable conditions in Panama. As Figure 2.5 indicated, homicide rates in Panama are lower than those of the Northern Triangle, but still quite high. Indeed, homicide rates in Panama are on par with those of Mexico, a country featuring prominently in the international media precisely due to its high levels of violent crime. From 2000 through 2008, homicide rates increased 90 percent in Panama (UNDP 2009). Panama has not witnessed outright clashes between rival factions of maras and organized crime (or between these criminal elements and government forces), which have led to a spike in murder rates elsewhere. However, Panama has long had connections to the transit of the drug trade, and associated money laundering activities. It has escaped some of the worst violence of the current crime crisis, but it is not immune. Panama has selected to confront these problems through a *mano amiga* approach, but this is not a logical outcome from a completely different reality of crime and punishment. It is a conscious policy choice.

To date, Panama's crime-fighting initiatives have succeeded in encouraging citizens to collaborate with the police, but it is important to remember that they have not succeeded in curbing the crime rate. Panama's rate of violent crime has continued to rise throughout the reform period, almost doubling during the first decade of the twenty-first century. Furthermore, there are indications that corruption remains a problem. While police corruption in Panama is low for the region, it is on the minds of the people. When asked to identify the main problem of justice administration in Panama, 51 percent of respondents blamed corruption, compared to the 26 percent that gave the next most frequent response, the slowness of justice (see Figure 5.4).

One more note of caution is due. This examination of Panama has found that citizens have responded positively to the *mano amiga* approach to fighting crime, and justice reforms that are civilian-oriented. However, this positive reaction could be tied to the Hawthorne Effect—citizens might be responding positively to a change in policing under democratization, but this novelty could wear off, particularly if citizens become disenchanted with the performance that accompanies the rhetoric. Still, as Chapter 4 demonstrated, increases in crime have not lead citizens to endorse extralegal justice enthusiastically. Extreme solutions have not found the political purchase in Panama as they have in other Central American countries. Rather, Chapter 5

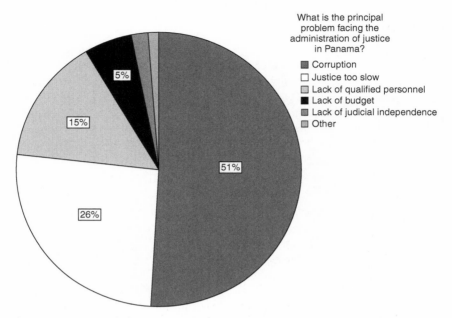

FIGURE 5.4 What is the Principal Problem Facing the Administration of Justice in Panama? (LAPOP 2010)

finds that there is more respect for using the law to address crime, as indicated by crime reporting trends. Panama's police reform may not be a runaway success, but it has appeared to encourage citizen reliance on the law and collaboration with the police.

Conclusion

On the surface, crime reporting rates are a valuable indicator of citizens' willingness to solve problems according to the rule of law. If citizens are going to rely upon the law to address issues related to their personal victimization by crime, reporting the incident to the authorities is the logical first step. This analysis has shown that in practice, crime reporting is more nuanced. Victims are motivated by practical matters, such as whether they considered the crime to be serious, and whether property was involved.

In countries caught in Bailey's (2009) security trap, people's perceptions of institutions matter a great deal. Crime reporting is not an automatic response to victimization, but rather, victims consider whether they can really trust the institutions entrusted with upholding the rule of law. In addition, this analysis suggests that the financial resources of citizens also factor into the equation, as wealthier citizens reporting property crimes also indicate that the police solicit bribes at significantly higher levels.

The evidence from Panama provides some examples of how countries can escape from the security trap. Panama's approach to soaring rates of violent crime has sought to strengthen the rule of law by encouraging police-community interactions, particularly when citizens find themselves victimized by crime. Data from Panama indicate that this type of community outreach might not reduce crime rates themselves, but it does foster respect for the law from a different perspective, by encouraging citizens to work with the justice system.

Can Panama's experience be generalized? Critics are quick to point out that Panama has historical differences from the other Central American countries, as detailed in Chapter 2. Economic development from colonial times has created distinct socioeconomic cleavages, but these cleavages have not historically exploded into violence as they have in other Central American countries. Indeed, as Caumartin (2007) emphasizes, the key reason police reform has been successful in Panama is because the broader political process reached consensus on the best way to reform. Political elites did not really politicize public security and crime control policy. Elite consensus avoided the sharp polarization crime has induced in other settings, where social outgroups are blamed for crime and marginalized, and the police act as border guards to keep these marginal groups from interacting with the more privileged parts of the population. This broader political backdrop might determine whether Panama's approach will work in different national settings.

Notes

[1] The ICVS informs the policies of major organizations, such as the United Nations Office on Drugs and Crime (UNODC).

[2] The number of respondents in each country indicating they had experienced some type of victimization was: Guatemala (261), El Salvador (294), Honduras (207), Nicaragua (254), Costa Rica (237), Panama (128). LAPOP also asked respondents to which institution they would report a crime. Overwhelmingly, respondents indicated the police; however, small percentages registered a preference for reporting crime to other institutions, such as the courts. The preferences for crime reporting ranked as follows: police (74 percent), judiciary (e.g., prosecutor) (15 percent), municipality (4 percent). An additional 4 percent indicated they would not report a crime, and less than 2 percent indicated the Church, media, human rights office, or other.

[3] In addition to the highest percentage of victims indicating they reported crime, other crime reporting trends are also positive in Panama. As Table 5.1 indicates, Panama registers the lowest percentage of crime victims stating that they did not report a crime because "it would not accomplish anything" and the highest percentage stating that they did not report the crime because it was not serious. When combined, these two findings indicate that a failure to report crime is due more to a lack of perceived seriousness, rather than the perception that relying upon the law to solve crime-related grievances is futile.

[4] Selected personnel from the defunct Panamanian Defense Forces were invited to be part of the new national police force (Caumartin 2007).

[5] International collaboration has featured prominently during this paradigm shift (Gosselin 2006). Civil society organizations like the American Bar Association (ABA) have collaborated with US agencies to socialize a variety of actors to the changes in the justice system. For example, the ABA has collaborated with the US Department of State's Bureau of International Narcotics and Law Enforcement Affairs to train "police, attorneys, judges and civil society on their roles and responsibilities within the criminal justice system . . . to better protect human rights and to help guarantee due process under the country's new, adversarial system" (accessed June 8, 2011 from http://apps.americanbar.org/rol/news/news_panama_interview_with_police_officers_0111.shtml).

[6] These slogans were listed on the PNP's webpage, accessed June 8, 2011 from www.policia.gob.pa/.

[7] These groups were listed on the PNP's website, accessed June 8, 2011 from www.policia.gob.pa/comunidad.html.

[8] In contrast, of the 261 respondents who stated that they felt a little unsafe or very unsafe around police officers, smaller percentages gave the following justifications: the police abuse their power (27 percent), the police abuse human rights (19 percent), my past experiences with the police were not good (8 percent), the police make me afraid (4 percent), other (5 percent).

[9] The Chronbach's alpha for this additive index was .806, indicating a very high degree of inter-item correlation.

6

Privatizing Security

Guatemala 'thieves' lynched over flour theft.

BBC, February 22, 2011(b)

El Salvador swoops on street gang.

BBC, July 13, 2006

As these BBC captions demonstrate, news of lynchings and mano dura crackdowns steal the headlines. These forms of extralegal justice are publicized to highlight the pernicious effects of crime and the precarious state of the rule of law in the region. There are more widespread, yet less sensational manifestations of these phenomena, however. A walk through the streets of most major cities in Central America showcases a very different threat to the rule of law. Visitors to San José, for example, are frequently struck by the extent to which homes and businesses are shrouded in fences, barbed wire, walls (frequently topped with broken glass), gates, and alarms. On some corners, a "watchiman" stands guard over a designated group of homes, as neighbors pool their resources to pay for their own private guard. Private security measures have proliferated even more rapidly than crime rates, as citizens seek to protect themselves through increasingly more sophisticated private security measures (Espinoza and Zúñiga 2003).

Of course, private security measures are not unique to Central America. Private security is ubiquitous in many parts of the world. In the United States, for example, the 1980s were marked by the rapid construction of gated communities, as fear of crime drove many affluent Americans to suburban gated enclaves (Blakely and Snyder 1997). Private security guards are frequently employed by businesses, and even neighborhoods (Thompson 2010). Since the 1980s, private security companies like Corrections Corporation of America run substantial portions of the American penal system. Private

Photo 6.1 *Salvador Allende Port, Managua*

Photo 6.2 *Guarded Entrance to Salvador Allende Port*

This sign graces the entrance to the *Puerto Salvador Allende*, or the Salvador Allende Port, on the lakefront of Managua, Nicaragua. Below the picture of the former Chilean President and revered leftist icon is a quote from Allende's last address to the Chilean people: "Go forward knowing that, sooner rather than later, the great avenues will open again and free men will walk through them to construct a better society." Ironically, as the second photograph illustrates, people are not free to walk the great avenue of the Salvador Allende Port. One must pay a modest admission, largely due to the provision of private security.

Photos by Author

security forces increasingly play a role in US international policing efforts, as private security companies like Blackwater are contracted by the US Department of State to provide security abroad.

Still, in Latin America the pace of private security growth has been remarkable. Since the 1980s, investments in private security measures have grown 10 percent each year, on average (Ungar 2007). Ungar (2007) estimates that there are currently about 1.6 million registered private security employees in Latin America, in addition to an estimated two million more working informally. From 2003 through 2007 alone, the number of legal private security guards grew 65 percent in the Latin American region as a whole (Cafferata 2010). In Central America, private security guards outnumber public security forces—the police—in every country (Silva 2003). Given the purchasing power needed to procure private services, not surprisingly wealthier countries like Panama and Costa Rica have higher rates of private security coverage even though their crime rates are considerably lower (UNODC 2007).

From a rule of law perspective, this is a disturbing trend. Piecemeal privatization of security might not raise alarm like deploying the military does, as people tend to worry less about security guards at the mall than the army patrolling the streets. Still, there are several reasons why current trends toward security privatization do not bode well for the strengthening of the rule of law. First, it is problematic to see the state relinquishing its monopoly on coercion. The fundamental job of the state is to provide security for the life and property of its citizens, and monopolizing the tools of coercion is the way in which the state fulfills this goal. As an influential United Nations report noted:

> There are serious problems with outsourcing a core function of government like security. All should be equal before the law, but private security makes no pretence of being unbiased. Given the high-level connections that many private security firms maintain, they can easily manipulate the system to the advantage of their clients, and they are highly unlikely to give testimony against them. Since private firms generally pay much better than the government, serving police personnel may regard their positions as a kind of audition for subsequent private employment, and treat acting security guards with corresponding deference. (UNODC 2007, 82)

Extensive reliance on private security confirms a disturbing trend in Central American democratization—unequal application of the law. As the state is perceived as incapable of providing the public good of security, people will try to satisfy their security needs in the marketplace when they have the financial means to do so. This leaves the poor to get by as they can. This dynamic reinforces the police's role as border guards, and can intensify patterns of social exclusion. When private security takes the form of gated communities, this trend is even more pronounced, and self-reinforcing. If wealthy citizens create their own private communities replete with private services, they have little value for state provision of these goods, and resist policies like taxation that would typically be used to finance the provision of public goods like security. In practice, this tends to crystallize a status quo of inequality, in which the affluent physically isolate themselves from the poor. Privatization can increase the fractionalization of communities according to socioeconomic cleavages. The United Nations Office of Drugs and Crime has expressed strong reservations about this trend:

> the national project of crime prevention requires the support of the wealthy and powerful, but when they can insulate themselves from the reality suffered by their less affluent countrymen, they have little incentive to deal with their grievances. In the end, the more numerous and better equipped private security system may make official law enforcement superfluous in the eyes of the people with the financial clout to demand reform. (UNODC 2007, 82)

Privatization unleashes a disturbing cycle and ultimately reinforces the security trap. Underfunded police and courts have trouble providing security, so affluent citizens seek to purchase security on the private market. Once citizens have invested in these private services and protected themselves, they have little incentive to finance public servants, and seek to decrease their contributions through mechanisms like taxation. With less revenue, the police and courts then have even fewer resources to address security concerns, perpetuating the cycle of this negative security equilibrium.

Security privatization raises additional problems of accountability. The third wave Central American democracies have found it difficult to establish effective mechanisms for holding public officials accountable. In their edited volume, Frühling, Tulchin, and Golding (2003) highlight the many challenges Latin American justice systems have confronted in their efforts to establish effective checks and balances on the power of public officials and servants. Since effective mechanisms to hold authorities accountable for their actions have proven elusive, there is little reason to suspect that there will be success in establishing these mechanisms for private security officials. This is especially the case when such large numbers of private security guards work informally, escaping official detection. All evidence suggests that states are ill-prepared to hold private security firms accountable for abuses of power. Private security forces lack the even weak oversight of their public servant counterparts, increasingly the likelihood that the campaign against crime will claim casualties in the form of human rights and civil liberties. Regulation of the private security industry is uneven, and even when regulatory statutes exist, they are often flouted, leading to weaknesses in both regulatory frameworks as well as in systems of monitoring and control (Cafferata 2010).

While security privatization poses numerous pitfalls for the rule of law, it is easy to see why such measures are appealing to a fearful public. In the high crime, low rule of law countries like Guatemala, El Salvador, and Honduras, citizens may perceive private security as the only lifeline out of a dire situation. Costa Rica boasts the lowest crime rate and best performing justice system, but residents accustomed to far less crime are disturbed by homicide rates that have risen 83 percent from 2000 through 2008. Crime has not been politicized to the same extent in Panama and Nicaragua, but the crime increases of the past decade could easily draw people to private responses, such as locks, alarms, and security guards. This chapter examines citizens' private responses to crime, untangling the ways in which personal experiences with crime and justice, as well as perceptions of crime and justice, can lead citizens to search for private solutions to public security problems.

Trends in Private Security

Privatization has been the buzzword in Latin America for the past two decades. When countries across Latin America defaulted on their loans in the 1980s, international creditors seized the opportunity to push for free market reforms. In order to restructure debt and maintain access to international credit lines, Latin American governments were obliged to enact neoliberal reforms. Privatization was a hallmark of these reforms, as state-owned enterprises found themselves on the auction block, awaiting private investors. Just as the 1980s marked the beginning of the third wave of democracy in Latin America, it also marked the transition to neoliberal economies, which minimized the role of the state in the economy to make room for private investors.

Despite this sweeping trend toward privatization, observers have still registered surprise at the extensive privatization of one critical area—public security. Typically the state jealously guards its monopolization of force, and is loathe to relinquish this monopoly to private actors. As Hobbes (1651, 2009) noted long ago, the primary function of the state is *salus populi* (the people's safety). In Central America the state has proven willing to share this function with private actors. Most notably, in 2006 the Honduran government invited private security forces to join the police and the military in a mano dura crackdown on crime, called Operation Thunder. This invitation drew swift condemnation from human rights organizations, especially Honduran Human Rights Commissioner Ramón Custodio, who criticized the government for failing to heed the important distinction between private and public security forces, as well as failing to provide security through the appropriate legal institutions, like the Ministry of Security (Mejia 2006). Given Honduras's human rights track record during these mano dura campaigns, human rights activists have strongly opposed adding new actors to the mix, particularly when such actors lack institutional oversight and horizontal accountability (Booth et al. 2010).

Such incidents reveal that far from viewing private security as a competitor, in some cases governments are willing to welcome the role of private security forces, particularly because in most cases private security forces are better equipped and more numerous. As Table 6.1 indicates, the number of licensed private security forces overshadows that of the police in every Central American country. Indeed, Table 6.1 underestimates the presence of private security, as it includes only licensed public security operators. In some countries, this number can easily be doubled when informal security

TABLE 6.1 Private vs. Public Security Forces

Country	Public security forces (per 100,000)	Private security forces (per 100,000)
Guatemala	50	124
El Salvador	293	386
Honduras	91	114
Nicaragua	135	169
Costa Rica	288	479
Panama	353	513

Source: These estimates are based upon Silva's (2003) work, and have subsequently been adjusted to account for population size.

workers are included in the tally. As Honduran Police Commissioner Simeón Flores noted, in addition to the 30,000 licensed private security officers allowed to legally practice their trade, "we have counted 150 companies that operate without a license, employing another 30,000 men who no one oversees or regulates, and who thus represent a danger to the country. We are identifying them in order to force them to legalise their situation" (Mejia 2006, 1).

Large private security companies that can deploy copious numbers of trained private police occupy one end of the private security spectrum. This type of private security provision is highly organized, fully armed and trained. Given the poorly outfitted police forces in countries like Honduras, these "ready to go" private security officers appear to be attractive alternatives to their own legally sanctioned police. Still, this is one end of a large spectrum. At the polar opposite end of the private security spectrum are very simple private security measures. At the most basic level, security privatization can be something as simple as a watch dog or burglary alarm.

To understand the full range of private security options, Ungar (2007) creates a typology based on two key dimensions: the mission of private security actors and the state's level of involvement. Ungar explains how the mission of private security agents can range from something very specific, like guarding a casino, to a broader mandate like maintaining public order in a neighborhood. To fulfill its mission, private security can take several different forms. Private security services can be technical in nature, such as installing alarms, locks, new lighting, and surveillance cameras. Alternatively, the private security mission could focus on controlling physical access to specific venues, such as the temporary guarding of entrances at major events to the long range patrol of gated communities. Sometimes the mission is of a more consultative nature, such as the training of personnel or the improvement of computer security. Finally, Ungar (2007) points to the growth of a more specialized type of mission involving high-risk situations like kidnappings and VIP protection. All of these different types of private security missions can range from very specific to open-ended.

In addition to the type and scope of mission, Ungar (2007) identifies a second dimension for understanding how private security forces operate—the level of state involvement. At one end of the spectrum, the state maintains a high level of control over private security, as occurs when police officers are hired to protect specific venues such as banks. On the other side of the continuum, private security forces can be completely autonomous from the state, and even evade regulation. Indeed, the relationship between the state and private security has become particularly murky, as substantial overlap between private and security forces has made it increasingly difficult to delineate between the two (Cafferata 2010). As Ungar notes:

> Amid the industry's growth, the private and public security spheres have increasingly overlapped, with public officials acquiring business interests in private firms, oversight by state agencies becoming corrupted, and public security monies going to private use. In many countries, private firms are often hired by—and are probably formed with the express intent to service—local governments. (Ungar 2007, 35)

To understand the range of private security options, and their implications for the rule of law, Figure 6.1 diagrams Ungar's (2007) typology. These four basic categories illustrate the many different forms private security can take. When people first think of private security, typically they think of it as involving a specific mission, such as guarding a bank, hotel, casino, or even a hospital. On the face of it, there is nothing particularly alarming about a private security guard monitoring the entrance of a tourist hotel. Indeed, an argument could be made that hotels should use revenue from the tourist industry to provide extra security, freeing up public funds to strengthen public security in nontourist areas, thus benefitting society more broadly. Such private security measures become problems from a rule of law standpoint when they are not subject to effective oversight, and when they supplant public police

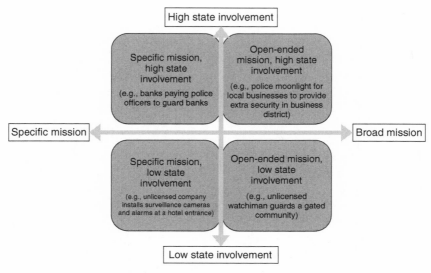

FIGURE 6.1 Ungar's (2007) Typology of Private Security

forces. If private security forces are better funded and outnumber those of the public sector, the risk emerges that private agents could carve out their own fiefdoms, and not turn problems over to public security forces when the rule of law needs to be applied. Furthermore, as the mission of private security becomes broader, the potential for private forces to act as border guards between social classes increases. It is one matter for a security guard to monitor a hotel entrance and ensure that only guests enter the premises. It is more problematic when entire streets are designated as private areas, and modest admission charges serve not just to pay for security, but also as an entry barrier for members of lower socioeconomic classes.

An example from Nicaragua illustrates this point. To generate tourist revenue, a group of investors sought to capitalize on Managua's lakefront property and develop a series of restaurants, artisan shops, and boat excursions around Lake Xolotlán. The historic center of Managua, the *Malecón*, seemed an excellent location for what was to be called the *Puerto Salvador Allende*, or Salvador Allende Port.[1] The venture faced numerous obstacles, however. Among other problems, the *Malecón* and other parts of the historic center of Managua did not host large numbers of tourists, and were known as crime hotspots. The security issue was resolved by constructing fencing around the Salvador Allende Port, and hiring security guards to patrol its entrance. The fee to enter the park is modest (well under USD $1), but poses barrier enough to the poorer classes. The Salvador Allende Port opened its gates in 2008 to paying customers, but the lakefront development project served to reinforce inequality, rather than develop a public space for people of Managua to enjoy as a whole. It is clear that without safety, such tourist development projects will not be successful. However, when private security measures carve out a small neighborhood from the city as a whole, barriers between the rich and poor are reinforced.

Similar issues emerge when examining the effects of private security measures that are open-ended with low state involvement, like gated communities. In a seminal work on the impact of crime and private security in São Paolo, Caldeira (2000) illustrates how in the process of ostensibly solving public security problems, gated communities ultimately end up creating new problems of their own. Caldeira documents how fear of crime can restrict public interactions and increase spatial segregation, primarily through the growth of gated communities that employ elaborate private security measures. Once behind guarded walls, residents are isolated from members of other socioeconomic groups, and do not consider legal authorities like the police to be in charge of their security. Private guards, under their employment, are responsible for keeping the peace. Residents retreat behind walls because they think they will be immune to problems of crime; however, as teenage residents of gated communities sometimes take advantage of the absence of police presence, property crime in these communities persists. Frequently, people living in gated communities do not view themselves as subject to an impartial law, but rather, as paying customers who expect to receive the goods to which they are entitled. If a teenage child breaks the law and steals a neighbor's goods, the incident is not considered to be a police matter, but rather one to be handled privately. Crime does not necessarily stop once people retreat behind the gates, it appears in different ways.

The migration to gated communities has additional ramifications, as it leads people to disengage from their neighbors and reduce their participation in their communities, weakening the bonds of civil society. Caldeira (2000) explains how crime and personal insecurity can erode interpersonal ties in society, leading communities to fracture according to socioeconomic lines. Indeed, frequently fear of crime is tied to perceptions of marginalized groups, and fear of crime solidifies already entrenched tendencies to keep certain socioeconomic groups at arms length through the construction of physical barriers such as walls and gated communities. Given the important role civil society and neighborhood networks can play in deterring crime and reducing public feelings of insecurity, this isolation can ultimately create more crime-related problems than it solves.

Similar problems emerge when examining reliance on other private security measures. On the face of it, alarms, watch dogs, and walls do not appear to threaten the rule of law. The key problem is that these measures ultimately isolate members of a community from one another, eroding interpersonal trust and heightening fear of crime. If members of a community retreat behind walls adorned with barbed wire, the chances crime will incur can actually increase, as the informal mechanisms of neighborhood vigilance are muted. Furthermore, when such private security measures seek to replace the legal authorities entrusted with upholding the rule of law, this ultimately enforces the negative equilibrium of the security trap, leaving citizens to opt out of interactions with the justice system in favor of their own purchased defense mechanisms.

Despite these problems, when citizens look around at the security status quo, it is easy to see how they might find private security measures soothing. If the police are not responsive (or worse, complicit with criminal activity), it makes sense to get a guard dog, build a wall, or install an alarm system. To understand why people turn to private security, and which measures they select, this analysis relies upon the 2008 LAPOP surveys, which included a series of extended questions targeting the issue of private responses to public security problems.

Private Responses to Public Insecurity (LAPOP 2008)

When deciding whether to invest in private security measures, people need to make a series of cost-benefit calculations. In these calculations, citizens need to weigh their level of fear against the cost of taking action on their own. How afraid do people need to be to take action? What types of crime are they afraid of? What is the best way to protect oneself? What is affordable? What is feasible? Citizens answer all of these questions as they think about how best to direct their financial investment into private security. As Barney points out, the adoption of one private security mechanism over another is very much contingent upon the cost involved:

> "For instance, locks, concrete walls, or broken glass are fairly inexpensive actions and tend to require low levels of expertise while weapons are likely difficult to acquire, house alarm installation can be complicated or expensive, and private security guards tend to be quite expensive related to the other methods listed" (2010, 5).

Due to the realities of these calculations, particularly the financial cost involved, frequently there is a disjuncture between the measures people think are best, and the ones they ultimately enact. Rico (2006) found that in surveys of Costa Rica, people rarely acted on the security measures they thought would be best. As Table 6.2 illustrates, people endorsed organizing the neighborhood as the best way to fight crime by a considerable margin—49 percent of people polled indicated this was the best way to protect themselves against crime. In contrast, only 3 percent thought that installing bars on windows was the best crime-fighting strategy. When it came to action, however, only 20 percent of respondents reported taking any action

TABLE 6.2 Disjuncture between Ideal and Action in Private Security Measures in Costa Rica

Security measure	Percentage identifying measure as best way to protect against crime (%)	Percentage actually taking that measure (%)
Organize neighborhood	48.6	19.8
Buy a watch dog	3.2	39.2
Install bars on windows	3.0	64.2
Buy a weapon	2.2	6.2

Source: Rico (2006)

toward organizing the neighborhood, whereas 64 percent stated that they put bars on the windows. Some of this disjuncture can be attributed to practical matters; someone might think that buying an alarm system is best, but lack the funds to do so. The disjuncture between the percentages of people who thought it best to organize the neighborhood and those who actually did so underscores a larger point, however. Such crime-fighting strategies might be well-received initially, but fail to garner support when it comes to action given the necessary costs involved in actually working together with neighbors. These costs are not necessarily financial, but rather investments of time and interpersonal contact. Interpersonal contact can be difficult to generate when people are afraid of crime, as this fear undermines interpersonal trust. Survey respondents might think that organizing the neighborhood is the best way to fight crime, but against a backdrop of high crime rates, do they trust their neighbors enough to work with them? For people with sufficient financial resources, purchasing security is typically easier. It is easier to buy bars for the windows than it is to organize the community, and the results are perceived to be more immediate. Unfortunately, investing in measures like alarms and bars further reduces the likelihood of the widely endorsed organization of the neighborhood. As more people retreat behind barred windows and turn on their alarms, fewer are left to interact with their neighbors and become involved in their communities.

To examine how people make the calculations to invest in private security, and what form these investments take, the 2008 LAPOP survey posed a series of questions to determine which measures people have taken, and what more they would like to do. Survey responses provide a great deal of insight into how citizens create private responses to satisfy the lack of a public good like security. For example, LAPOP asked respondents: "In the past twelve months, have you taken any security measures to protect yourself against crime in your home? (1) yes (0) no." Figure 6.2 provides the percentage of respondents in each country who reported taking private security measures in the past year, grouped by income. These percentages reflect only those who took new action in the past year; it does not take into account security measures purchased in prior years, like alarms, that would still be present in homes. People who answered "no" to this question might very well have private security measures in place, but these measures could have been adopted more than a year ago.

Since purchasing private security measures is dependent upon income, Figure 6.2 groups national percentages according to income levels. Respondents were grouped into quartiles depending upon the number of material goods they possessed: (1) bottom 25 percent, (2) 26–50 percent, (3) 51–75 percent, (4) top 25 percent.[2] People owning the highest number

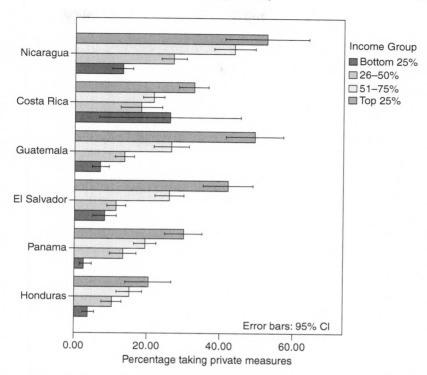

FIGURE 6.2 Percentage Taking Private Security Measures in Past Twelve Months, by Country and Income (LAPOP 2008)

of goods were placed in the top 25 percent, while those owning a relatively small number were in the bottom 25 percent of respondents. As Figure 6.2 indicates, income is far more decisive in determining who has taken private action than nationality.

Figure 6.2 illustrates that wealth is a decisive factor in determining who relies on private security measures. Wealthy people in Nicaragua, Guatemala, and El Salvador registered similar levels of purchasing private security measures, despite Nicaragua's comparatively lower crime rate. Costa Rica had a much higher national rate of private security acquisition, but when income is taken into account, rates of purchasing private security measures are statistically the same among the wealthy of Panama and Costa Rica.

After identifying the respondents who had invested in private security measures, LAPOP posed a follow-up question to determine what types of measures were most popular: "What security measure did you take in your home to protect yourself from crime?" Respondents indicated the type of private security they had purchased, and these responses were later grouped into seven categories. After recording the first response, LAPOP asked if respondents had purchased a second measure; 9 percent identified a second form of security in which they had invested, and this second response was also coded into one of seven categories. Table 6.3 lists these categories, as well as the percentage in each country that invested in each. As respondents were allowed to give multiple responses to this question, the country totals can exceed 100 percent.

Respondents varied in terms of how they invested in private security; however, overall purchases were more concentrated in less expensive measures. Of course, the actual price tag of these private security measures can vary tremendously depending upon scope and quality, but overall, installing bars and barbed wire tends to be less expensive than installing an alarm, purchasing a weapon, or hiring a private security service. These latter three measures had the lowest frequencies, proving either less popular or less feasible than installing more basic physical barriers around one's home, like broken glass on top of walls.

TABLE 6.3 Types of Private Security Acquisitions (LAPOP 2008)

Private security measure	Guatemala (*N*=281) (%)	El Salvador (*N*=298) (%)	Honduras (*N*=164) (%)	Nicaragua (*N*=410) (%)	Costa Rica (*N*=373) (%)	Panama (*N*=274) (%)
Bars or additional walls	26.3	25	51	28	58	77
Barbed wire, electric fencing, or broken glass	9	25	40	20	26	22
Alarms	8	5	7	3	10	5
Chains or steel barriers	26	29	27	39	33	22
Weapon	6	8	10	6	7	4
Private security service	3	6	3	7	6	1
Other	23	28	9	37	13	9

Note: Respondents were able to list two private security measures, leading country totals to exceed 100% in some cases.

Data Analysis of Private Security Investments

What leads citizens to turn to private security measures? This analysis relies upon the same theoretical framework of Chapters 4 and 5 and seeks to determine whether investments in private security can be linked to perceptions and experiences with crime and justice. For example, is privatization driven by first-hand experiences with victimization? Or is it attributable to perceptions of crime in the immediate environment, or country as a whole? What role does the justice system play in increasing the appeal of private security measures? Do we see cross-national differences? These questions

TABLE 6.4 Variables and Hypotheses Predicting Private Security Measures

	Independent variables	Hypotheses
Crime	Victimization	Victims will be more likely to adopt private security measures than nonvictims.
	Fear of crime in the neighborhood	As fear of crime in the neighborhood increases, reliance on private security will increase.
	Fear of crime in the country	As fear of crime in the country increases, reliance on private security will increase.
Institutional performance	Ability to punish criminals	As people's trust that the justice system will punish criminals increases, reliance on private security will decrease.
	Experience with police corruption	People who have experienced police corruption will be more willing to rely on private security.
Individual attributes	Gender	Women will be more reliant on private security than men.
	Age	Older respondents will be more reliant on private security than younger cohorts.
	Income	As income increases, reliance on private security will increase.
	Education	As education increases, reliance on private security will increase.
	Size of municipality	As the size of the municipality increases, reliance on private security will increase.
	Indigenous dummy variable (Guatemala only)	In Guatemala, indigenous respondents will be less reliant on private security than ladinos.

were the bases for analyses of extralegal justice and reporting crime. This analysis extends this theoretical framework to examine the privatization of security. Table 6.4 reviews the variables associated with this theoretical framework and states the anticipated relationships between these variables and the dependent variable—respondents' decision to invest in private security. As Figure 6.2 illustrated, investment in private security is measured dichotomously; respondents either purchased a private security measure in the past twelve months (1) or they did not (0).

Table 6.5 reports the results of this binary logistic regression analysis for all countries. Many of the results are remarkably consistent across the countries, particularly considering how much cross-national variation existed in analyses of support for extralegal justice and crime reporting. When examining the adoption of private security measures, respondents followed several similar patterns in different national contexts. In every country, both personal experience with crime and fear of future victimization in one's neighborhood was positively associated with the adoption of private security measures. Victims of crime in the past year were significantly more likely than nonvictims to invest in private security in the prior year. Likewise, as respondents' fear of crime in their immediate environment increased, they became more likely to purchase items for their security. Personal experiences and local perceptions consistently shaped people's willingness to turn to private security.

Perceptions of crime in the country mattered in four cases: Costa Rica, Nicaragua, Panama, and Honduras. In these countries, perceptions that crime was threatening the country as a whole increased people's willingness to rely upon private security. However, in Guatemala and El Salvador, respondents' perceptions at the national level did not translate into private action. This difference could be due to the fact that the surge in sensationalist, violent crime happened earlier in Guatemala and El Salvador, so people with economic means might have invested in private security at an earlier point in time, and not made as many investments in the past year.

The impact of the justice system on private security investments was less consistent. In terms of personal experiences, respondents with corrupt encounters with police were significantly more likely to turn to private security measures in Guatemala, El Salvador, Honduras, and Costa Rica. However, there was no relationship between police corruption and private security in Panama and Nicaragua. In the three high crime/low rule of law countries, experiences with corrupt police appear to have added to the perception that one cannot rely upon justice institutions for protection, leading people to turn to private alternatives. The significant results in Costa

TABLE 6.5 Reliance on Private Security Measures

	Independent variables	Guatemala	El Salvador	Honduras	Costa Rica	Nicaragua	Panama
Crime variables	Victimization	.523**	1.067***	.891***	.669***	.966***	1.214***
		(.183)	(.165)	(.214)	(.168)	(.165)	(.221)
	Fear of crime in the neighborhood	.256**	.396***	.243*	.333***	.522***	.645***
		(.085)	(.076)	(.109)	(.074)	(.072)	(.093)
	Fear of crime in the country	−.051	.131	.635***	.269*	.748***	.612***
		(.116)	(.152)	(.141)	(.111)	(.139)	(.133)
Institutional performance	Ability to punish criminals	−.179*	−.046	−.004	.164*	.041	.115
		(.083)	(.076)	(.104)	(.068)	(.067)	(.085)
	Experience with police corruption	.600**	.501*	1.016***	.888***	.113	.318
		(.209)	(.233)	(.252)	(.223)	(.223)	(.335)
Individual attributes	Gender	.080	.163	.036	−.151	.236	.006
		(.159)	(.149)	(.189)	(.136)	(.136)	(.151)
	Age	.046	.057*	.124**	.026	.036	.087**
		(.028)	(.026)	(.037)	(.022)	(.026)	(.026)
	Income	1.644***	1.365**	.997*	1.035*	1.778***	2.179***
		(.445)	(.434)	(.467)	(.430)	(.374)	(.455)
	Education	.092***	.089***	.110***	.044*	.068***	.043
		(.022)	(.019)	(.027)	(.018)	(.018)	(.024)
	Size of municipality	.147*	.051	.072	.131**	.081	.023
		(.061)	(.056)	(.069)	(.040)	(.046)	(.053)
	Indigenous dummy variable (Guatemala only)	.742***					
		(.181)					
	Nagelkerke pseudo *R* squared	.238	.247	.230	.125	.276	.221
	N	1302	1474	1423	1365	1422	1409

* *p*<.05; ** *p*<.01; *** *p*<.001

Note: Binomial logistic regression coefficients with standard errors in parentheses.

Rica demonstrate that this relationship is not found only in the context of high crime rates, but also when crime increases suddenly. In the context of Costa Rica, where citizens are disturbed with the justice system's inability to curb the recent tide of rising crime rates, police corruption can further cement these feelings of frustration and encourage people to invest in private security.

Perceptions that the justice system would punish criminals followed the hypothesized relationship only in the case of Guatemala. In Guatemala, as perceptions that the police would punish criminals increased, respondents were less likely to purchase private security measures. This relationship was not replicated in any other country. People's private security purchases were not tied to their perceptions of the justice system. Even people who perceive the justice system as performing adequately prefer not to take their chances, and still invest in private security when they have the means to do so. Indeed, in Costa Rica, perceptions of the justice system were positively related to private security purchases—as people perceived the system as doing better, they were *more* likely to invest in private security. The significance of this positive relationship is most likely a statistical artifact; there does not appear to be an intuitive reason why people would invest in private security because they trusted the justice system more. This finding is best interpreted as illustrating that trust in the justice system is not enough to stave off private security in Costa Rica. Again, if people fear crime or experience it firsthand, and have the financial means, why take chances on the justice system? People may perceive it is a safer bet to purchase security for themselves.

The socioeconomic variables performed unevenly across the countries, as they did in earlier analyses of support for extralegal justice and reporting crime. The key exception here is income. The most important variable in determining whether respondents purchased private security measures in the past year was income. Far more important than the crime or justice variables was respondents' wealth. In every case, income was significant and had the largest impact on the dependent variable in terms of magnitude. Table 6.6 illustrates the size of the impact of income on private security purchases vis-à-vis the other independent variables that performed consistently across countries—victimization and fear of crime in the neighborhood. To fully interpret the logistic regression results, it is necessary to take the antilog of the logistic regression coefficient reported in Table 6.5 and discuss the exponentiated (b). Given the sizeable effects of income, this extended interpretation of the statistical results is most helpful. As Table 6.6 explains, the smallest impact of income is in the case of Honduras, where an increase in income renders respondents 171 percent more likely to purchase private

TABLE 6.6 Exponentiated (*B*) Slope Coefficients by Country

Country	Exponentiated (*B*) for income	Exponentiated (*B*) for victimization	Exponentiated (*B*) for fear of crime in neighborhood
Guatemala	5.178	1.688	1.291
El Salvador	3.915	2.908	1.486
Honduras	2.711	2.438	1.275
Nicaragua	5.919	2.629	1.685
Costa Rica	2.814	1.952	1.396
Panama	8.833	3.365	1.906

security. The largest impact of income is in Panama, where an increase in income leaves respondents almost eight times (or 783 percent) more likely to invest in private security. In contrast, victimization made respondents 144 percent more likely to buy private security measures in Honduras and 237 percent more likely in Panama. These contrasts indicate that while significant and important, the effects of victimization and fear of crime are small compared to those of income. People who have the money to spend on private security will do so, regardless of the other factors involved. Rationally speaking, it is the safest bet. When money is not scarce, people who can purchase security will do so. The United Nations Office on Drugs and Crime was more blunt in its assessment: "Vigilantism is for the poor. The rich can afford their own police" (UNODC 2007, 82).

Behavior Modifications

For those who cannot afford the financial investments of private security, behavioral modifications also offer private solutions to public security problems. Bailey and Flores-Macías describe how crime can generate "attitudes of distrust of the government and of others" and that this distrust "leads to a variety of behavioral adjustments" (Bailey and Flores-Macías 2007, 18). Among other things, these behavioral adjustments include: restricting access to neighborhoods, reduced participation in civic activities, and abstention from voting. Smulovitz (2003) reaches similar conclusions in her analysis of crime's effects on civil society in Argentina. She finds that in addition to encouraging people to migrate to gated communities, acquire weapons, and hire private security services, crime can also induce simpler changes in people's behavior, such as leaving home less frequently. Smulovitz (2003) argues that these simpler behavioral changes have important repercussions, as reductions in civic participation and engagement in the community can further erode civil society and interpersonal trust, reinforcing cycles of fear and retreat. While this is an important caution, the empirical results associating fear of crime with retreat from the community are mixed. In an analysis of the Latin American region as a whole, Bateson (2009) finds that crime victimization is associated with *increased* civic and political participation.

Figure 6.3 displays different ways in which crime can lead respondents to change their behavior. To examine these types of retreats from civil society, or behavioral changes, LAPOP asked respondents: "For fear of being a victim of crime, in the past twelve months have you . . ."

- Limited the places you go shopping?
- Limited the places you go to for recreation?

These two items were combined into an additive index to measure crime-induced behavioral change, ranging from (0) no change at all through (2) changes in both shopping and recreational habits.[3]

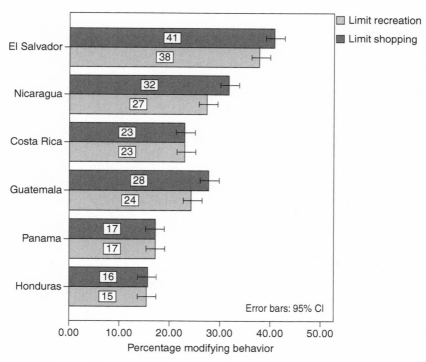

FIGURE 6.3 Behavior Modification (LAPOP 2008)

TABLE 6.7 Behavior Modification (LAPOP 2008)

	Independent variables	Guatemala	El Salvador	Honduras	Costa Rica	Nicaragua	Panama
Crime variables	Victimization	.910***	.884***	1.524***	.534**	.782***	.576**
		(.166)	(.140)	(.173)	(.160)	(.148)	(.214)
	Fear of crime in the neighborhood	.590***	.543***	.405***	.402***	.415***	.821***
		(.073)	(.057)	(.088)	(.071)	(.062)	(.087)
	Fear of crime in the country	.203*	.446***	.731***	.152	.614***	.450***
		(.102)	(.104)	(.109)	(.100)	(.109)	(.118)
Institutional performance	Ability to punish criminals	-.115	-.032	.024	.068	.092	-.023
		(.069)	(.054)	(.084)	(.065)	(.057)	(.080)
	Experience with police corruption	.492*	.457*	1.080***	.355	.337	.604
		(.198)	(.210)	(.221)	(.220)	(.197)	(.314)
Individual attributes	Gender	-.122	-.222*	-.040	.024	.151	-.049
		(.136)	(.110)	(.150)	(.129)	(.116)	(.142)
	Age	.035	-.054**	-.004	-.012	.005	.017
		(.024)	(.019)	(.030)	(.021)	(.022)	(.025)
	Income	1.024**	.951**	.990**	.719	.354	1.074**
		(.381)	(.323)	(.369)	(.408)	(.325)	(.410)
	Education	.032	.021	.023	.025	.050**	-.001
		(.019)	(.014)	(.022)	(.018)	(.016)	(.023)
	Size of municipality	.290***	.062	.300***	.192***	.149***	.126*
		(.051)	(.041)	(.055)	(.038)	(.040)	(.050)
	Indigenous dummy variable (Guatemala only)	.235					
		(.151)					
	Nagelkerke pseudo R squared	.289	.224	.311	.105	.188	.176
	N	1287	1473	1405	1358	1407	1395

* $p < .05$; ** $p < .01$; *** $p < .001$

Note: Ordinal logistic regression coefficients with standard errors in parentheses.

Table 6.7 displays the statistical results of an analysis of behavioral modification. The theoretical expectations of the crime, justice, and socioeconomic
variables are the same as in the analysis of private security measures. However,
since behavioral modifications do not rely as extensively on purchasing power,
one would expect to see income have less of an impact on the dependent variable. As the results in Table 6.7 indicate, the relationship between crime and
behavior modification is strong and consistent across all of the countries. In
every case, both personal experience with crime and perceptions of crime
in the neighborhood significantly alter respondents' behavior. Respondents
who have been victimized by crime or who fear crime in their neighborhoods
are significantly more likely to change their daily behaviors, limiting the
places they go shopping and engage in recreation. In every country except
Costa Rica, fear of crime at the national level also significantly alters respondents' behavior. As behavior modification is the easiest change respondents
can make to address their level of insecurity, behavior modification is most
consistently tied to victimization and fear of crime.

Consistently, perceptions of the justice system were not tied to respondents' behavioral changes. In every case, perceptions that the justice system
could sanction criminals were unrelated to the changes people made in their
daily lives due to insecurity. Respondents indicated that they acted far more
on their experiences with and perceptions of crime than on views toward the
justice system. Personal experiences with police corruption were significant
only in the high crime/low rule of law countries, where they significantly
raised the likelihood that respondents would alter their behavior and limit
some of their activities. In the remaining countries, people did not tie their
experiences with police to the need to change their daily routines.

The socioeconomic variables of gender, age, and education tended not to be
significant, with a few exceptions. In contrast, both income and size of municipality had more of an effect on behavioral change. While income did not have
the large impact it had in the model predicting private security acquisition, it
did significantly increase the likelihood of changing behavior in Guatemala,
El Salvador, Honduras, and Panama. Intuitively, it makes sense that wealthier
people would have more options to change their daily routines and find new
places for shopping and recreation. While behavioral change would not necessarily be out of the reach of poorer respondents, practical limitations might
make such changes a little more difficult. In addition, the size of the city also
significantly affected behavioral change (except in El Salvador), as citizens in
larger cities were more likely to change their daily routines. Once again, this
is likely due to practicality, as larger cities offer more options for shopping
and recreation. Also, larger cities tend to make respondents more sensitive to
crime, and thus more likely to change their behavior.

Conclusion

The results of this data analysis indicate that people are very likely to respond to fear of crime and victimization with investments in private security if they have the financial means to do so. This relationship holds regardless of national context. The analysis of private security does not demonstrate the same level of cross-national variation as the analyses of support for extralegal justice and reporting crime. Intuitively, it makes sense that private security measures would be similar across very different national contexts. In the case of extralegal justice, people need to consider whether they will bend the law to give more power to authorities or their fellow citizens. Thus, there are two points to consider: Is the law more important than capturing criminals, particularly given the nature of the rule of law in the country? Are people willing to give more power to authorities like the police, or to their fellow citizens? Answers to the latter depend upon views toward the agent in question. In the case of the police, citizens are frequently caught in between a rock and a hard place. Crime leads them to look for alternatives, but granting extra power to corrupt and/or abusive police might not seem like much of an option. Likewise, attitudes toward fellow citizens will shape people's willingness to extend extra powers to them to engage in vigilante justice. In these scenarios, people have to decide whether to bend or break the law, and then to which agent to give the extra power to sanction suspected criminals.

In contrast, private security does not pose the same dilemma. It is perfectly legal to build walls, install alarms, erect barbed wire, and in some cases purchase weapons. The consideration is not whether to bend or break the law, but whether people can financially afford to make these investments. In most cases, such action does not empower additional actors. Installing bars on the windows merely creates a physical barrier between the home and the outside world, it does not give fellow citizens or the police extra power to act against criminals. In the case of hiring private security guards, people do empower another agent, but the action is still perfectly legal. Also, private security guards are viewed as apolitical actors—they are hired to guard a hotel, street, or bank, and are paid according to their ability to do so. Questions of competence are typically dealt with financially—the more money someone has, the better security guard they can hire.

When such action is beyond the financial means of respondents, there are smaller ways in which people can privately address crime. Simple changes in behavior can lead people to perceive that they have reduced the likelihood of victimization. Such behavioral changes are more closely tied to experiences with and perceptions of crime, rather than broader perceptions of justice institutions as a whole.

Taken together, these results indicate that the greatest threat to the rule of law might be a comparatively quieter one—privatization. Privatization does not immediately strike observers as undermining the rule of law, as it involves legal behavior, and in many cases, modest behavior at that. Still, if privatization trends continue at the current pace and supplant legal authorities, the rule of law will not be an impartial arbiter of state and society relations. Rather, public security will be available to the highest bidder, thus reinforcing already entrenched patterns of inequality and social exclusion. If the state cannot provide public security, it fails in its basic function. If private security agents cannot be held accountable, they become little more than border guards between the social classes. As people retreat behind fortified walls, community ties and interpersonal trust deteriorate. In many different ways, the widespread privatization of security reinforces the negative equilibrium of the security trap.

The increasing privatization of security has picked up pace without much fanfare, until recently. In June 2011, a tragedy did put private security at the center of international media attention, when a security guard in Costa Rica fatally shot an American teenager on vacation (CNN 2011). This tragedy grabbed the headlines, as it underscored the depth of the security problem, as well as the pitfalls of private solutions. Costa Rica has sought to insulate its tourist industry, on which it is heavily reliant, with private security forces (Millet and Stiles 2008). It is quite common for private security guards to patrol hotels, resorts, and other vacation destinations. The quality of security guards varies tremendously, however, as does regulation of the industry, and enforcement of this regulation. In this case, the security guard in question did not have a permit to carry the gun he fired, as required by national law. When the teenager and his friends tried to return to their rooms before sunrise after sneaking out past curfew to visit friends in another part of the hotel, the security guard mistook them for intruders and opened fire. The guard was charged with simple homicide and incarcerated until his trial. This oversight came too late to avoid tragedy, however, as regulatory capability has not kept pace with the growth in the private security industry, in Costa Rica as well as the rest of Central America. Private security appears to be a feasible fix to an intractable problem; however, it faces several potential pitfalls of its own and detracts from rule of law promotion efforts instead of enforcing them.

Notes

1 The website for the Salvador Allende Port contains photographs, a history of the project, as well as detailed financial records for the investments in the locale: www.epn.com.ni/Puerto-Salvador-Allende.aspx.
2 Chapter 4 details how this measure of income was constructed.
3 The Chronbach's alpha for this index was .844. LAPOP included additional measures of crime-induced behavioral change; however, many of these items did not apply as readily to all respondents (e.g., due to fear of crime, did you have to close your business? Change neighborhoods?). A lower Chronbach's alpha confirmed that these items measured phenomenon in addition to behavioral change; consequently they were excluded from the analysis.

7

Conclusion

I thanked President Obama, as I do it right now in public, for his decision to visit the tomb of Monsignor Romero and the kindness of his invitation to accompany him in this historic visit. As I have said, Monsignor is the spiritual guide of this nation, and the visit that you are going to carry out to the tomb of Monsignor implies for us a recognition of a leader, an international leader like President Obama, to the message of Óscar Romero and the universal validity of his message.

Salvadoran President Mauricio Funes, March 2011

In a visit to El Salvador in March of 2011, American President Barack Obama and Salvadoran President Mauricio Funes visited the tomb of Archbishop Óscar Romero on the 31st anniversary of his murder. Romero was an advocate for the poor and an outspoken critic both of the Salvadoran military government as well as US support for this repressive regime. Funes and Obama's joint visit to honor Romero marked several historic milestones. First, it served as a reminder of how far El Salvador had progressed from its violent past. Funes's political party, the FMLN, had fought against the military government throughout the 1980s. In 2009, Funes led the FMLN to electoral victory, marking the first peaceful transition of power in the presidency from the ruling party ARENA to the political opposition of the FMLN. The widespread acceptance of this transfer of power both at home and abroad underscored a crucial point—democracy is now the only game in town. Elections are the mechanisms by which power is now contested. Obama heralded this milestone, praising Funes: "I want to commend you for your courageous work to overcome old divisions in Salvadoran society and to show that progress comes through pragmatism and building consensus. You've articulated a vision of economic growth and social progress that is inclusive of all segments of Salvadoran society."[1] In contrast to the past, when the United States supported dictatorship in order to oppose the FMLN, the United States now welcomed democracy and leaders like Funes.

Whatever problems plague contemporary democracy in El Salvador and its Central American neighbors, it is important to acknowledge how far political development has come. Citizens have a voice in the decision-making process, and leaders are held accountable for their actions through regular, competitive elections. As this book has indicated, leaders are not always held accountable through other mechanisms, however. The judiciary in particular has served as only a weak check on the power of elected officials, and impunity remains problematic for elected officials in higher office as well as for the state bureaucrats on the streets, like police officers. Democratic elections are the norm, but the rule of law continues to be a work in progress.

During a joint press conference, Obama and Funes acknowledged the work that remains to be done for democracy and the rule of law to thrive, announcing the creation of the Central American Citizen Security Partnership, which aims to build upon previous regional security agreements and targets $200 million to the region to strengthen the rule of law. According to Obama, this program represents "a new effort to confront the narco-traffickers and gangs that have caused so much violence in all of our countries, and especially here in Central America . . . We'll help strengthen courts, civil society groups and institutions that uphold the rule of law." These remarks underscore the sobering reality of democracy in El Salvador, but also Central America more broadly—it is impossible to discuss strengthening the rule of law, the missing piece of democratization, without addressing the toll of the crime epidemic.

As both Funes and Obama acknowledged, crime continues to take a steady toll throughout Central America. Most obvious is the toll that violent crime has taken on human life. The extraordinarily high homicide rates of the Northern Triangle in particular make crime a human rights issue. Just as observers decried the horrific loss of life in the region during the civil wars and military dictatorships of the 1980s, so they now denounce the disregard for human life and personal security endemic in the crime crisis today. Organizations like the World Bank have also pointed to the economic costs of the crime wave:

Beyond the trauma and suffering of individual victims, crime and violence carry staggering economic costs at the national level. Indeed, some experts estimate these costs at close to eight percent of regional GDP if citizen security, law enforcement and health care are included. Crime and violence also drag down economic growth, not just from the victims' lost wages and labor, but by polluting the investment climate and diverting scarce government resources to strengthen law enforcement rather than promote economic activity. (Serrano-Berthet and Lopez 2011, ii)

Honduras provides clear examples of how crime jeopardizes economic development by frightening away foreign investment, as its fledgling textile industry suffered a heavy blow when investors responded to a string of kidnappings by moving their factories elsewhere. In a region historically beset by problems of poverty, such economic losses are no trifling matter. The Latin American region as a whole has shown remarkable resilience in confronting the 2008 economic crisis. Still, economic progress faces a growing threat from the crime crisis (Sanchez-Bender and León 2011, World Bank 2011).

Migration is another consequence of crime. As Dammert and Bailey point out, "crime and violence have become significant push factors for outmigration from Latin America to the United States" (2006, 3). Income from remittances already fuels migration northward. Indeed, given the large numbers of Central Americans working abroad, particularly in the United States, analysts have come to agree that many Central American countries are now exporting their people. As Booth et al. explain, "By the 1990s, whereas coffee and bananas were once the foundations of Central American economies, migrants to the United States had become the new monocrop" (2010, 235). Remittances comprise 18–20 percent of GDP in El Salvador, Honduras, and Nicaragua, and approximately 13 percent of GDP in Guatemala (Booth et al. 2010, 236). While remittances are considerably less in Costa Rica and Panama, they did increase during the 2000s.[2] Remittances provide strong incentives for migration, and crime provides further impetus for the hike north. Of course, the effects of emigration, such as family disintegration and the risk of deportation, further exacerbate the crime crisis by eroding family and community ties. The UNDP (2009) notes that the Northern Triangle countries, for example, have suffered more from emigration's negative effects than the other countries in the region.

While analysts acknowledge the broad toll that crime takes on so many aspects of life in Central America, they repeatedly find themselves returning to the theme of governance, where crime and the rule of law have interacted in a self-reinforcing negative cycle. Most importantly, criminal elements took advantage of institutional weaknesses to set up shop in several of the third wave Central American democracies. Criminal organizations actively exploited institutional weaknesses during the initial transition to democracy in the 1990s, joined by additional criminal elements that flocked to the isthmus to evade US-backed crackdowns in Colombia, the Caribbean, and Mexico (Meyers and Ribando Seelke 2011). Once entrenched, criminal actors have systematically undermined efforts to reform the rule of law and its corresponding institutions, and have had particular success in stymieing reform in Guatemala and Honduras. Ineffective reforms make it easier for crime to continue unabated, perpetuating this negative pattern. Even international efforts like the UN's CICIG have found it difficult to confront actors like organized crime and officials accustomed to impunity. As the World Bank's recent report noted:

> Crime and violence also weaken key institutions. Existing evidence indicates that drug trafficking increases corruption levels in the criminal justice systems of some Central American countries and tarnishes the legitimacy of state institutions in the public's mind. On average, victims of crime tend to: (i) have less trust in the criminal justice system; (ii) support taking the law into their own hands in larger numbers; and (iii) believe less strongly that the rule of law should always be respected. (Serrano-Berthet and Lopez 2011, ii)

This caution highlights an additional concern at the level of the citizenry. Indeed, when examining the impact of crime on democratic governance, observers have increasingly expressed concern about citizens' reactions to the crime wave and weak justice institutions, and what these reactions mean for the rule of law and democratic governance more broadly. Extralegal police action, vigilante justice, and domestic military patrols pose problems for democratic governance, yet such measures have proven popular in some cases given the magnitude of the crime crisis. Once again, the problems of crime and the rule of law take the form of a self-perpetuating negative cycle: if political culture does not strongly embrace the rule of law, it will be easier for people to engage in criminal activities on the one hand, and for extralegal crime fighting measures to garner support on the other. Both criminal activity and extralegal measures further erode the rule of law, rendering citizens even more supportive of illegal and extralegal justice. Bailey (2009) referred to such situations as negative equilibriums, or security traps.

This book has focused squarely on such concerns and assessed the various ways in which crime and justice shape citizens' attitudes and behaviors toward the rule of law. The empirical analysis of survey data presented here paints a much more nuanced view of the relationships among crime, justice, and public support for the rule of law. Chapter 4 found that both personal experiences with and perceptions of crime and justice can lead people to support extralegal solutions to the crime crisis, in the form of vigilante justice and Dirty Harry-inspired official misconduct. This is not the inevitable outcome of the crime crisis, or weakened institutions, however. Crime victims do not immediately turn to extralegal justice. Citizens who are disenchanted with the justice system do not automatically endorse extrajudicial sanctions of suspected criminals. The potential is there for this to occur, but personal experiences and perceptions of crime and justice do not always lead to the endorsement of extralegal alternatives. Indeed, in the countries in which crime has not been as politicized, such as Panama and Nicaragua, this translation between negative experiences and perceptions and support for extralegal action is stunted. For example, Chapter 5 found that in these two countries, as well as in Costa Rica, people tended to report crime regardless of their experiences with or perceptions of the justice system as a whole. Rather than disregard the law and look for alternative solutions, victims were willing to turn to the justice system by reporting crime.

These empirical findings do not dispute the linkages among crime, justice, and support for extralegal action. The potential is most certainly there for victims to support Dirty Harry solutions to fighting crime, or community forms of vigilante justice. However, these empirical results do provide a way to put a positive spin on these linkages. The potential is there for crime and institutional weakness to further erode public support for the rule of law, but this is not a foregone conclusion. Politicians might increase this likelihood with punitive rhetoric or policies, or they could ameliorate such tendencies with comprehensive policies that target crime prevention, not just sweeping, punitive crackdowns. Once again, Panama and Nicaragua offer some intriguing insights. Despite the fact that crime rates are rising, and justice institutions (particularly in the case of Nicaragua) remain in need of reform, politicians have by and large emphasized preventive crime-fighting strategies, like Panama's mano amiga. In these countries, crime victims are less likely to endorse extralegal measures to fight crime, compared to the other countries in the region.

These national level variations in support for extralegal justice and crime-reporting drive home the importance of studying citizens' reactions to crime and justice in their appropriate national contexts. As Chapter 2 highlighted, these reactions occur in very different political environments. Both the magnitude of the crime crisis as well as the strength of justice institutions vary considerably across these cases. Chapter 4 also explained how politicians have presented citizens with very different options for fighting crime. Against these distinct national backdrops, it is easy to see why victims might turn to extralegal justice in some circumstances, yet not others. It is imperative to ground citizens' reactions in their appropriate environment, as doing so provides a more complete picture of how citizens become socialized to respect the rule of law, or encouraged to disregard it.

There is widespread agreement that rule of law promotion involves not just constitutional amendments and institutional reform, but also the resocialization of legal authorities and average people. This resocialization occurs in a specific context. Citizens are not taught the new and improved rules of the democratic game so they can go off and internalize them on their own. Rather, the process of democratization ushers in a new set of rules and norms that serve as a foundation for democratic governance and the rule of law. These norms and rules govern citizens' behavior toward each other, as well as between them and their government. During the democratization process, citizens must learn how to navigate this new framework. As O'Donnell (2006) reminds us, these rules are both formal and informal, so citizens need to think of how best to adapt to the new status quo with both formal and informal mechanisms in mind. It does little good for one citizen to adapt to the new rules of the game if no one else does. If everyone else bribes the police to get out of traffic tickets, it is not much use to be the lone holdout. To draw upon O'Donnell's analogy once again, motorists in certain parts of certain cities would be foolish to adhere to formal traffic laws at night: "If you do this, you are subjecting yourself to serious risks. The first is being run over by the car behind you; of course the driver of this car does not expect you to stop. The second risk is that without, or before, or even more, after the accident, you will be robbed" (2006, 285). As this analogy illustrates, citizens' respect for the law is formed at least partly according to the incentives afforded by the political environment.

Lyne (2008) applies this logic to understand a different phenomenon, the failure of policy-based platforms to materialize across new democracies. To understand variations in development policy, Lyne embeds micro-level voting behavior in a larger structural context and argues that this context explains why voters' preferences for public goods do not always translate into votes for policy-based platforms. If votes are cast in the context of pervasive clientelism, citizens who vote for collective goods may find themselves excluded from clientelist benefits. Lyne illustrates how electoral strategies that seem self-defeating in policy-based systems are actually quite rational in clientelist systems and notes that this same logic might explain the failure of reforms to transform the rule of law in Latin America. Lyne's work offers important insights into the provision of other types of public goods, such as public security. If citizens are trapped in what Bailey (2009) called a negative equilibrium, they would be foolish to rely upon the formal rule of law to solve problems, as they would be among the very few doing so, and the system would not respond to such efforts. Informal coping strategies emerge to deal with institutional weakness or corruption, and the threat posed by the crime crisis. Citizens' unwillingness to respect the rule of law is not necessarily indicative of a lack of a legal culture. Rather, it signals that people are responding to their environments, and in their current environments, a rational response might be to circumvent the law instead of uphold it.

Chapter 3 demonstrated that when learning to navigate their environments, citizens do not rely upon objective assessments of contemporary or historical trends. They operate according to their own impressions of the status quo, and their place in it. Perceptions of justice differ depending upon people's experiences, expectations, their place in the socioeconomic hierarchy, and evaluations of alternatives. Of course, perceptions are not completely disconnected from objective realities. One would be hard pressed to argue that impunity did not exist in Guatemala, for example. Still, it can explain why cross-national public attitudes do not match assessments of international entities, for example. In the case of Costa Rica, people have higher expectations of their political system, and the justice system's inability to confront crime and corruption has led many to register displeasure. Thus, comparisons of cross-national performance do not lead to higher public evaluations in the system that performs best in the region. Rather, respondents have low evaluations of the system because it does not perform according to high expectations. The object of comparison is the past performance, not other countries in the region.

When citizens seek to address problems like crime according to their perceptions of the justice system and broader political environment, in some environments, support for extralegal justice might appear to be one of the few viable alternatives for addressing problems like crime. While there is important cross-national variation, the empirical analyses in Chapter 4 found that crime victims in Guatemala, El Salvador, Honduras, and even Costa Rica registered significantly more support for some forms of extralegal justice. Still, Chapter 4 also illustrated that victims in Panama and Nicaragua did not follow this pattern, opening the door to more positive reactions to crime that might allow citizens to escape from the security trap. Empirical evidence from Chapter 6 offers a more grim assessment in some respects, however. While crime victims, and those who fear crime more generally, do not automatically endorse extralegal justice, they are willing to privatize justice. What is most striking about the empirical analyses of this book is that the one area in which there is very little cross-national variation is in the area of security privatization. When citizens think about how to best navigate their environments, across all contexts private security is appealing. The reliance on private security has only recently been subject to empirical examination by scholars and practitioners. The results of Chapter 6 indicate that this new focus is timely and very much warranted. Observers have worried that popular support for extralegal justice might undermine the rule of law, but it appears that private security poses an even greater threat. Private security measures are typically legal, but overreliance on them leads private security forces to supplant public ones, leading justice and security to belong to the highest bidder. An impartial law cannot effectively govern relationships in society and between society and government if it is enforced by private entities responsible to their employers, not the public good. On another note, the exponential growth of the private security field belies arguments that there is not enough money for effective law enforcement and criminal justice. If there is money to pay private security guards, there should be money to pay police officers. It seems the difference is not in the availability of resources, but rather in political will. Rather than investing in public security through taxation, wealthy individuals are investing in private security through personal contracts. While currently understudied, private security is a crucial area for future research on the rule of law.

So how can citizens respond to crime and justice in ways that allow them to escape from the security trap and foster a positive equilibrium for state-society relationships? Given current trends, responses will depend as much on what happens within Central American countries as what happens abroad. It is impossible to address the issue of crime and the rule of law without considering the broader regional problem. Officials both within Central America as well as in the United States have increasingly acknowledged that the weakness of the rule of law and the ability of criminal elements to capitalize on these weaknesses have created an international security problem. This problem is intensified by the realities of the US War on Drugs. The US focus on halting the supply of drugs and blocking transit routes has meant that the violence has shifted geographically to evade US controls. The crackdown on Colombia shifted power to the Mexican cartels, and the subsequent crackdown in Mexico and on transit routes in the Caribbean led the drug trade and corresponding violence to shift to Central America (Meyers and Ribando Seelke 2011). The United States' focus on the supply side of the War on Drugs has increased the violence within Latin American countries. Central American countries face yet additional hurdles in mounting a credible offensive against maras and organized crime, as both the demand for drugs and the supply of weapons originates largely outside their borders. While the United States has acknowledged its role in the regional conflict as both a consumer of drugs and exporter of arms, current solutions have not dramatically departed from the status quo. Despite calls for creative and effective dialogue on drug policy, the United States, at least for the time being, appears wedded to fighting the supply side war, albeit with promises of more weapons (Global Commission on Drug Policy 2011). In 2008, the United States launched the Mérida Initiative, which sought to replicate Plan Colombia primarily in Mexico, with spillover effects in the other Central American countries (Bailey 2011). The Mérida Initiative included the Central American Regional Security Initiative (CARSI), pledging "equipment, training, and technical assistance to support immediate law enforcement and interdiction operations," while also seeking to "strengthen the capacities of governmental institutions to address security challenges as well as the underlying economic and social conditions that contribute to them" (Meyers and Ribando Seelke 2011, ii). Still, if CARSI pays lip service to the latter underlying economic and social conditions, and concentrates more of its scarce resources to militarized confrontation of organized crime, there is little hope of overcoming the security trap. Indeed, former President Jimmy Carter issued a plea in June of 2011 to "call off the global drug war," noting that in its current form, the War on Drugs:

> Entailed enormous expenditure of resources and the dependence on police and military forces to reduce the foreign cultivation of marijuana, coca and opium poppy and the production of cocaine and heroin. One result has been a terrible escalation in drug-related violence, corruption and gross violations of human rights in a growing number of Latin American countries. (Carter 2011)

Carter endorsed the report of the Global Commission on Drug Policy (2011), which advocated replacing the militarized supply side war against drugs with major changes in the policies of countries that are consumers of drugs. In drug producing or transit countries, the Global Commission on Drug Policy advocated more preventive models of policing. As Table 7.1 indicates, there is support within Central American countries for such alternative models, as most respondents attributed crime increases to things like lack of youth programs and poverty, not a lack of force. If leaders wanted to endorse such measures, there would be room to do so in a way that would be well-received by at least some segments of the domestic population. In Obama and Funes's 2011 meeting in El Salvador, both leaders indicated they were at least open to the preventive and holistic approach to addressing crime within Central America. It remains to be seen if action will match rhetoric.

TABLE 7.1 Reasons for Increases in Crime (LAPOP 2008)

Country	Lack of police (%)	Lack of justice (%)	Poverty (%)	Lack of youth programs (%)
Guatemala	21	24	30	26
El Salvador	21	9	25	45
Honduras	13	14	52	21
Nicaragua	26	9	26	40
Costa Rica	26	16	18	40
Panama	23	11	21	45

In the search for appropriate models to address both the occurrence of crime and public fear of crime, and present viable alternatives to extralegal measures or private security, it is helpful to examine cases that defy expectations. In a classic exchange, famed fictional detective Sherlock Holmes points to the need to examine the case of "dogs that do not bark." In "Silver Blaze" Sir Arthur Conan Doyle (1894) records this famous exchange:

Scotland Yard detective: "Is there any other point to which you would wish to draw my attention?"
Holmes: "To the curious incident of the dog in the night-time."
Scotland Yard detective: "The dog did nothing in the night-time."
Holmes: "That was the curious incident."

To identify alternative models of addressing public security that strengthen citizens' support for the rule of law, it is helpful to examine cases in which crime has not led to heightened support for extralegal justice. Here, Nicaragua is a surprising exception to the general trends in the region. It has evaded the worst of the crime crisis, even with its legacy of internal conflict. Nicaraguans are also less likely to react to crime and fear of crime with support for extralegal measures. It is notable that Nicaragua has pioneered a preventive and holistic model of public security in the major city of León, which has served as a model for the rest of the country (Espinoza and Herrera 2009). The Nicaraguan model offers important insights, as it addresses both crime itself as well as fear of crime, and the implications the latter have for the rule of law and democratic governance more broadly.

Preventive and holistic models address both fear of crime and actual crime, and citizen involvement (when not corrupted) can encourage different reactions to crime that might allow for an escape from the security trap. They also address the root causes of crime in the first place. Three decades ago President Carter famously declared, "We know that a peaceful world cannot long exist, one-third rich and two-thirds hungry." A large amount of empirical evidence backs up this view. In a seminal work, Muller and Seligson (1987) demonstrate empirically that inequality breeds insurgency. Large gaps between the rich and poor foster violence. When writing their article, Muller and Seligson were addressing the civil wars, as well as smaller clashes between military governments and their people, that plagued the region throughout the Cold War. Now that the Cold War is over, the violence has persisted. The clashes are no longer between communists or left-leaning guerrillas and right-wing military dictatorships. The fighting now involves criminal elements of varying levels of organization that fight amongst themselves, against government forces, or even against unarmed civilians. The root causes of this violence remains the same, however—poverty and inequality. Preventive and holistic models have the advantage of not just reacting to the occurrence of crime, but actually addressing the long-standing economic forces that have precipitated conflict in the region in the past as well as the present day.

Notes

[1] The text of both Funes's and Obama's remarks were accessed June 20, 2011 from the *Washington Post's* website: http://projects.washingtonpost.com/obama-speeches/speech/602/.

[2] Costa Rica is an exception here, as it serves as a major destination point for Nicaraguan immigration. Rather than dispatching large numbers of migrants, Costa Rica hosts them, particularly in domestic, agricultural, and private security sectors.

Appendix

Latin American Homicide Data Sources and Years

Country	Homicide rate	Source	Year of homicide estimate
Argentina	5.24	United Nations Office on Drugs and Crime (UNODC)	2006
Bolivia	4.85	United Nations Office on Drugs and Crime (UNODC)	2006
Brazil	22	Ministério da Justiça do Brasil	2008
Chile	1.6	Chilean Ministry of the Interior and Public Security	2008
Colombia	38.8	Policía Nacional de Colombia	2007
Costa Rica	11	United Nations Development Program (UNDP)	2008
Ecuador	17.8	Instituto Nacional de Estadística y Censos de Ecuador	2008
El Salvador	52	United Nations Development Program (UNDP)	2008
Guatemala	48.4	United Nations Development Program (UNDP)	2008
Honduras	58	United Nations Development Program (UNDP)	2008
Mexico	18	Instituto Ciudadano de Estudios sobre la Inseguridad (ICESI)	2010
Nicaragua	13	United Nations Development Program (UNDP)	2008
Panama	19	United Nations Development Program (UNDP)	2008
Paraguay	12.33	United Nations Office on Drugs and Crime (UNODC)	2006
Peru	5.54	United Nations Office on Drugs and Crime (UNODC)	2006
Uruguay	4.7	United Nations Office on Drugs and Crime (UNODC)	2006
Venezuela	48.0	Organization of American States (OAS)	2007

References

Amaya, Edgardo Alberto. 2006. "Security Policies in El Salvador, 1992–2002." In *Public Security and Police Reform in the Americas,* edited by John Bailey and Lucía Dammert. Pittsburgh: University of Pittsburgh Press, 132–147.

American Bar Association Rule of Law Initiative (ABA ROLI) 2011. *Promoting the Rule of Law: Panama.* Accessed June 8, 2011 from http://apps.americanbar.org/rol/latin_america/panama.html.

Amnesty International 2003. El Salvador: Open Letter on the Anti-Maras Act. Accessed on June 1, 2011 at www.amnesty.org/es/library/asset/AMR29/009/2003/es/3fb7905f-d65d-11dd-ab95-a13b602c0642/amr290092003en.pdf.

Anderson, Christopher J. 2007. "The End of Economic Voting? Contingency Dilemmas and the Limits of Democratic Accountability." *Annual Review of Political Science* 10: 271–296.

Appialoza, Martín and Lucía Dammert. 2011. "Diálogo entre expertos: La pelea política en seguridad es por adueñarse de las víctimas del delito." *MDZ Diario de Mendoza,* March 14, 2011. Accessed April 22, 2011 at www.mdzol.com/mdz/nota/279746-dialogo-entre-expertos-la-pelea-politica-en-seguridad-es-por-aduenarse-de-las-victimas-del-delito/.

Arana, Ana. 2005. "How the Street Gangs Took Central America." *Foreign Affairs,* May/June.

Archibold, Randal and Damien Cave. 2011. "Drug Wars Push Deeper Into Central America." *The New York Times.* March 23, 2011, A1.

Arias, Enrique Desmond, and Mark Ungar. 2009. "Community Policing and Latin America's Citizen Security Crisis." *Comparative Politics* 41(4):409–429.

Arias Sánchez, Óscar. 1990. "Panama, Without an Army." *New York Times,* January 9, 1990.

Azpuru, Dinorah. 2008. "The 2007 Presidential and Legislative Elections in Guatemala." *Electoral Studies* 27 (3): 562–566.

Azpuru, Dinorah. 2006. *The Political Culture of Democracy in Guatemala: 2006.* United States Agency for International Development (USAID) Democracy Audit. Accessed June 1, 2011 at www.vanderbilt.edu/lapop/ab2006/guatemala1-en.pdf.

Bailey, John. 2011. "The U.S. Homeland Security Role in the Mexican War against Drug Cartels." *Prepared Statement for the House Committee on Homeland Security, Subcommittee on Oversight, Investigations, and Management,* Washington, DC, March 31, 2011.

Bailey, John. 2009. "Security Traps' and Democratic Governability in Latin America: Dynamics of Crime, Violence, Corruption, Regime, and State."

Criminality, Public Security, and the Challenge to Democracy in Latin America, ed. Marcelo Bergman and Laurence Whitehead. Notre Dame: University of Notre Dame Press, 251–276.

Bailey, John and Gustavo Flores-Macías. 2007. "Violent Crime and Democracy: Mexico in Comparative Perspective." *Paper Prepared for Delivery for the Annual Meeting of the Midwest Political Science Association.* Chicago, IL.

Bailey, John and Lucia Dammert. 2006. *Public Security and Police Reform in the Americas.* Pittsburgh: University of Pittsburgh Press.

Bailey, John and Matthew Taylor. 2009. "Evade, Corrupt, or Confront? Organized Crime and the State in Brazil and Mexico." *Journal of Politics in Latin America* 2: 3–29.

Barney, Richard. 2010. "Private Reactions to Public Insecurity in Central America." *Paper prepared for presentation at the 2010 annual meeting of the New England Political Science Association,* Newport, RI April 23–24.

Bateson, Regina (2009). "The Political Consequences of Crime Victimization in Latin America." *Paper Presented at Midwest Political Science Association's Annual Meeting,* Chicago, IL.

Bautista, Francisco Javier. 2008. La inseguridad en la agenda electoral municipal. Accessed May 20, 2010 at www.franciscobautista.com/?z=7#I) Sobreseguridadypolicía.

BBC. 2011a. "Guatemala First Couple's Divorce on Hold." *BBC news online,* April 2, 1011, Accessed May 6, 2011 at www.bbc.co.uk/news/world-latin-america-12948675.

BBC. 2011b. "Guatemala 'thieves' lynched over flour theft." *BBC news online,* February 22, 2011. Accessed July 12, 2011 from www.bbc.co.uk/news/world-latin-america-12546971.

BBC 2006. "El Salvador swoops on street gang." *BBC news online,* July 13, 2006. Accessed July 12, 2011 from http://news.bbc.co.uk/2/hi/americas/5177616.stm.

Belton, Rachel Kleinfeld. 2005. *Competing Definitions of the Rule of Law: Implications for Practitioners,* Washington, DC, Carnegie Endowment for International Peace.

Bergman, Marcelo. 2006. "Crime and Citizen Security in Latin America: The Challenges for New Scholarship." *Latin American Research Review* 41(2): 213–227.

Bergman, Marcelo and Laurence Whitehead. 2009. "Introduction: Criminality and Citizen Security in Latin America." In *Criminality, Public Security, and the Challenge to Democracy in Latin America,* edited by Marcelo Bergman and Laurence Whitehead. Notre Dame: University of Notre Dame Press, 1–26.

Blakely, Edward, and Mary Gail Snyder. 1997. *Fortress America: Gated Communities in the United States.* Washington, DC: Brookings Institution Press.

Blumstein, Alfred. 2007. "The Roots of Punitiveness in a Democracy." *Journal of Scandinavian Studies in Criminology and Crime Prevention* 8: 2–16.

Booth, John A. 1998. *Costa Rica: Quest for Democracy.* Boulder: Westview Press.

Booth, John, Christine J. Wade, and Thomas W. Walker. 2010. *Understanding Central America: Global Forces, Rebellion, and Change (fifth edition).* Boulder: Westview Press.

Bratton, William and William Andrews. 2001. "Driving out the Crime Wave: The Police Methods that Worked in New York City Can Work in Latin America. *Time Magazine,* July 23, 2001.

Briscoe, Ivan. 2007. "Guatemala: a Good Place to Kill." *openDemocracy* 34854.

Briscoe, Ivan. 2006. "Fending off the Iron Fist: Crime and the Left in Latin America." *openDemocracy,* April 20, 2006.

Cafferata, Fernando Gabriel. 2010. "Privatisation of Security in Latin America: Review." *Global Consortium on Security Transformation.* Working Paper No. 3. Accessed June 12, 2011 from www.securitytransformation.org/images/ publicaciones/160_Working_Paper_3_-_Privatisation_of_Security_in_Latin_ America_-_Review.pdf.

Caldeira, Teresa P. R. 2000. *City of Walls: Crime, Segregation, and Citizenship in São Paulo.* Berkeley, CA, University of California Press.

Call, Charles T. 2003. "Democratisation, War and State-Building: Constructing the Rule of law in El Salvador." *Journal of Latin American Studies* 35 (4): 827–862.

Candina, Azún. 2006. "The Institutional Identity of the Carabineros de Chile." In *Public Security and Police Reform in the Americas,* edited by John Bailey and Lucía Dammert. Pittsburgh: University of Pittsburgh Press, 75–93.

Carothers, Thomas. 2006. "The Rule-of-Law Revival." In *Promoting the Rule of Law Abroad: In Search of Knowledge,* edited by Thomas Carothers. Washington, DC, Carnegie Endowment for International Peace, 3–13.

Carothers, Thomas. 2003. "Promoting the Rule of Law Abroad: The Problem of Knowledge." *Rule of Law Series Working Papers* No. 34, Carnegie Endowment for International Peace.

Carter, Jimmy. 2011. "Call Off the Global Drug War." *The New York Times,* June 16, 2011. Accessed June 17, 2011 from www.nytimes.com/2011/06/17/ opinion/17carter.html?_r=2&hp.

Caumartin, Corinne. 2007. "Depoliticisation' in the Reform of the Panamanian Security Apparatus." *Journal of Latin American Studies* 39: 107–132.

Ceobanu, Alin M., Charles H. Wood, and Ludmila Ribeiro. 2011. "Crime Victimization and Public Support for Democracy: Evidence from Latin America." *International Journal of Public Opinion Research* 23(1): 56–78.

Chevigny, Paul. 1999. "Defining the Role of the Police in Latin America." In *The (Un)Rule of Law and the Underprivileged in Latin America,* edited by Juan E. Méndez, Guillermo O'Donnell, and Paulo Sérgio Pinheiro. Notre Dame: University of Notre Dame Press, 49–70.

Chevigny, Paul. 2003. "The Control of Police Misconduct in the Americas." In *Crime and Violence in Latin America: Citizen Security, Democracy, and the State,* edited by Hugo Frühling, Joseph S. Tulchin and Heather A. Golding. Baltimore: Johns Hopkins University Press, 45–68.

Chilean Ministry of the Interior and Public Security. 2009. Tasas de Homicidios Dolosos. Accessed June 12, 2011 at seguridadciudadana.gob.cl.

Chinchilla Miranda, Laura. 2003. "Experiences with Citizen Participation in Crime Prevention in Central America." In *Crime and Violence in Latin America: Citizen Security, Democracy, and the State,* edited by Hugo Frühling, Joseph S. Tulchin and Heather A. Golding. Baltimore: Johns Hopkins University Press, 205–232.

Chinchilla Miranda, Laura. 2002. Public Security in Central America. Accessed May 20, 2010 at http://pdba.georgetown.edu/Pubsecurity/ch2.pdf.

CNN Wire Staff. 2011. "Guard Faces Charges in Case of U.S. Student Killed in Costa Rica." June 3, 2011. Accessed June 15, 2011 from http://articles.cnn.com/2011-06-03/world/costa.rica.student.killed_1_costa-rica-security-guard-arenal?_s=PM:WORLD.

Comisión Internacional contra la Impunidad en Guatemala (CIGI). 2009. "Two Years of Work: A Commitment to Justice." *United Nations Report.* Accessed June 1, 2011 at http://cicig.org/uploads/documents/report_two_years_of_work.pdf.

Córdova Macías, Ricardo, José Miguel Cruz, and Mitchell Seligson. 2007. "The Political Culture of Democracy in El Salvador." *United States Agency for International Development (USAID) Democracy Audit,* Accessed June 2, 2010 at www.vanderbilt.edu/lapop/.

Correa, Jorge. 1999. "Judicial Reforms in Latin America: Good News for the Underprivileged?" In *The Rule of Law and the Underprivileged in Latin America,* edited by Juan Méndez, Guillermo O'Donnell and Paulo Pinheiro. Notre Dame, University of Notre Dame Press, 255–277.

Cruz, José Miguel. 2009. "Public Insecurity in Central America and Mexico." *AmericasBarometer Insights Series,* No.28, Accessed May 24, 2011 at www.vanderbilt.edu/lapop/insights/I0828en.pdf.

Cruz, José Miguel. 2008. "Violence and Insecurity as Challenges for Democratic Political Culture in Latin America." Accessed June 2, 2010 at sitemason.vanderbilt.edu/files/iicjwk/Cruz.pdf.

Cruz, José Miguel. 2006. "Violence, Citizen Insecurity, and Elite Maneuvering in El Salvador." In *Public Security and Police Reform in the Americas,* edited by John Bailey and Lucía Dammert. Pittsburgh: University of Pittsburgh Press, 148–168.

Cruz, José Miguel. 2003. "Violencia y democratización en Centroamérica: el impacto del crimen en los regímenes de posguerra." *América Latina Hoy* 35: 19–59.

Cruz, José Miguel. 2000. "The Impact of Crime on Democratization in El Salvador." *Paper presented at the XXII International Congress of the Latin American Studies Association,* Miami, FL., March 16–18.

Dakolias, Maria. 2001. "Legal and Judicial Reform: The Role of Civil Society in the Reform Process." In *Rule of Law in Latin America: The International Promotion of Judicial Reform,* edited by Pilar Domingo and Rachel Sieder. London: Institute of Latin American Studies, 80–98.

Dammert, Lucía and Mary Fran T. Malone. 2010. "A Convenient Scapegoat: The Impact of Economic Insecurities on Fear of Crime in Latin America." *Paper Presented at the 2010 International Studies Association Annual Meeting,* New Orleans, LA.

Dammert, Lucía and Mary Fran T. Malone. 2006. "Does It Take a Village? Policing Strategies and Fear of Crime in Latin America." *Latin American Politics and Society* 48 (4): 27–51.

Danner, Mark. 1993. *The Massacre at El Mozote.* New York: Vintage Books.

De Mesquita Neto, Paulo. 2006. "Public-Private Partnerships for Police Reform in Brazil." In *Public Security and Police Reform in the Americas*, edited by John Bailey and Lucía Dammert. Pittsburgh: University of Pittsburgh Press, 44–57.

Diamond, Larry. 1999. *Developing Democracy: Toward Consolidation*, Baltimore, Johns Hopkins University Press.

Djankov, Simeon, Rafael La Porta, Florencia Lopez-de-Silanes, and Andrei Shleifer. 2001. "Legal Structure and Judicial Efficiency: the Lex Mundi Project." *World Bank Background Paper for 2002 World Development Report.*

Dodson, J. Michael and Donald W. Jackson. 2004. "Horizontal Accountability in Transitional Democracies: The Human Rights Ombudsman in El Salvador and Guatemala." *Latin American Politics & Society* (46) 4: 1–27.

Dodson, J. Michael and Donald W. Jackson. 2001. "Judicial Independence and Instability in Central America." In *Judicial Independence in the Age of Democracy: Critical Perspectives from around the World*, edited by Peter H. Russel and David M. O'Brien. Charlottesville, VA, University Press of Virginia, 251–272.

Doyle, Arthur Conan. 1894. "Silver Blaze" in *The Memoirs of Sherlock Holmes*.

Duce, Mauricio, Claudio Fuentes, and Cristián Riego. 2010. "The Impact of Criminal Procedure Reform on the Use of Pretrial Detention in Latin America." Accessed May 17, 2011 at www.cejamericas.org/portal/index.php/en/virtual-library/virtual-library/search_result.

Duce, Mauricio and Rogelio Pérez Perdomo. 2003. "Citizen Security and Reform of the Criminal Justice System in Latin America." In *Crime and Violence in Latin America: Citizen Security, Democracy, and the State*, edited by Hugo Frühling, Joseph S. Tulchin and Heather A. Golding. Baltimore: Johns Hopkins University Press, 69–92.

Espinoza, Ana Yancy and Nidia Zúñiga. 2003. *La Seguridad Privada en Centro América.* Fundación Arias para la Paz y el Progreso Humano and Diálogo Centroamericano. Accessed June 12, 2011 from www.revistazo.com/12_04/seguridad_privada_ca.pdf.

Easton, David. 1975. "A Re-Assessment of the Concept of Political Support." *British Journal of Political Science* 5 (4): 435–457.

The Economist. 2007. "Ballots, Bullets and Business: Elections in Guatemala and Jamaica Illuminate the Battle between Democratic Politics and Organized Crime."

The Economist. 2010. "Guatemala and Organised Crime: Reaching the Untouchables." March 11, 2010.

Eijkman, Quirine A. M. 2006. "Around Here I Am the Law! Strengthening Police Officers' Compliance with the Rule of Law in Costa Rica." *Utrecht Law Review* 2(2): 145–176.

Ellingwood, Ken. 2008. "Mexico Safety Chief's Tough Job: Policing the Police." *Los Angeles Times*, September 15, 2008.

Espinoza, Braulio. 2004. *La Oratoria Forense: Una Estrategia del Juicio Oral.* León: Universidad Nacional Autónoma de Nicaragua UNAN-León.

Espinoza, Braulio and Andrés Herrera. 2009. *Triada de la Seguridad Ciudadana en León, Nicaragua.* Editorial Universitaria, UNAN-León.

Fernández García, María Cristina. 2004. "Lynching in Guatemala: Legacy of War and Impunity." *Working Paper, Weatherhead Center for International Affairs*

Harvard University. Accessed June 2, 2011 at www.wcfia.harvard.edu/fellows/papers/2003-04/fernandez.pdf

Finkel, Jodi. 2008. *Judicial Reform as Political Insurance: Argentina, Peru, and Mexico in the 1990s.* Notre Dame, University of Notre Dame Press.

Foweraker, Joe, and Roman Krznaric. 2009. "The Uneven Performance of Third Wave Democracies: Electoral Politics and the Imperfect Rule of Law in Latin America." In *Latin American Democratic Transformations: Institutions, Actors, and Processes,* edited by William Smith. Malden, MA: Wiley-Blackwell, 53–78.

Freedom House Organization. 2010. *Freedom in the World 2010.* Accessed June 1, 2011 at www.freedomhouse.org.

Frühling, Hugo. 2003. "Police Reform and the Process of Democratization." In *Crime and Violence in Latin America: Citizen Security, Democracy, and the State,* edited by Hugo Frühling, Joseph S. Tulchin and Heather A. Golding. Baltimore: Johns Hopkins University Press, 15–44.

Frühling, Hugo, Joseph S. Tulchin and Heather A. Golding. 2003. *Crime and Violence in Latin America: Citizen Security, Democracy, and the State.* Baltimore: Johns Hopkins University Press.

Fuchs, D. 1999. "The Democratic Culture of Unified Germany." In *Critical Citizens: Global Support for Democratic Governance,* edited by Pippa Norris, New York: Oxford University Press, 123–145.

Gaviria, Alejandro and Carmen Pages. 1999. "Patterns of Crime Victimization in Latin America." *Inter-American Development Bank Working Paper No. 408,* Accessed June 1, 2011 at http://papers.ssrn.com/sol3/papers.cfm?abstract_id=192590.

Global Commission on Drug Policy. 2011. *War on Drugs: Report of the Global Commission on Drug Policy.* Accessed June 20, 2011 from www.globalcommissionondrugs.org.

Godoy, Angelina Snodgrass. 2006. *Popular Injustice: Violence, Community and Law in Latin America.* Palo Alto: Stanford University Press.

Godoy, Angelina Snodgrass. 2002. "Lynchings and the Democratization of Terror in Postwar Guatemala: Implications for Human Rights."*Human Rights Quarterly* 24 (3): 640–661.

González, Luis E. and Rosario Quierolo. 2009. "Understanding 'Right' and 'Left' in Latin America." *Paper presented at the 2009 meeting of the Latin American Studies Association,* Rio de Janiero, Brazil, Accessed June 1, 2011 at http://lasa.international.pitt.edu/members/congresspapers/lasa2009/files/GonzalezLuis.pdf.

Gosselin, Donald S. 2006. "Ongoing Paradigm Shift in Panamanian Policing." *Crime & Justice International* 22(94): 15–22.

Grimmett, Richard. 2004. "Instances of Use of United States Armed Forces Abroad, 1798 – 2004." *Foreign Affairs, Defense, and Trade Division, Congressional Research Service.* Washington DC: Library of Congress.

Gutiérrez, Raúl. 2008. "Hard-Line Policies Vs. Rule of Law." *Inter Press Service News Agency (IPSNEWS).* Accessed June 2, 2011 from http://ipsnews.net/news.asp?idnews=43517.

Hammergren, Linn A. 2007. *Improving Judicial Performance in Latin America,* University Park, PA: Penn State Press.

194   *References*

Hammergren, Linn. 2002. "Fifteen Years of Judicial Reform in Latin America: Where We Are and Why We Haven't Made More Progress." USAID, Global Center for Democracy and Governance, www.undp-pogar.org/publications/judiciary/linn2/latin.pdf (accessed September 10, 2011).

Helmke, Gretchen and Steven Levitsky. 2006. *Informal Institutions and Democracy: Lessons from Latin America.* Baltimore: Johns Hopkins University Press.

Herrera, Andrés (2006). *Heaven Can Wait: Studies on Suicidal Behavior among Young People in Nicaragua.* Umea: University Umea Press.

Herrera, Andrés and Braulio Espinoza (2008). *La Seguridad Ciudadana en el Municipio de León, Nicaragua.* Editorial Universitaria, UNAN-León.

Hinton, Mercedes S. 2006. *The State on the Streets: Police and Politics in Argentina.* Boulder: Lynne Rienner Publishers.

Hobbes, Thomas. 1651 [2009]. *Leviathan (Oxford World's Classics).* Edited by J. C. A. Gaskin. New York: Oxford University Press.

Hudson, Andrew and Alexandra W. Taylor. 2010. "The International Commission against Impunity in Guatemala: A New Model for International Criminal Justice Mechanisms." *Journal of International Criminal Justice* 8: 53–74.

Huhn, Sebastian. 2009. "The Culture of Fear and Control in Costa Rica: The Talk of Crime and Social Changes." *GIGA Research Programme, Violence, Power, and Security* No. 108. Hamburg: German Institute of Global and Area Studies. Accessed June 2, 2011 at http://giga-hamburg.academia.edu/SebastianHuhn/Papers/141546/The_Culture_of_Fear_and_Control_in_Costa_Rica_II_The_Talk_of_Crime_and_Social_Changes.

Huhn, Sebastian. 2008. "Discourses on Violence in Costa Rica, Nicaragua, and El Salvador: Social Perceptions in Everyday Life." *GIGA Research Programme, Violence, Power, and Security* No. 81. Hamburg: German Institute of Global and Area Studies. Accessed June 2, 2011 at http://giga-hamburg.academia.edu/SebastianHuhn/Papers/124962/Discourses_on_Violence_in_Costa_Rica_El_Salvador_and_Nicaragua_Social_Perceptions_in_Everyday_Life.

Huntington, Samuel. 1993. *The Third Wave: Democratization in the Late Twentieth Century.* Norman: University of Oklahoma Press.

Instituto Ciudadano de Estudios sobre la Inseguridad (ICESI 2010). Tasas de Homicidios Dolosos. Accessed June 12, 2011 from www.icesi.org.mx/documentos/estadisticas/estadisticasOfi/denuncias_homicidio_doloso_1997_2010.pdf.

Instituto Nacional de Estadística y Censos de Ecuador (INEC). 2011. Tasas de Homicidios Dolosos. Accessed June 12, 2011 from www.inec.gov.ec.

International Crime Victims Survey (ICVS) (1989–2005). International Crime Victims Survey Database. Accessed June 2, 2011 at http://rechten.uvt.nl/icvs/news.htm.

Justice Studies Center of the Americas (CEJA-JSCA) 2008–2009. Report on Judicial Systems in the Americas (Fourth Edition). Accessed May 17, 2011 from www.ceja.cl/reporte/2008-2009/.

Justice Studies Center of the Americas (CEJA-JSCA) (2006–2007), Report on Judicial Systems in the Americas (Third Edition), www.cejamaericas.org (accessed September 10, 2011).

Kaufmann, Daniel, Aart Kraay, and Massimo Mastruzzi. 2009. Governance Matters VIII: Aggregate and Individual Governance Indicators 1996–2008, Accessed June 2, 2010 from http://papers.ssrn.com/sol3/papers.cfm?abstract_id=1424591.

Krause, Krystin. 2009. "Iron Fist Politics in Latin America: Politicians, Public Opinion, and Crime Control." *Paper presented at the XXVIII International Congress of the Latin American Studies Association, Rio de Janeiro, Brazil.* June 11–14.

Lacey, Marc. 2009. "After Losing Honduras, Ousted Leader Wins International Support." *The New York Times,* June 30, 2009, A6.

Lafree, Gary and Andromachi Tseloni. 2006. "Democracy and Crime: A Multilevel Analysis of Homicide Trends in Forty-Four Countries, 1950-2000." *The Annals of the American Academy of Political and Social Science* 605 (1): 25–49.

Latin American Public Opinion Project (LAPOP). 2010. Americasbarometer datasets from 2004–2010. www.vanderbilt.edu/lapop.

Latin American Public Opinion Project (LAPOP). 2008. Americasbarometer Dataset 2008 wave. www.vanderbilt.edu/lapop (accessed September 10, 2011).

Llana, Sara Miller. 2008. Can Mexico's Calderón stop the killings? *Christian Science Monitor,* September 2, 2008.

Lyne, Mona M. 2008. *The Voter's Dilemma and Democratic Accountability: Latin America and Beyond.* University Park, Pennsylvania: The Pennsylvania State University Press.

Mainwaring, Scott, and Frances Hagopian. 2005. "Introduction: The Third Wave of Democratization in Latin America." In *The Third Wave of Democratization in Latin America: Advances and Setbacks,* edited by Frances Hagopian and Scott Mainwaring. New York: Cambridge University Press, 1–13.

Malkin, Elisabeth. 2010. "Strains in Guatemala's Experimental Justice System." *The New York Times,* July 4, 2010, A4.

Malkin, Elisabeth. 2009. "Honduran President Is Ousted in Coup." *The New York Times,* June 28, 2009, A1.

Malone, Mary Fran. 2010a. "Does Dirty Harry Have the Answer? Citizen Support for the Rule of Law in Central America." *Public Integrity* 13(1): 59–80.

Malone, Mary Fran. 2010b. "The Verdict Is In: The Impact of Crime and Reform on Public Trust in the Justice System." *Journal of Politics in Latin America* 3: 99–128.

Malone, Mary Fran T. 2004. *Respect for the Law in Latin America.* Ph.D. Dissertation, Department of Political Science, University of Pittsburgh, Pittsburgh.

McAllister, I. 1999. "The Economic Performance of Governments." In *Critical Citizens: Global Support for Democratic Governance,* edited by Pippa Norris. New York: Oxford University Press, 188–203.

Mejía, Thelma. 2006. "A Violent Death Every Two Hours." *IPS News.* October 27, 2006. Accessed June 14, 2011 from http://ipsnews.net/news.asp?idnews=35275.

Méndez, Juan E. 1999. "Institutional Reform, Including Access to Justice: Introduction." In *The (Un)Rule of Law and the Underprivileged in Latin America,* edited by Juan E. Méndez, Guillermo O'Donnell, and Paulo Sérgio Pinheiro. Notre Dame: University of Notre Dame Press, 221–226.

Mendoza, Carlos. 2006. "Structural causes and diffusion processes of collective violence: Understanding lynch mobs in post-conflict Guatemala." *Paper presented at the 2006 Meeting of the Latin American Studies Association,* San Juan, Puerto Rico, March 15–18. Accessed June 2, 2011 at www.nd.edu/~cmendoz1/collectiveviolencelasa2006.pdf.

Meyer, Peter J. and Clare Ribando Seelke. 2011. "Central America Regional Security Initiative: Background and Policy Issues for Congress." Congressional Research Service. Accessed June 14, 2011 from www.fas.org/sgp/crs/row/R41731.pdf.

Millet, Richard L. 2009. "Crime and Citizen Security: Democracy's Achilles Heel." In *Latin American Democracy: Emerging Reality of Endangered Species,* edited by Richard L. Millet, Jennifer S. Holmes, and Orlando J. Pérez. New York: Routledge, 252–264.

Millet, Richard L. and Thomas Shannon Stiles. 2008. "Peace without Security: Central America in the 21st Century." *Journal of Diplomacy* Winter/Spring 2008.

Ministério da Justiça do Brasil. 2011. Anuário do Fórum Brasileiro de Segurança Pública. Accessed June 12, 2011 from http://portal.mj.gov.br/Senasp/data/Pages/MJCF2BAE97ITEMIDC5C3828943404A54BF47608963F43DA7PTBRIE.htm.

Moodie, Ellen. 2008. *El Salvador in the Aftermath of Peace: Crime, Uncertainty and the Transition to Democracy.* Philadelphia: University of Pennsylvania Press, 2010.

Muller, Edward and Mitchell Seligson. 1987. "Inequality and Insurgency." *American Political Science Review* 81(2): 425–452.

Nagle, Luz E. 2009. "The Rule of Law in Latin America." In *Latin American Democracy: Emerging Reality of Endangered Species,* edited by Richard L. Millet, Jennifer S. Holmes, and Orlando J. Pérez. New York: Routledge, 80–100.

Nowalski, Jorge. 2006. "Human Security and Sustainable Livelihoods in Central America: the Case of the Maras." In *National and Human Security Issues in Latin America: Democracies at Risk,* edited by Satya Pattnayak and Lowell Gustafson. Lewiston, NY: The Edwin Mellen Press, 205–232.

Observatorio Centroamericano sobre Violencia. 2006. Tasas de Homicidios Dolosos en Centroamérica y República Dominicana por 100,000 Habitantes (1999–2007). Accessed June 1, 2011 at www.ocavi.com/docs_files/file_378.pdf.

O'Donnell, Guillermo. 2006. "Afterword: On Informal Institutions, Once Again." In *Informal Institutions and Democracy: Lessons from Latin America,* edited by Gretchen Helmke and Steven Levitsky. Baltimore: Johns Hopkins University Press, 285–289.

O'Donnell, Guillermo. 1999. "Polyarchies and the (Un)Rule of Law in Latin America: A Partial Conclusion." In *The (Un)Rule of Law and the Underprivileged in Latin America,* edited by Juan E. Méndez, Guillermo O'Donnell, and Paulo Sérgio Pinheiro. Notre Dame: University of Notre Dame Press, 303–338.

O'Donnell, G. 1998. "Horizontal Accountability in New Democracies." *Journal of Democracy* 9 (3): 112–126.

Organization of American States (OAS), 2005. Resolution 892: Support for Nicaragua. Accessed May 6, 2011 at www.oas.org/consejo/resolutions/res892. asp.

Pain, Rachel. 2000. "Place, Social Relations and the Fear of Crime: a Review." *Progress in Human Geography* 24 (3): 365–387.

Pallais, Elise. 2009. "Rule of Law in Nicaragua: The Consequences of Governing by 'El Pacto'." *Wake Forrest University School of Law Working Paper Series.* Accessed May 4, 2011 from ssrn.com/abstract=1440944.

Palmer, Steven and Iván Molina. 2006. *The Costa Rica Reader: History, Culture, Politics.* Durham: Duke University Press.

Peffley, Mark, and Hurwitz, Jon (2010). *Justice in America: The Separate Realities of Blacks and Whites.* New York: Cambridge University Press.

Pegram, Thomas. 2008. "The Human Rights Ombudsman and Democracy in Latin America." *Paper presented at the Seminario de Investigación, Programa de Doctorado Procesos Políticos Contemporáneos,* Universidad de Salamanca, January 24.

Pérez, Orlando. 2003. "Democratic Legitimacy and Public Insecurity: Crime and Democracy in El Salvador and Guatemala." *Political Science Quarterly* 118 (4): 627–644.

Pérez, Orlando. 2000. "Drugs and Post-Intervention Political Economy in Haiti and Panama." In *The Political Economy of Drugs in the Caribbean,* edited by Ivelaw L. Griffith. New York: Palgrave, 138–161.

Pérez-Liñan, Aníbal. 2007. *Presidential Impeachment and the New Political Instability in Latin America.* New York: Cambridge University Press.

Policía Nacional de Colombia. 2007. Tasas de Homicidios Dolosos. Accessed June 12, 2011 from http://oasportal.policia.gov.co/portal/page/portal/UNIDADES_POLICIALES/Direcciones_tipo_Operativas/Direccion_de_Investigacion_Criminal/Documentacion/REVISTA%202008.

Popkin, 2000. *Peace without Justice: Obstacles to Building the Rule of Law in El Salvador.* University Park: The Pennsylvania State University Press.

Prensa Libre. 2011. "Repuntan linchamientos en tres meses del 2011." *Prensa Libre,* April 1, 2011. Accessed April 22, 1011 from http://prensalibre.com/noticias/Repuntan-linchamientos-meses_0_454754548.html.

Prillaman, William C. 2000. *The Judiciary and Democratic Decay in Latin America: Declining Confidence in the Rule of Law,* Westport, CT, Praeger Press.

Reuters 2010. "14 Killed on Sports Field in Honduras." *The New York Times,* October 30, 2010, A8.

Ribando Seelke, Clare. 2011. "Gangs in Central America (updated)." Congressional Research Service (CRS), Washington, DC: The Library of Congress. Accessed June 2, 2011 from www.fas.org/sgp/crs/row/RL34112.pdf.

Ribando, Clare. 2005. "Gangs in Central America." Congressional Research Service (CRS), Washington, DC: The Library of Congress. Accessed June 2, 2011 from www.fas.org/sgp/crs/row/RS22141.pdf.

Rico, José María. 2006. *(In)seguridad ciudadana en Costa Rica: balance de la situación.* San José: Programa de las Naciones Unidas para el Desarrollo (UNDP). Accessed July 12, 2011 from www.pnud.or.cr/images/stories/downloads/pdf/Cuaderno01.pdf.

Rico, José María and Laura Chinchilla. 2002. *Seguridad ciudadana en América Latina: hacia una política integral.* Mexico City: Siglo Veintiuno Editores.

Rodley, Nigel. 1999. "Torture and Conditions of Detention in Latin America." In *The (Un)Rule of Law and the Underprivileged in Latin America,* edited by Juan E. Méndez, Guillermo O'Donnell, and Paulo Sérgio Pinheiro. Notre Dame: University of Notre Dame Press, 25–41.

Rogers, Tim. 2011. "Nicaragua Opposition Unites to Contest Legality of President Ortega's Candidacy." *The Christian Science Monitor.* March 23, 2011, Accessed May 12, 2011 from www.csmonitor.com/World/Americas/2011/0323/Nicaragua-opposition-unites-to-contest-legality-of-President-Ortega-s-candidacy.

Rogers, Tim. 2010. "Nicaragua Wakes up to Daniel Ortega's New 'Sandinista Constitution'." *The Christian Science Monitor.* September 21, 2010, Accessed May 12, 2011 from www.csmonitor.com/World/Americas/2010/0921/Nicaragua-wakes-up-to-Daniel-Ortega-s-new-Sandinista-Constitution.

Rohter, Larry. 1998. "The Guerrilla Poet, Lionized but Still Elusive." *New York Times,* June 9, 1998.

Rohter, Larry. 1997. "At Peace, Guatemala Is Ready for Visitors." *New York Times,* March 23, 1997.

Rose, R., D. Shin, and N. Munro. 1999. "Tensions between the Democratic Ideal and Reality: South Korea." In *Critical Citizens: Global Support for Democratic Governance,* edited by Pippa Norris. New York: Oxford University Press, 146–168.

Rosenberg, Mica. 2007. "Vigilantes Target Gangs as Guatemala Tires of Crime." *Reuters,* September 19, 2007.

Salas, Luis. 2001. "From Law and Development to Rule of Law: New and Old Issues in Justice Reform in Latin America." In *Rule of Law in Latin America: The International Promotion of Judicial Reform,* edited by Pilar Domingo and Rachel Sieder. London: Institute of Latin American Studies, 17–47.

Sanchez-Bender, Marcela and César León. 2011. "Crime and Violence: a Staggering Toll on Central American Development." *World Bank Press Release* No. 2011/409/LAC.

Sarles, Margaret. 2001. "USAID's Support of Justice Reform in Latin America." In *Rule of Law in Latin America: The International Promotion of Judicial Reform,* edited by Pilar Domingo and Rachel Sieder. London, Institute of Latin American Studies, 47–69.

Schor, Miguel. 2005. "Constitutionalism Through the Looking Glass of Latin America." Suffolk University Law School Faculty, Publications, Paper 19. Accessed May 2, 2011 from http://lsr.nellco.org/cgi/viewcontent.cgi?article=1028&context=suffolk_fp&sei-redir=1#search="schor+rule+of+law+latin+america.

Seligson, Mitchell. 2006. "Costa Rica." *Latin American Politics and Development* (sixth edition), edited by Howard J. Wiarda and Harvey F. Kline. Wesport: Westview Press, 442–455.

Seligson, Mitchell. 2005. "Democracy on Ice: The Multiple Challenges of Guatemala's Peace Process." *The Third Wave of Democratization in Latin America: Advances and Setbacks,* edited by Frances Hagopian and Scott Mainwaring. New York: Cambridge University Press, 202–234.

Seligson, Mitchell and John Booth. 2010. "Crime, Hard Times, and Discontent." *Journal of Democracy* 21(2): 123–135.

Seligson, Mitchell and Dinorah Azpuru. 2001. "Las dimensiones y el impacto político de la delincuencia en la población guatemalteca." In *Población del istmo 2000: Familia, migración, violencia y medio ambiente*, edited by Luis Rosero Bixby. San José: Centro Centroamericano de Población, 277–306.

Serrano-Berthet, Rodrigo and Humberto Lopez. "Crime and Violence in Central America: A Development Challenge." *The World Bank's Sustainable Development Department and Poverty Reduction and Economic Management Unit, Latin America and the Caribbean Region.* Accessed June 20, 2011 from http://siteresources. worldbank.org/INTLAC/Resources/FINAL_VOLUME_I_ENGLISH_ CrimeAndViolence.pdf.

Shifter, Michael. 2011. "Central America's Security Predicament." *Current History* 110 (733): 49–53.

Sibaja, Harold, Enrique Roig, Anu Rajaraman, Aurora Bolaños, Aurora Acuña. 2006. "Central America and Mexico Gang Assessment, Annex 5: Nicaragua Profile." Washington DC: US Agency for International Development. Accessed June 2, 2011 from www.usaid.gov/locations/latin_america_caribbean/democracy/nicaragua_pro- file.pdf

Silva, José Adán. 2003. "Policía en Desventaja ante Seguridad Privada." *La Prensa.* March 3, 2003. Accessed June 14, 2011 from http://archivo.laprensa.com.ni/ cronologico/2003/marzo/03/nacionales/nacionales-20030303-18.html.

Smith, Peter H. and Melissa R. Ziegler. 2009. "Liberal and Illiberal Democracy in Latin America." In *Latin American Democratic Transformations: Institutions, Actors, and Processes*, edited by William Smith. Malden, MA, Wiley-Blackwell, 13–34.

Smulovitz, Catalina. 2003. "Citizen Insecurity and Fear: Public and Private Responses in Argentina." In *Crime and Violence in Latin America: Citizen Security, Democracy, and the State*, edited by Hugo Frühling, Joseph Tulchin, and Heather Golding. Baltimore: Johns Hopkins University Press, 125–152.

Sokolon, Marlene and Mary Fran T. Malone. 2011. "Democracy's March through History." In *Achieving Democracy: Democratization in Theory and Practice*, edited by Mary Fran T. Malone. New York: Continuum Books, 3–28.

Staats, Joseph L., Shaun Bowler, Shaun, and Jonathan Hiskey. 2005. "Measuring Judicial Performance in Latin America." *Latin American Politics & Society* 47 (4): 77–106.

Sullivan, Mark. 2011. "Panama: Political and Economic Conditions and U.S. Relations." *Congressional Research Service (CRS), Foreign Affairs and National Defense Division.* Accessed June 8, 2011 from assets.opencrs.com/rpts/ RL30981_20110422.pdf.

Sullivan, Mark P. 1997. "Panama-U.S. Relations: Continuing Policy Concerns." *Congressional Research Service (CRS), Foreign Affairs and National Defense Division.* Accessed May 7, 2011 from http://www.fas.org/man/crs/92-088.htm.

Thompson, Brian. 2010. "One NJ Neighborhood Opts for Private Police Force." NBC New York, December 22, 2010. Accessed June 13, 2011 from www.nbcnewyork.com/news/local/One-NJ-Neighborhood-Opts-for-Private- Police-Force-112341519.html.

Tulchin, Joseph S. and Heather A. Golding. 2003. "Introduction: Citizen Security in Regional Perspective." In *Crime and Violence in Latin America: Citizen Security, Democracy, and the State*, edited by Hugo Frühling, Joseph S. Tulchin, with Heather A. Golding. Baltimore: Johns Hopkins University Press.

Tyler, Tom. 1990. *Why People Obey the Law*. New Haven: Yale University Press.

Ungar, Mark. 2009. "La Mano Dura: Current Dilemmas in Latin American Police Reform." In *Criminality, Public Security, and the Challenge to Democracy in Latin America*, edited by Marcelo Bergman and Laurence Whitehead. Notre Dame: University of Notre Dame Press, 93–118.

Ungar, Mark. 2007. "The Privatization of Citizen Security in Latin America: from Elite Guards to Neighborhood Vigilantes." *Social Justice* 34(3/4): 20.

Ungar, Mark. 2002. *Elusive Reform: Democracy and the Rule of Law in Latin America*. Boulder, CO, Lynne Rienner Publishers.

United Nations Development Program (UNDP). 2009. Informe sobre el desarrollo humano para América Central 2009-2010: Abrir espacios y la seguridad ciudadana y el desarrollo humano. Accessed May 20, 2010 from hdr.undp.org/es/informes/regionalreports/americalatinacaribe/name,19660,es.html.

United Nations Office on Drugs and Crime (UNODC). 2011. *Tenth Survey of Crime Trends and Operations of Criminal Justice Systems*. Accessed June 12, 2011 at www.unodc.org/documents/data-and-analysis/CTS10%20homicide.pdf.

United Nations Office on Drugs and Crime (UNODC). 2007. "Crime and Development in Central America: Caught in the Crossfire." *United Nations Publication*. Accessed June 14, 2011 from www.unodc.org/documents/data-and-analysis/Central-america-study-en.pdf.

United States Agency for International Development. 2002. Achievements in Building and Maintaining the Rule of Law: MSI's Studies in LAC, E&E, AFR, and ANE, Office of Democracy and Governance. Accessed June 2, 2010 from www.usaid.gov/our_work/democracy_and_governance/publications/pdfs/pnacr220.pdf.

United States Department of State. 2010. *Human Rights Reports*. Washington, DC. Accessed May 18, 2011 from www.state.gov/g/drl/rls/hrrpt/2010/wha/index.htm.

Walker, Lee Demetrius. 2009. "Judicial Separation amidst Declining Judicial Confidence: Evidence from Central America." *Paper Presented at the Southern Political Science Association's Annual Meeting*, New Orleans, LA.

Walklate, Sandra L. 2001. "Fearful Communities?" *Urban Studies* 38 (5–6): 929–939.

Whitehead, Laurence. 2009. "Citizen Insecurity and Democracy: Reflections on a Paradoxical Configuration." In *Criminality, Public Security, and the Challenge to Democracy in Latin America*, edited by Marcelo Bergman and Laurence Whitehead. Notre Dame: University of Notre Dame Press, 277–314.

Wolf, Sonja. 2011. "Mano Dura: Gang Suppression in El Salvador." Accessed June 8, 2011 from http://sustainablesecurity.org/article/mano-dura-gang-suppression-el-salvador.

Wolf, Sonja. 2010. "Public Security Challenges for El Salvador's First Leftist Government." North American Congress on Latin America (NACLA).

World Bank. 2011. "Crime and Violence: A Staggering Toll on Central American Development." *World Bank Press Release* No. 2011/409 LAC. Accessed June 20, 2011 from http://web.worldbank.org/WBSITE/EXTERNAL/NEWS/0,,co ntentMDK:22881633~pagePK:64257043~piPK:437376~theSitePK:4607,00. html.

World Bank. 2002. "Legal and Judicial Sector Assessment Manual." *The World Bank,* Washington D.C. Accessed May 12, 2011 from www.gsdrc.org/go/ display/document/legacyid/1038.

Index